RICHARD ALLEN

The Trains We Rode

Volume 11

The Trains We Rode

VOLUME II
NORTHERN PACIFIC — WABASH

Lucius Beebe & Charles Clegg

HOWELL
-NORTH
BOOKS

BERKELEY, CALIFORNIA • 1966

FRONT ENDPAPER

The Pennsylvania Railroad's all-coach *Jeffersonian* between New York and St. Louis rolls down Collinsville Hill as it nears St. Louis on a hot August morning in 1940 at sixty miles an hour under a dense trail of smoke exhaust for its portrait by William Barham.

BACK ENDPAPER

The Denver & Rio Grande Western's combined freight and passenger depot at Glenwood Springs, Colorado, about 1910. No motor car mars the bucolic atmosphere of a vignette of country railroading and beyond the brass-bound trunks on the platform *The Scenic Limited's* observation car is visible as the westbound train clears the station. (*Western Collection, Denver Public Library.*)

THE FRONTISPIECE

This original painting by Howard Fogg, executed for THE TRAINS WE RODE depicts the Boston & Maine - Maine Central's resoundingly named all-Pullman *Boston & Mount Desert Limited Express* of 1888. This summer-only parlor car candy run was the immediate predecessor and inspiration for the shortly-to-be inaugurated *Bar Harbor Express* and *State of Maine* which were to make history for more than half a century out of New York and Boston on the Maine coastal resort runs. Here *The Mount Desert* with the Boston & Maine's fine locomotive *Columbia* on its drawbar rolls three Pullman parlor cars, a diner and head end through the New England countryside for a rendezvous with railroad immortality.

THE TRAINS WE RODE, Volume II

© Copyright 1966 by Howell-North Books, a corporation, all rights reserved. No part of this book may be reproduced in any manner without permission in writing, except in the case of brief quotations embodied in critical articles and reviews.

Printed and bound in the United States of America

Library of Congress Catalog Card No. 65-25208

Published by Howell-North Books
1050 Parker Street, Berkeley, California 94710

NORTHERN PACIFIC

Acknowledgments

MANY OF THE contributors of photographs and other good offices to this book have been previously acknowledged as having monumented their claims to the authors' gratitude in Volume I of THE TRAINS WE RODE. At risk of repetition, however, and perhaps in the acknowledgment of a double debt, they wish to record the generosity of John P. Ahrens, Richard H. Kindig, Richard Steinheimer, Henry R. Griffiths, Jr., Dr. Philip R. Hastings, Gerald M. Best, Alfred W. Johnson, Arthur D. Dubin, Richard Allen, Ron Ziel, Donald Duke, the late Herb Arey, James Shea of Southern Pacific and Edmund C. Schafer of Union Pacific, William Kratville, Everett De Golyer and The De Golyer Foundation of Dallas, John Barriger, Richard Cook, Douglas C. Wornom, John H. White, Jr., of The Smithsonian Institution, A. E. Brown, Gus E. Payne of the Pennsylvania Railroad, Fred Jukes, Lesley Suprey, Mrs. Alys Freeze of the Western Collection, Denver Public Library, Andrew Merrilees, William J. Rugen, Joseph H. Cobb of the Maine Central and Conductor Carl A. Henry of the same carrier, Professor George Hilton of U.C.L.A., Alden MacIntyre, Mrs. Thomas V. Braband of the Mariners Museum, Newport News, O. Winston Link, Elmer L. Onstott, Laurence Breed Walker, Jay Allen, R. Loren Graham of Marine Photo Service, Arthur D. Fay of the Peabody Museum, Salem, Charles Porter Atherton, Esq. and Jim Shaughnessy.

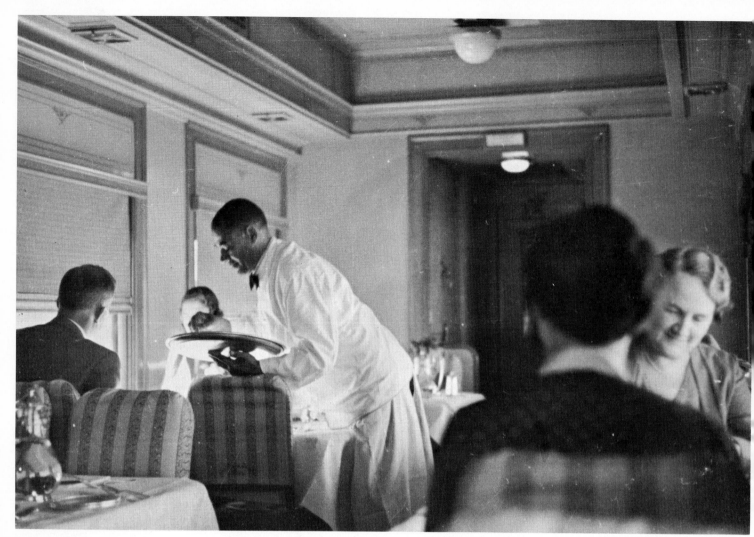

SOUTHERN PACIFIC

The real charm of a train is self-contained and has very little to do with its destination . . .
The real joy to be had from riding them begins where their usefulness ends.

John Mason Brown

Publisher's Note

*T*HIS IS THE TWELFTH BOOK we have published written by Lucius Beebe and through a long and pleasant period of working with him we became very fast friends. He was a "pro" in every sense, a prodigious worker and a great admirer of other "pros".

As publication of a new book neared, his enthusiasm mounted. He would watch the presses, check on the shipping department and especially be interested in how prepublication orders were coming in.

In our office and in our plant his excitement was contagious. He earnestly hoped his affection for the great age of railroads would be spread to many others through his books. A proof that he achieved this is the numerous letters received from his fans bemoaning his untimely death.

During the preparation of THE TRAINS WE RODE, Volume II, there was no one in our organization who was not keenly aware of his absence. They missed his vigorous step, his anticipation of examining the first copy, his constant telephone calls for progress reports on "the work". His railway books were his most cherished, even though sales figures might be greater on his books on other subjects.

Beebe was an impatient researcher, and the "nuts and bolts" railfan found occasional mistaken details in his writing. Serious historians too, would take issue with him over the matter of exact dates. Yet all segments of the railroad-devoted public were grateful to him for preserving the essence of railroading — the smell of the coal smoke, the hiss of the steam, the thrill of a journey aboard the cars. Above all, he brought a picture to them of the workings of huge railroad empires — and of the moguls who manipulated the destinies of these empires.

The day before his fatal heart attack was spent in our office discussing the fact that such an unbelievable wealth of marvelous material was being uncovered that he thought we should consider changing our format to three volumes. Mr. North, on seeing some of this material, could do nothing but agree. When Beebe returned home that evening, he began to tear apart and reorganize the "dummy", delighted with the prospect of enlarging on some sections considered "closed" and enjoying the prospect of adding whole new sections.

It was in this mixed-up state that the material came back to us to again to put together as one volume. Hence it is larger than Volume I. We have made every effort to arrange the material as we believe Mr. Beebe would have wanted it, and if we've guessed wrong, please bear with us. One mystery remains, and that is how he planned to include a railroad whose name starts with "M" in a volume with only roads from "N" to "Z". He undoubtedly had a logical explanation.

Charles Clegg's contribution to this authors' team was his masterful photo restoring and reproduction. He knew nothing of the literary end nor of the plans for order of contents.

Therefore, we decided to use only the parts of the book that Lucius Beebe completed, and make no attempt to fill in with other writers' work. First of all, there is not and never will be another Beebe and an imitation of him would immediately be recognizable. Second of all, this is the book of which he was the most proud. It is both our obligation and pleasure to publish it as we believe would suit him best.

HOWELL-NORTH BOOKS

Berkeley, California
October, 1966

Table of Contents

The North Coast Limited Was
The Glory of the Northern Pacific

Here *The North Coast Limited* is shown double headed against a scenic background of mountains and waterways near Yakima for its portrait as the very style and archetype of a great transcontinental name train. Opposite, resplendent with the first electric lighting system on any train west of the Missouri, is one of its buffet-lounges which may well have known the tread of the copper kings. (*Above: Everett De Golyer Collection; Opposite: Library of Congress.*)

AT NO TIME in its long and sometimes glamorous history was *The North Coast Limited* freighted with great financial destinies comparable to those that rode its staterooms during the years 1905-1907 when the fearful war of the copper kings raged between F. Augustus Heinze and the representatives of Standard Oil and John D. Rockefeller for the control of Montana copper. Beginning in the sixties as a gold and silver camp, Butte by the turn of the century had exhausted its precious metals but was found to be sitting atop the world's greatest single deposit of almost pure copper. Previous contenders for this truly colossal bonanza had been Marcus Daly and William A. Clark, but Daly died in 1900 and Clark, having achieved his life's ambition of election to the United States Senate, had sold his vast holdings to H. H. Rogers and William Rockefeller. Heinze, strictly an adventurer collected the better part of Daly's holdings and in the ensuing decade Butte was the scene of warfare, treachery and legal chaos that attracted international attention to Montana. *The North Coast Limited,* throughout these skirmishes and alarms, operated as an extension of Wall Street and Boston's State Street. Titans of finance and their general staffs, the highest paid legal talent in the land and financial writers from as far afield as London foregathered nightly in its diners and lounges and held secret conclave in private drawing rooms. On one occasion the Rockefeller interests, speaking through Thomas W. Lawson, the publicity broker of the age, claimed Heinze had sold his Butte holdings to a New York stock jobber and was claiming mines in which he held no equity. $5,000,000 in stock certificates were hastily jammed into a suitcase by a Heinze lieutenant and rushed aboard *The North Coast* to be displayed in a Butte bank next day to refute the story. At length, when the smoke of battle cleared, Heinze was found to be a ruined man and the copper wealth of Montana became a Rockefeller barony under the name of Anaconda. But while it lasted the Pullmans of *The North Coast Limited* had been the setting for as much concentrated melodrama as ever, in an E. Phillips Oppenheim novel, rode the *Simplon-Orient Express* or *The Blue Train* en route to Monte Carlo.

467

NO TRAIN was more abundantly heir to the tradition of the Old West and its immense distances of time and space than *The North Coast Limited.* When it went into service toward the end of 1900, at first as a summer-only vacation run and soon thereafter as an all-year round name train of continental consequence, the Western frontier had only been officially declared closed for a decade and evidences of the cattle trade that was still its most romantic preoccupation were on every hand. On the page opposite the scene at the top antedates *The North Coast Limited* by nearly a decade and was taken in 1891 at Gardiner, Montana, by the great William Henry Jackson as the spring wagon from the O K Ranch came down to meet the cars. Below: *The Limited* was twenty years old and institutional when it paused at Garrison, Montana, on a summer's day in 1920 while the Butte connection waited on the depot track across the platform. *(Above: Southern Pacific; Opposite: Everett De Golyer Collection; Northern Pacific.)*

HAD NOT THE MONAD been adopted as the heraldic symbol of the Northern Pacific, an alternate might reasonably have been a fine bushy set of whiskers such as adorned many of the carrier's principals and patrons in the years of its greatest excitements during the wars of the copper kings. Most celebrated of these, beyond all peradventure, was the Visigothic facade of Senator William Andrews Clark *(opposite)* archboodler of Montana's epic scuffles for fortune and preferment around the copper smelters of Butte.

Almost as magnificent was the beard of Thomas F. Oakes, President of the Northern Pacific *(right)* who, in a generation of railroad executives who looked the part, guided its destinies at a time when, as shown below, *The North Coast Limited* headed out of Missoula, Montana, shortly after the turn of the century behind two primordial locomotives with steam chests big enough to serve as kennels for St. Bernards. *(Everett De Golyer Collection.)*

AT THE CENTURY'S turn, when the Pullmans of the *North Coast Limited* were awash with financial notables ranking from Tom Lawson to William Rockefeller and representatives of the Rothschilds, the most celebrated patron of its ample buffet was fiercely acquisitive and boundlessly ambitious William A. Clark *(left)* who began life selling tobacco and mining tools and ended as one of the wealthiest of United States senators when that body was known as the most exclusive rich man's club in the world. In a time when silver and gold were the preoccupation of the mining world, Clark foresaw the day when the immense copper resources underlying Butte would dominate the world market for the red metal.

His smelting works, shown below in a contemporary engraving by the celebrated team of Western artists, Tavernier & Frenziny, made him incalculably wealthy so that, not without scandal, he was able to become senator and the greatest single figure in copper until the coming, many years later, of Daniel Jackling of Utah.   *(Brown Bros.)*

Three "Seeing America" Trains

Through the Storied Northwest

North Coast Limited	Northern Pacific Express	Puget Sound Limited
From Chicago via C. & N. W.- Northern Pacific	From Chicago via C. B. & Q.- Northern Pacific	From St. Louis via C. B. & Q.- Northern Pacific

Electric-lighted service of highest order and latest type, with dining car meals that are world-famous---identifying "Northern Pacific" as the "Route of the Great BIG Baked Potato": the line with its own bakery and butcher shops and a poultry and dairy farm.

Low Fares---Summer 1912

To Yellowstone Park and North Pacific Coast. Specially Low Fares on certain dates, account Annual Rose Festival and Grand Lodge of Elks at Portland, Golden Potlatch Carnival at Seattle and Carnival of Nations, Tacoma.

Stop off at Spokane and visit beautiful Hayden Lake.

Northern Pacific Ry

Illustrated literature on request with full particulars of fares and service.
A. M. CLELAND, General Passenger Agent
Saint Paul

Original, direct and only line to Gardiner Gateway— Official entrance to Yellowstone Park
Panama Pacific International Exposition—San Francisco, 1915

THE SUPERBLY matched and polished Circassian walnut, the marquetry and blue velvet of *The North Coast Limited* library-lounge-buffet car shown at the immediate left (another elevation of the same interior is depicted on an adjacent page) knew the aggressive whiskers of Senator William A. Clark and the other battle-scarred veterans of the wars of the copper kings. Its brocaded velvet valances and tulip-shaded electroliers lent it a beauty remarkable even in a period of splendid Palace Cars from Pullman. The restrained delight of the patrons on the observation platform of *The North Coast Limited* shown opposite dates from the 1930s, while below *The Limited* is shown running against a background of wilderness beside the Green River in the Cascades where, between Seattle and Stampede Pass it crosses the river eleven times. *(Above, Two Photos: Northern Pacific; Below: Everett De Golyer Collection.)*

AT THE FAR MARGIN of the opposite page a Northern Pacific travel ad for the summer of 1912 lists three name trains, *The North Coast Limited*, *The Northern Pacific Express* and *The Puget Sound Limited*. It is worth noting that while the flagship of the N.P. fleet left Chicago over the connecting iron of the Chicago & North Western, the two secondary trains departed via the Burlington. The last line of type at the bottom looks forward three years hence to the Panama Pacific Exposition at San Francisco, while "the BIG Baked Potato" is a capitalized feature on the diner. *(Arthur D. Dubin Collection.)*

473

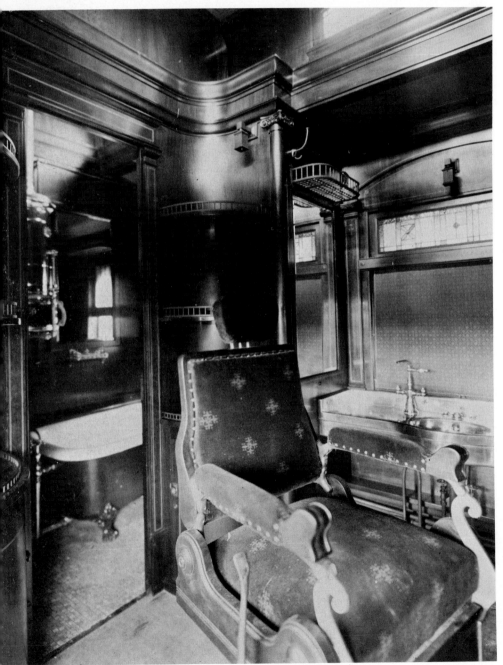

AMONG THE IDENTIFYING hallmarks of a train of pedigree in the great years of luxury travel one of the foremost status symbols was, of course, the barbershop, usually located in the forward combination baggage buffet car and attended by a talented tonsor whose professional expertise included not only the use of a straight razor at accelerated speeds over dubious roadbeds with an acceptable average of casualties, but a wide range of conversational versatility. It was a time when politics dominated the barbershop colloquies of the land and the man of lather and lilac water who aimed to please became adept at sizing up the political complexions buried under the hot towels and adapting himself to them. On a railroad train the maintenance of a barbershop was the ultimate in elegance because the economic facts of patronage of a one-man operation were precarious and the owning carrier usually ran the establishment at a loss. On the other hand, the company was apt to be better than average and the tips on a flyer such as *The North Coast Limited* more rewarding than elsewhere. Thus when, after his defeat in the Presidential campaign of 1916 by Woodrow Wilson, Charles Evans Hughes and Mrs. Hughes took a nice vacation at Yellowstone to recoup from the fatigues of campaigning, the *North Coast* barber was assured of at least one singe and trim job on the most exalted imaginable plane. American police still wore helmets at the time and Spokane (*opposite*) was no exception. (*Opposite: Arthur D. Dubin Collection; Left: Northern Pacific.*)

474

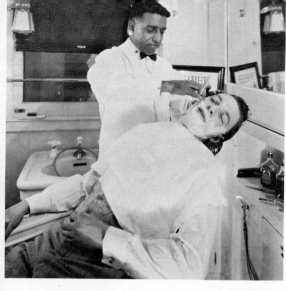

A LATER, and presumably more degenerate age saw
The Limited's barbershop shorn of its plush and finely grained
and polished woodwork in favor of devisings of sanitation
that could have been encountered in any good hospital.
Senator Clark and his contemporaries would not, it is safe to say,
have approved.   *(Northern Pacific.)*

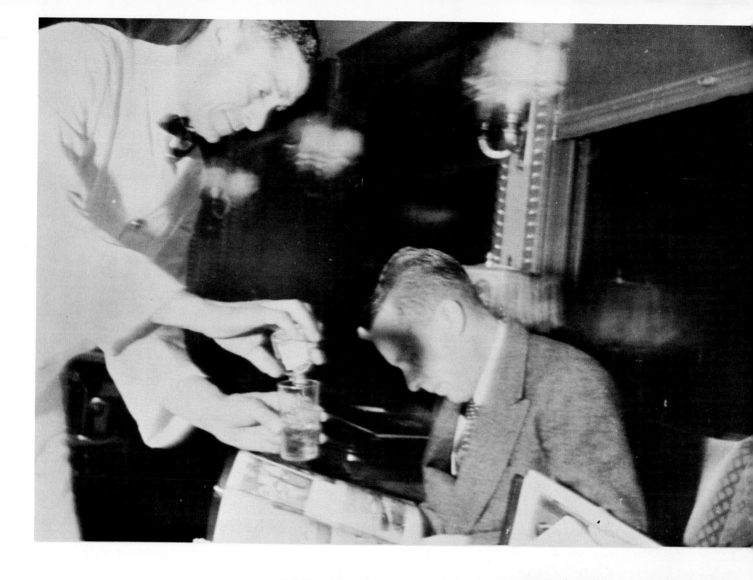

COCKTAIL TIME, "The Hour" of the immortal Bernard De Voto, on the lounge cars of *The North Coast Limited* was an unhurried sacrament. Time was on the side of the Martinis. Wherever the cars were at six in the evening, they wouldn't get there until tomorrow and the diner crew had nothing to do but await the convenience of the patrons. The radio console in the club car was a hallmark of opulence in the 1930s. From earliest times the image of the Northern Pacific *(opposite)* was that of big time railroading reflected in the vast distance it traversed and the big sky above its right of way. Its rear end, posed at Livingston, Montana, in 1924 was the profile of luxury in the age of Pullman Standard. *(Four Photos: Northern Pacific.)*

477

ACCORDING TO Sinologists as well as on the word of Arthur D. Dubin, foremost student of American train heraldry and railroad insignia, the black and white figure which is the Northern Pacific's heraldic device, the monad, was created in 1017 A.D., by Chinese philosopher Chow Lien Ki to represent the eternal forces of light and darkness, life and death, good and evil. Who adapted it to the Northern Pacific's use is not known but Dubin maintains that its first appearance in company literature was in 1900 in connection with the inaugural of *The North Coast Limited*. Since then, the monad has been associated with the N.P. the way the legendary mountain goat symbolized the Great Northern and the keystone the Pennsylvania. On some runs the monad was incorporated with the train name on drumhead heralds as on the *Yellowstone Comet* opposite. On the streamlined *North Coast Limited* solarium it was subordinated to the Mars light which, *faute de mieux*, rode the drawbar. *(Three Photos: Northern Pacific.)*

AS THE IRON of the Northern Pacific was laid ever westward to become the second transcontinental carrier, its architect Henry Villard made a practice of taking trainloads of notables out to the end of track where they lived sumptuously aboard specially appointed Palace Cars and were sluiced with rare vintages while witnessing the tribal dances and other ceremonies of the Crows and other relatively tame Indians. In lesser degree, perhaps, than they figured in the promotional advertising of the Santa Fe, Indians still were one of the picturesque assets of the Northern Pacific until well into the twentieth century and, at appropriate stops along the way, gathered around *The Yellowstone Comet* in an age of Brownie cameras and high button boots as suggested here and on the opposite page. *(Two Photos: Northern Pacific.)*

479

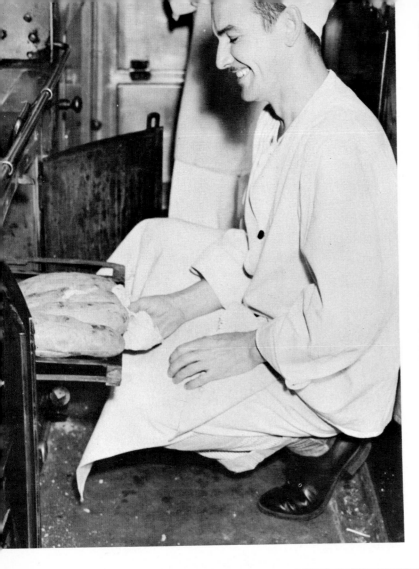

IN THE YEAR 1930 when the photographs on these two pages were taken, no varnish run in the pages of *The Official Guide* more dazzlingly lived up to the concept of what a classic transcontinental should be. From the pilot of its long barreled 4-8-4 locomotives to the illuminated heraldry that rode the tailgate of its observation, it was Pullman Standard, the finest construction the world of car-building has ever known, and, as of the year mentioned, fitted entirely with roller bearing trucks. Its pedigree was without reproach, reaching back to the days when the Northern Pacific was truly a pioneer carrier and the Old West a remembered reality. Its patrons had been the overlords of feudal estates, mines, ranches and timberlands and its amenities were tailored to those who wanted the best and nothing else. Just as its competing Great Northern made a symbol of the huge Wenatchee apple and promoted the Red Delicious of Lake Chelan on its menus, so the Northern Pacific featured "great big Idaho baked potaoes" as evidenced in the photograph opposite. At one time in the regime of William Jeffers the Union Pacific undertook to appropriate the symbolism of the Idaho potato but without notable success. It was too well established in the public awareness as a Northern Pacific property. The train's beaming chefs did nothing to dispel the illusion of good things to come at mealtimes. Above, *The North Coast Limited* threads its way along the Yakima River in Washington State. *(Four Photos: Northern Pacific.)*

THROUGHOUT its long and honored annals, *The North Coast Limited*, like flagship runs on other mainline carriers, was assigned the newest and finest equipment as it came from the drawing boards of Budd, Pullman and A.C.F., while earlier equipment was handed down to secondary trains. Thirty-seven new sleepers and public cars ordered from Pullman just before the market debacle of 1929 was the last large order for Standard equipment before the advent of streamlining. After the 1941 war a streamlined, Diesel-powered *North Coast* carried the North Coast fleet pennon first hoisted before the century's turn. Wall-to-wall carpeting, cheerful murals and private banquettes characterized the diner *(opposite)* while, as portrayed on this page the buffet lounge car *Traveller's Rest* was decorated with portraits of Meriwether Lewis and William Clark from originals by Wilson Peale. Below the great Northwestern pathfinders are shown with Sacajawea in the style of the artists of the period. *(Four Photos: Northern Pacific.)*

AT the top of the page, the streamlined *North Coast Limited* gets a window-wash during its long run across the continent. *(Rail Photo Service.)*

Like the Erie, The Nickel Plate-Lackawanna Provided an Alternate Route to Chicago

WHILE, in the great years of passenger transport by rail which climaxed in 1922 and again reached all-time highs during the necessitous times of the 1941 war, the vast majority of travelers between New York and Chicago took passage on one of the big three, the Pennsylvania, the New York Central or the Baltimore & Ohio, an agreeable alternative routing was available on slower cardings and at differential rates over the Erie and the Nickel Plate-Delaware, Lackawanna & Western. Through coaches and Pullmans were exchanged, usually during the night, at the Lackawanna's western terminal at Buffalo with the Nickel Plate where the components of the Lackawanna's flagship, *The Lackawanna Limited*, were integrated to the *Nickel Plate Limited* for the run terminating at La Salle Depot beside Lake Michigan. The Nickel Plate's unnamed No. 7 absorbed the Lackawanna's sun par-

lor-buffet-lounge-sleeper and conventional Pullman from Newark from *The Chicago Limited* while through elements of *The Western Special* were routed over the Michigan Central in the consist of *The Wolverine* west of Buffalo. Sleepers from the Lackawanna's other consequential name train, *The White-light Limited*, terminated at Buffalo, as did Pullmans in *The Buffalo Mail*. In the mid-thirties *The Lackawanna Limited* was a fine thing to see as is suggested in its likeness taken on a winter day near Summit, New Jersey. Opposite, one of the Lackawanna's Hoboken ferry boats operating out of Barclay Street in lower Manhattan is depicted in the North River through the rigging of a passing vessel of greater tonnage. *(Below: Lucius Beebe; Opposite: Everett De Golyer Collection.)*

LIKE THE OTHER coal-haul carriers, the Reading, Lehigh Valley, Central of New Jersey and the New York, Ontario & Western, the Delaware, Lackawanna & Western, running from Hoboken, New Jersey, to Buffalo where it made through connections for Chicago with the Nickel Plate and the Michigan Central, burned anthracite in a vast fleet of both camelback and conventional locomotives in freight and passenger service. Opposite in an atmospheric scene of 1900, the Lackawanna local discharges mail and express at Stroudsburg, Pennsylvania, while the town hack waits at the depot platform for business. Below, in a winter pastoral of snowy fields and split-rail fences, *The Buffalo Mail* snakes across the gelid countryside of the Southern Tier. Stone coal, the anthracite of the Lehigh, was the basis of the Lackawanna's century-long prosperity as it had been for the Reading and as was attested by the folk-ballad of sootless Phoebe Snow. Shown in this homely old-time scene, anthracite was delivered in a thousand communities in the East in half-ton tipcarts drawn by gentle draft horses over the cobblestone pavements of the turn of the century. (*Three Photos: Everett De Golyer Collection.*)

BY 1935 *The Lackawanna Limited* had cut two hours from the schedule of *The Chicago Limited* as shown opposite and made the connection west of Buffalo via the Nickel Plate instead of the Michigan Central. A train of distinctive character if not overwhelming style, it was favored by loyal partisans to whom a split second schedule was less of a consideration than an old fashioned daylight ride through the superlative setting of the Poconos and the countryside of the Southern Tier. *(Everett De Golyer Collection.)*

(Via Michigan Ce	*nt. R.R.)*	
Lv. **Chicago** *(C.T.)*	*9 00 P M	
Lv. **Kalamazoo** *(C.T.)*	11 54 P M	
Lv. **Detroit** *(E.T.)*	– –	
Ar. **Buffalo** *(E.T.)*	9 18 A M	
..............**See**	**Note** ⊙	
(Via Nickel Plate.)	....	
Lv. **Chicago**	*7 30 P M	
Lv. **Fort Wayne** ..	10 58 P M	
Lv **East Cleveland** ..	4 13 A M	
Lv. **Erie**	6 22 A M	
Ar. **Buffalo**	8 10 A M	
..............**See**	**Note** ⊙	
Lv. **Buffalo**	*9 30 A M	
Ar. **Elmira**	12 45 P M	
Lv. **Ithaca**	12 25 P M	
Lv. **Oswego**	10 45 A M	
Lv. **Syracuse**	12 00 Noon	
Ar. **Binghamton** .	2 05 P M	
Ar. **Scranton**	3 30 P M	
Ar. **Philadelphia** .	8 34 P M	
(30th Street Sta.)	....	
Ar. **Newark**	6 40 P M	
Ar. **New York**	7 12 P M	
....	....	
....	....	

Dining Car for meal service on Nickel Plate No. 4.
Coaches........Chicago to Buffalo

Note ⊙—Nickel Plate connection discontinued September 8th.

No. 6—LACKAWANNA LIMITED.
Daily
Runs via Blairstown and Newark.
Observation Parlor Lounge Car..Buffalo to New York.
Sleeping Car...Chicago to New York—Drawing-room, via M.C. No. 40.
Club Lounge....Chicago to Buffalo.
Parlor Car....Oswego to N.Y.—D.R.
Individual Seat Coaches, Buffalo to New York.
Oswego to New York.
Dining Car.....St. Thomas to Buffalo.
Buffalo to New York.
Coaches........Chicago to Buffalo.
Syracuse to Binghamton.
Ithaca to Owego.
(Lackawanna Limited train No. 6 will be held not to exceed 40 minutes for connection with Michigan Central No. 40 at Buffalo).

(Via Nickel Plate No. 4.)
Last trip from Chicago Sept. 8th.
Sleeping Car...Chicago to New York—Compartment, D.R.

IN THE YEAR 1913 when the young lady in the long skirts and picture hat was being solicited as a patron of the Lackawanna's *Chicago Limited*, twenty-seven hours between New York and Lake Michigan via the Michigan Central connection west of Buffalo was not as long a schedule as it might have been thought a decade or so later. *The Broadway* and *The Century* were then twenty hour trains and the Lackawanna made no pretense of being in direct competition with them. After all, it was less than ten years since Lackawanna passengers on the way to its New Jersey terminal via the company ferry who did not wish to incur the expense of a growler or hansom cab had taken the horse cars, one of the last remaining lines in Manhattan, down Twenty-third Street to the ferry slip as shown below. (*Everett De Golyer Collection.*)

ERIE-LACKAWANNA'S Train No. 10 stands in snowy Binghamton, New York in December 1963 with nine head-end cars and a rider coach for a portrait of silent midnight. *(Richard Allen.)*

LOOKING down-harbor toward The Narrows and the
Statue of Liberty, a Lackawanna ferry in its slip
on the Jersey shore of the North River forms a twilight
vignette of marine tranquility. At the left Erie-Lackawanna
Train No. 43 ends its run for the day at Binghamton,
while on the page opposite Charles B. Chaney
photographed *The Lackawanna Express* in the Jersey
Meadows in 1921.   (*Above: Everett De Golyer Collection;
Right: Richard Allen; Opposite: The Smithsonian
Institution.*)

491

PHOTOGRAPHED AT EAST ORANGE, New Jersey, at Christmas 1939, *The Lackawanna Limited* is heading westbound behind 4-8-4 No. 1106 and 4-8-4 No. 1504 running tandem to carry the holiday tonnage. Ordinarily a ten car consist, the Lackawanna's pride was conventionally handled between Hoboken and Scranton by a single high wheeled 4-8-4, but for the occasion shown here, the carrier's candy run required a helper. Pullman sleepers, a sun-lounge cafe car, two coaches, a diner and head-end revenue were all present and accounted for. On the page opposite: like all consequential railroads at the time, the Lackawanna maintained ticket agencies and travel bureaus at strategic points around New York and its suburbs where prospective patrons could be gentled amidst opulent surroundings by the subdued rustle of coated paper brochures advertising the rich resources of watering places at distant remove. This ticket desk was at the Lackawanna's Travel Bureau at 500 Fifth Avenue in the mid-thirties, a location calculated to skim the cream of the mid-town carriage trade with a minimum of inconvenience. In the below vignette, *The Pocono Express* nears the New York end of its run behind an identifying camelback at approximately the same period.   (*Below: Robert Le Massena; Opposite: Lackawanna Railroad, Everett De Golyer Collection.*)

NO COMPETITION IN THE FIELD OF SPEED to the *Broadway* or *Century,* but characterized by solid comfort on an unpretentious schedule was the Chicago-New York run on The Nickel Plate Railroad's *Nickel Plate Limited* with connecting sleepers east of Buffalo in The Delaware, Lackawanna & Western's *Lackawanna Limited*. Twenty-three hours between La Salle Street and downtown New York was required aboard the *Limited's* eight section-solarium-lounge cars, the western end of the haul through the industrial heartland of the Midwest and the eastern leg through the Poconos which unhurried travelers felt were as rewarding as the scenery along the Central's Water Level Route. Here *The Nickel Plate Limited,* eastbound at Hammond, Indiana, in 1944 rolls against the background of summer thunderclouds piling in an August sky for a court portrait of minor royalty by Richard J. Cook.

THE NICKEL PLATE'S
passenger operations embodied in
the *Nickel Plate Limited*
represented, in microcosm, the
grand manner that was implied by
its name. On its Train No. 9,
too, the Cleveland-St. Louis overnight, a stylish company herald
rode the tailgate of the
observation-sleeper, *Kitchi-Gammi
Club* and its companion car,
The Carlton Club, with the same
assurance more august insignes
marked the goings of *The
Super Chief* or *Liberty Limited.*
Its Pullman-built diners were
among the earliest with high-speed
trucks and waiters filled
coffee cups to the brim to demon-
strate their effectiveness.
*(Left: Richard J. Cook; Below:
Timken Roller Bearings.)*

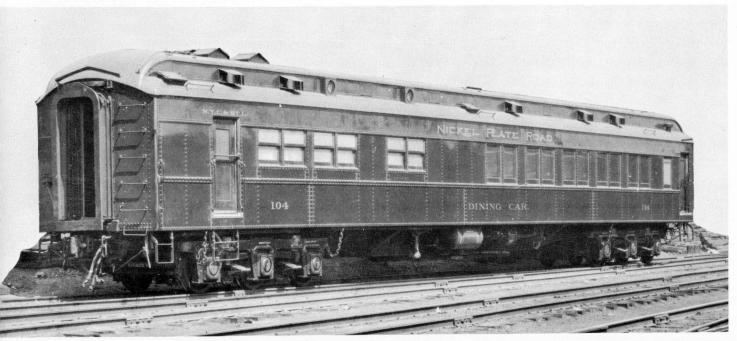

WARMED by the traditional cannonball stove of railway legend, the Nickel Plate operator at Angola, New York, gets his lineup from the dispatcher in the year 1958. Ninety-one years earlier another pot-bellied stove had made melancholy history at Angola when it fired the wreckage of the Lake Shore & Michigan Southern's *New York Express* with the loss of fifty lives in what came to be known to history as "The Angola Horror." Below, *The Nickel Plate Limited* departs Englewood, Illinois, with through Pullmans for the Lackawanna interchange at Buffalo against the identifying background of the Englewood gas works in the mid-thirties. *(Right: Philip R. Hastings; Below: De Golyer Foundation, Collons Collection.)*

THE THROUGH Pullmans between Hoboken and Chicago via the *Lackawanna Limited* and the Nickel Plate was not the only through run over these connecting carriers in the mid-thirties. A sleeper went west in the Lackawanna's *Western Special* to be picked up at Buffalo by the Nickel Plate's No. 7 and returned in *The Lackawanna Special,* shown here double heading through Summit, New Jersey, in the early morning hours for a pre-breakfast arrival at its Hoboken terminal. At the left the Nickel Plate depot at Conneaut, Ohio, in May of 1965 listed only two through passenger trains that paused at this once important stop, mute testimony to the carrier's ensmalled traffic and a desolate time. *(Above: Everett De Golyer Collection; Left: Richard J. Cook.)*

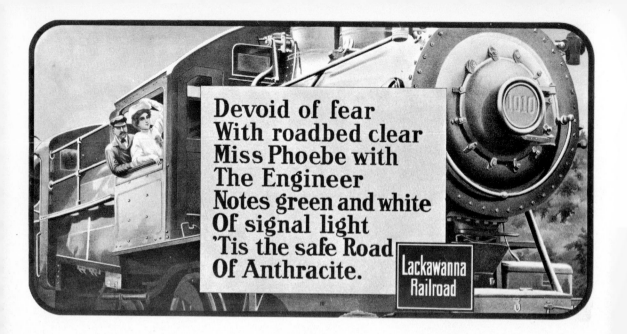

Devoid of fear
With roadbed clear
Miss Phoebe with
The Engineer
Notes green and white
Of signal light
'Tis the safe Road
Of Anthracite.

Lackawanna
Railroad

ONE OF THE FEW trains in *The Official Guide* to be named for a woman, the Erie-Lackawanna *Phoebe Snow* was a postdated tribute to the imaginary heroine of the Lackawanna's earliest skirmishes with promotion and publicity long before its merger with Erie. To focus attention on the carrier's antiseptic aspects as an anthracite burning railroad, a now forgotten genius, shortly after the turn of the century, confected no fewer than sixty four-line jingles about a mythical Miss Phoebe Snow whose garments remained stainless although exposed to all known vicissitudes of travel in the age of steam.

No friend of the dry cleaning industry, where rival soft coal burning roads were felt to have a vested interest, the Lackawanna made abundant capital of Miss Phoebe until she at length entered the national lexicon of popular awareness along with Buster Brown and the Flora Dora Girls. Years later, after the merger with Erie, the name seemed a natural for the carrier's new, stylish streamliner on the Buffalo-Hoboken daylight run, and the sleeping princess of advertising was re-animated fifty years after her first incarnation. At the right *The Phoebe Snow* is shown at Binghamton, New York, running six hours off schedule with the Christmas mails in 1956. *(Above & Right: Lackawanna Railroad; Photograph: Richard Allen.)*

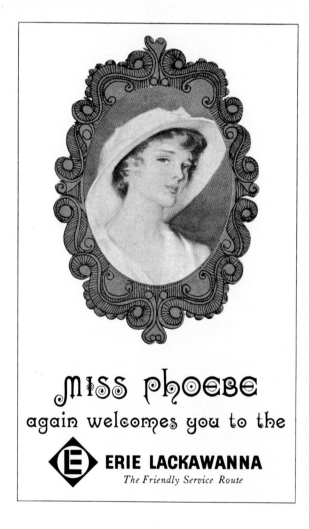

Miss Phoebe
again welcomes you to the

Ⓔ ERIE LACKAWANNA
The Friendly Service Route

The Folk-legend Became Reality

PRIMARILY a de luxe run between New York and Cincinnati with through cars from Washington via the Big Four to Louisville, St. Louis and Chicago, The Chesapeake & Ohio's *George Washington* was one of the great name trains of the Tidewater lexicon of railroading. The C & O owned both The Homestead at Hot Springs, Virginia, and The Greenbrier sixty odd miles away at White Sulphur and its candy trains, like those of the Florida East Coast, gave patrons a foretaste of the excellence they might expect at company hotels. In a pre-diner age, mammy types had sold Southern delicacies at depots where the cars paused. (*Lucius Beebe.*)

500

THE CAREFULLY CULTIVATED atmosphere of the Old South in ante-bellum times with which the Chesapeake & Ohio invested its hotel properties was also part of the facade of its three crack name trains, *The George Washington, The F.F.V.* and *The Sportsman.* The food aboard the dining cars and hand picked crews of cheerful and personable Pullman porters suggested old days on the plantation in the best Gone With the Wind tradition. The railroad never committed itself as to whether F.F.V. stood for Fast Flying Virginian or First Families of Virginia. It was agreeable to either interpretation and the aristocratic ways it suggested.

DURING A brief skirmish with airflow design, *F.F.V.* in the summer of 1947 poses at Hinton, West Virginia, for a profile photograph by Gene Huddleston for Rail Photo Service.

NO more effective tailgate insigne was ever devised for a crack varnish run than the simple portrait of the Founding Father which rode without further remark or identification at the end of *The George Washington's* observation lounge. (*Rail Photo Service.*)

501

LIKE MANY MEN of small stature, Robert R. Young had Napoleonic ideas and admired to surround himself with the great names of the world. Among them were the Duke and Duchess of Windsor at White Sulphur, and also many other headliners to add to the resort's century old and well established luster. Here the Windsors arrive aboard his private car No. 28 which, after his death, became the property of Mrs. Joan Payson, sister of John Hay Whitney, thus maintaining continuity with names that made news. *(Two Photos: Chesapeake & Ohio.)*

NO RAILROAD, not even the Southern Pacific and Del Monte or the Santa Fe and its Harvey Houses, was ever more closely associated with the hotel business than was the Chesapeake & Ohio through the agency of The Greenbrier at White Sulphur Springs. General Robert E. Lee had arrived aboard the cars in 1867 and from then until the time of Robert R. Young both its financial and social rating were beyond reproach. The only thinkable way to achieve The Greenbrier was *The George Washington,* while patrons of its rival, The Homestead came on *The F.F.V.* Snobbism rode the C.&O. stylishly and unabated. "You can see it on the train," a stately dowager told Cleveland Amory. "The people you want to be with are all going to The Hotel." The spring house is an ancient symbol of the allegedly therapeutic quality of the waters. *(Two Photos: Chesapeake & Ohio.)*

503

COMPANION TRAIN to the Chesapeake & Ohio's *George Washington* and *The Fast Flying Virginian* was *The Sportsman* with sleepers from Tidewater and Washington for Pittsburgh, Cincinnati and Detroit, the last of which terminals was reached over the iron of the subsidiary Pere Marquette. Above, its Pullman sleeper lounge is shown leaving Alexandria, just across the Potomoc from Washington and below is its Detroit section shortened to a mere five-car consist at the end of the run. *(Above: Lucius Beebe; Below: Rail Photo Service.)*

THE EXTENT to which the Chesapeake & Ohio Railroad was involved in the business of innkeeping represented by the Greenbrier Hotel at White Sulphur Springs, West Virginia, was the precise parallel of the commitment of the Southern Pacific in Del Monte on Monterey Peninsula or of Henry M. Flagler's Florida East Coast in the Flagler hotels at St. Augustine, Palm Beach or other resorts of the Florida littoral. Their affairs were interdependent, the *George Washington* providing the means of transport for arriving guests and departing patrons of the Greenbrier taking passage on *The Fast Flying Virginian*. It was a pattern of partnership of lodging and transport common to California, Florida, Colorado, New Jersey and wherever resorts were available via the cars in the age of Pullman. (*Two Photos: Chesapeake & Ohio.*)

505

THE CAFE-CHAIR CAR depicted below, a rare and exotic product of Pullman, was outshopped in June 1905 for the Great Central Route, a brief lived consolidation of the Cincinnati, Hamilton & Dayton, the Pere Marquette (to which No. 1008 was assigned and initialled) and the Chicago, Cincinnati & Louisville, a pattern of transport reaching from Cincinnati to Northern Michigan and from Buffalo west to Springfield, Illinois. No. 1008 ran in its *East Coast Flyer* between Chicago and Grand Rapids until the venture ended ingloriously in 1907. *(Arthur D. Dubin Collection.)*

SUNSET ON A SUMMER'S EVENING in the early thirties illuminates the smokebox (*opposite*) of the engine assigned to the Pere Marquette's Train No. 9, *The Resort Special* as it loads at the Fort Street Station in Detroit for the overnight run to Bay View with sleepers and a diner-lounge from Chicago it will pick up at Grand Rapids. Near its Bay View, Michigan, terminal, hard by the Straits of Mackinac, it will pass through the town of Petoskey, in the thirties a junction point of less consequence than it had been in 1908 when the photograph was taken that is reproduced above. Petoskey was then also on line of the Grand Rapids & Indiana and very much of a railroad community. (*Opposite: Ewing Galloway; Above: Smithsonian Institution.*)

SPECIAL ASPECTS of fascination in the character or operations of a single railroad have sometimes so fetched the imagination of individual photographers that their work has become specifically associated with one carrier almost to the exclusion of all others. O. Winston Link, a New York commercial photographer of great distinction, happily while steam still ruled this essentially Tidewater and coal haul road, fell in love with the Norfolk & Western, and tokens of his devotion are the two photographs appearing here and on the opposite page. Opposite, behind a bullet-nosed 4-8-4 the Norfolk & Western's *Powhatan Arrow* on the all day long run between Norfolk and Cincinnati with coaches only emerges westbound from Montgomery Tunnel twenty-seven miles west of Roanoke. Here Trains No. 1 and 2 with New York Pullmans from the Pennsylvania connection via the Shenandoah Valley route for Roanoke, Virginia, meet at Hager Tower, Hagerstown, Maryland. The time is January 1948. *(Two Photos: O. Winston Link.)*

DINERS, on the Norfolk & Western's two crack trains of the thirties, *The Pocahontas* and *The Cavalier* were informal and their cuisine Southern rather than Lucullan but could be entirely satisfying eaten against the incomparable backdrop of the N & W's scenic runs. Below: at Hagerstown, Maryland, the head-end crew of No. 129 climb down from the dual service streamlined engine cab preparatory to turning it over to the night crew who will take it south with Pullmans from the Pennsylvania interchange. (*Right: Norfolk & Western; Below: Jim Shaughnessy.*)

HERE, in pre-streamlined times, The Norfolk & Western's pride and companion train to *The Cavalier*, *The Pocahontas* provides an impressionist vignette of speed and power in a great name train in action. (*Norfolk & Western Magazine.*)

THE CHICAGO & NORTH WESTERN'S second passenger depot in Chicago, photographed in the opposite reproduction at the time of the 1893 Chicago World's Columbian Exposition is remarkable not only for its institutional architecture which made it as familiar a landmark as The Rookery, Potter Palmer's magnificent hotel or Marshall Field's store, but for the variety of surface transport in the picture. Visible are the ubiquitous stages of the Parmelee Transfer which shuttled between all Chicago railroad terminals then as today, an electric street car, a private brougham just coming off the bridge and at the extreme left, the public hack rank of coupes and hansoms. Not identifiable in the press of traffic, but unquestionably present in this, Chicago's year marked with a star, were the scrupulously maintained fleet of private hansoms kept on duty at the North Western Depot to meet incoming transcontinental trains by the enterprising Marshall Field. They were there to meet arriving Western millionaires from the Comstock or from Texas and to transport them directly to Field's world famous store before they could be induced to patronize the competition and, in many cases, before they even registered at their hotels. (*Library of Congress.*)

SHOWN immediately above on the fine summer morning of July 8, 1898, in a photograph from the archives of the State Historical Society of Wisconsin is the Chicago, St. Paul, Minneapolis & Omaha Railroad's Train No. 1 at an unidentified water stop. Notable are the two women at trackside attired in sunbonnets and the prudent country skirts of that now remote day. At the bottom of the page opposite the North Western's *Duluth-Superior Limited* approaches its Chicago terminal near Grand Avenue with a wooden diner next to the observation car with its identifying drumhead. (*The De Golyer Foundation, Roland Collons Collection.*)

THE RAILROAD DEPOT coaches of Parmelee Transfer, a Chicago Institution as venerable as the water works, were an integral part of city travel in the years when all transcontinental traffic paused to pay toll to the town's hotels, restaurants and public facilities before it continued east or west. In the mid-twenties inter-station traffic rode aboard an opera-coach type omnibus entered from the rear end. *(John Barriger.)*

IN THE YEARS of Vanderbilt domination of the Chicago & North Western, the antecedent trains to *The North Western Limited, The Short Line Limited* and *The Vestibuled Limited* had, of course, carried luxury equipment from the shops of Webster Wagner, reflecting the Vanderbilt alliance with the great rival and competitor of George M. Pullman. By the year 1898 when *The North Western Limited* had come to be known by the name it was to carry as flagship of the *North Western* fleet for five full decades to come, equipment was still by Wagner but the following year Wagner was absorbed by Pullman and from then on Pullman sleepers, diners and buffets rode in the train that its owning carrier was pleased to call "The Best in The West." By the late thirties when the photographs of and aboard *The North Western Limited* were taken, it was an all-Pullman run of truly continental dimension with the bulk of its equipment assigned to the through run between Chicago and the Twin Cities with set-out Pullmans from Milwaukee and Fond du Lac and a connecting sleeper for Duluth. What the management was pleased to call "limousine solarium" lounges *(right)* had replaced the open observation platform of tradition and motive power was sometimes the handsome green shrouded streamlined 4-8-4s usually reserved for the Omaha run. *(Above: Everett De Golyer Collection; Right: The De Golyer Foundation, Roland Collons.)*

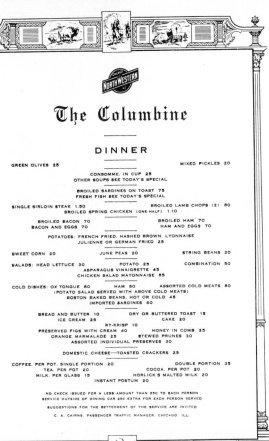

The Columbine

DINNER

GREEN OLIVES 25   MIXED PICKLES 20

CONSOMME. IN CUP 25
OTHER SOUPS SEE TODAY'S SPECIAL

BROILED SARDINES ON TOAST 75
FRESH FISH SEE TODAY'S SPECIAL

SINGLE SIRLOIN STEAK 1.50   BROILED LAMB CHOPS (2) 80
BROILED SPRING CHICKEN (ONE-HALF) 1.10

BROILED BACON 70   BROILED HAM 70
BACON AND EGGS 70   HAM AND EGGS 70

POTATOES: FRENCH FRIED. HASHED BROWN. LYONNAISE
JULIENNE OR GERMAN FRIED 25

SWEET CORN 20   JUNE PEAS 20   STRING BEANS 20

SALADS: HEAD LETTUCE 30   POTATO 25   COMBINATION 50
ASPARAGUS VINAIGRETTE 45
CHICKEN SALAD MAYONNAISE 85

COLD DISHES: OX TONGUE 80   HAM 80   ASSORTED COLD MEATS 80
(POTATO SALAD SERVED WITH ABOVE COLD MEATS)
BOSTON BAKED BEANS. HOT OR COLD 45
IMPORTED SARDINES 60

BREAD AND BUTTER 10   DRY OR BUTTERED TOAST 15
ICE CREAM 25   CAKE 20
RY-KRISP 10
PRESERVED FIGS WITH CREAM 40   HONEY IN COMB 25
ORANGE MARMALADE 25   STEWED PRUNES 30
ASSORTED INDIVIDUAL PRESERVES 30

DOMESTIC CHEESE—TOASTED CRACKERS 25

COFFEE. PER POT. SINGLE PORTION 20   DOUBLE PORTION 35
TEA. PER POT 20   COCOA. PER POT 20
MILK. PER GLASS 15   HORLICK'S MALTED MILK 20
INSTANT POSTUM 20

NO CHECK ISSUED FOR A LESS AMOUNT THAN 25C TO EACH PERSON
SERVICE OUTSIDE OF DINING CAR 25C EXTRA FOR EACH PERSON SERVED

SUGGESTIONS FOR THE BETTERMENT OF THE SERVICE ARE INVITED

C. A. CAIRNS. PASSENGER TRAFFIC MANAGER. CHICAGO. ILL.

AT THE APOGEE of its vast and diffused passenger operations when, in the mid-1930s, there was still a Vanderbilt on the board of directors to maintain continuity with its once proud estate as a Vanderbilt line, the Chicago & North Western operated a roster of name trains at least comparable to the fleet of varnish flyers of the Southern Pacific and the Pennsylvania. Excepting *The North Western Limited,* few of the name trains running exclusively over the North Western's left hand iron, *The Corn King, The Iron & Copper Country Express, The Iron Range Express, The Victory, The Rochester-Minnesota Special, The Viking* or *The Mondamin* could be termed de luxe runs. Luxury rode, rather, on its connecting trains via Union Pacific out of Omaha, *The Overland Limited, The Portland Rose, The Columbine, The Los Angeles Limited, The Mountain Bluebird* and, later *The City* streamliners until they were diverted to the Milwaukee. At the top opposite *The Corn King* arrives at Chicago behind one of the North Western's massive Class H, 4-8-4s. Below, *The Columbine* before the days of its elaborate Union Pacific solarium lounges, whose menu is shown adjacent, pauses at Boone, Iowa, on its Denver run. *The Continental Limited,* shown above through the arches of Mannheim Road viaduct at Bellwood, Illinois, in 1926 was an accommodation train to Portland and the northwest. *(Opposite, Two Photos: The De Golyer Foundation, Roland Collons; Above: Alfred W. Johnson.)*

517

RIDING THE NORTH WESTERN'S Omaha Line in 1902 sometimes provided excitement not listed on the operating timecard as when the Duluth Excursion was derailed on August 31 of that year. Salvaging their trunk from the wrecked baggage car while waiting for the town hack to pick them up was a lark for youths in the derby hats and knee pants of the then current fashion. Almost as much fun as a Methodist Church bake sale was the contretemps *(below)* on the Omaha Line near Belle Plaine, Minnesota, in December 1902. Even the Ladies' Aid meeting couldn't get the turnout occasioned by a nice train wreck. *(Two Photos: Wisconsin Historical Society, J. Foster Adams Collection.)*

ANOTHER contretemps on
The Omaha Line saw
The North Western's ten
wheeler No. 326 appropriately
carrying the white markers
of a special when it was
assigned to unsnarl
the Duluth Excursion train
wreck of 1903. (*Wisconsin
Historical Society.*)

519

WISCONSIN dairy products in ample profusion were assured to patrons of The Soo Line who were prompt to the summons when the dinner chimes sounded through the cars. Three eggs for breakfast were available for the asking, and the butterfat content was high all down the menu. A carrier subject to the caprices of seasonal traffic The Soo overnight between Chicago and the Twin Cities (below) regularly double headed in summer months with as many as twenty Pullmans and coaches on the drawbar of the road engine. (Right: Soo Line; Below: Leslie V. Suprey.)

IN THE MID-1930s when these photographs were taken along the Minneapolis, St. Paul & Sault Ste. Marie Railway, more usually known as The Soo, its overnight trains between Chicago and the Twin Cities were not name trains and ran as numbers only. Bucking the competition of the North Western, the Burlington, and the Milwaukee, all of which ran crack name trains in this densely trafficked area, The Soo had a loyal following who rode its no-nonsense cars, coaches, Standard sleepers, and well-conducted lounges and diners on schedules devoid of urgency through the Wisconsin farmlands.

No. 1 is shown above double-heading out of Fond du Lac in classic pose by Leslie Suprey, The Soo's official jongleur and cameraman. The beaver insigne at the left rode the observation car *Fernie* via The Soo and the Canadian Pacific all the way to Vancouver in *The Soo-Dominion*.

521

The Metropolitan

Nos. 25 and 25-155—THE METROPOLITAN.
(Tables 4, 5, 6.)

Lounge Car....	Pittsburgh to St. Louis—(10 S.). (Via Dayton.)
Sleeping Cars..	New York to St. Louis—(12 S., D. R.) (Via Dayton.)
	Indianapolis to St. Louis—(12 S., D.R.). (Open 8 00 p.m.)
	Pittsburgh to Louisville—(12 S., D R.). (Via Dayton (To No. 306 at Indianapolis.
	Pittsburgh to Detroit—(12 S., D. R.). (In No. 15-10 from Pittsburgh.)
	Columbus to St. Louis—(12 S., D. R.). (Via Dayton (Open 10 00 p.m.)
Parlor Cars.....	New York to Philadelphia—(Fountain Lounge).
	New York to Pittsburgh.
	Pittsburgh to Columbus—(Lounge Cafe).
	Pittsburgh to Cleveland (via Salem). (On No. 323.)
Parlor Coach...	Washington to Pittsburgh (in No. 15, arriving Pittsburg 6 05 p.m.).
Dining Cars ...	New York to Pittsburgh.
	Terre Haute to St. Louis.
Cafe Coach	Washington to Harrisburg
Coaches........	New York to Pittsburgh.
	Pittsburgh to St. Louis.

The Standard Railroad of The World

FOR UPWARDS of a century the Pennsylvania Railroad was rated by social historians as "the best gentleman's club in Philadelphia," a reference to the impeccable backgrounds, either acquired or inherited, of the long succession of magnificoes who served the carrier as president: Tom Scott, George Roberts and, most urbane and patrician of them all, the great Alexander Cassatt. All but forgotten in this refulgent tally were the founding fathers in the era of brass knuckles such as J. Edgar Thompson for whom the vast steel mills were named on the outskirts of Pittsburgh, and Andrew Carnegie, a one-time division superintendent whose destiny pointed elsewhere. As the best club in Philadelphia, it was only fitting that the Pennsylvania should occupy clubrooms suitable to its estate, and by and large the name trains of its passenger fleet in the great years of railroad travel served the purpose with distinction. No matter if a cynical commentator remarked of the Pennsy varnish: "When you've seen one, you've seen them all." The carrier spoke of itself as "The Standard Railroad of The World" and the superlative implied a degree of operational standardization over the vast network of high speed tracks that ranged from Montauk Point to St. Louis and from Louisville to the Straits of Mackinac. To the partisan of the Pennsylvania's special cachet of adequacy this uniform facade was no discouragement. It was a highballing organization. Its crack name trains to St. Louis and Chicago rolled double-headed across the countryside of Illinois and Indiana at speeds verging on a hundred miles an hour, and even when leaving the massive complex of Penn Station in Manhattan, the last car was a blur by the time it passed the end of the platform. Its most highly regarded name trains, *The Broadway Limited, The Liberty Limited* and *The Spirit of St. Louis*, each of them on a run explicitly in competition with rival carriers, had about it a character that was instantly perceptible to the seasoned traveler. Excepting on *The Broadway* its cuisine was seldom of an order to flutter pulses, at least within the memory of living men, although at the turn of the century there is evidence to suggest that its dining cars were conducted along more opulent lines. They had to be, if for no other reason than that a great deal of the road's traffic was in direct competition with the Baltimore & Ohio where the food was certifiably wonderful. When it came to passenger equipment, the Pennsylvania took a back seat to nobody and from the time of its primordial *Pennsylvania Limited* whose livery was so flamboyant it was known as "The Yellow Kid," down to the ultimate Tuscan red and cool beige interiors of its last *Broadway* the physical properties of its more regarded varnish runs were the envy of less affluent carriers. Where other carriers in the naming of their trains ran to regional history, folklore, mythology, zoology and horticulture, the Pennsy was patriotic: *The Liberty Limited, The Union, The Congressional, The General, The Admiral, The Jeffersonian, The Spirit of St. Louis, The American, The Senator* and *The Rainbow* (named for an Army division) all bearing witness to the road's essential patriotism. Now and then, as in the case of *The Red Bird, The Golden Arrow, The Gotham Limited* and *The Mercantile Express* it voided this generality, but mostly its lexicon was that of the national legend. It was a railroad steeped in protocol so that its stationmaster in New York, Big Bill Egan, like his English opposite numbers, as often as not appeared for duty in the silk top hat and morning attire of formal observance. And if the conductors of the Pennsylvania at one stage in the game enjoyed a widespread reputation for arrogance, were they not, after all, inheritors vicariously of the mantle of George Roberts and A. J. Cassatt, the symbol and operative authority of "The Standard Railroad of The World"?

BLACK STAR

523

Pennsylvania Limited

HOLIDAY

BILL OF FARE

1883-4.   **HOLIDAY MENU.**   1883-4

BLUE POINTS ON HALF SHELL.

Terrapin Soup.
Kennebec Salmon with Green Peas.
Potatoes a la Parisienne.

Boiled Leg of Lamb, caper sauce.   Boiled Capon, cream sauce.

Ribs of Beef with brown potatoes.

Turkey, cranberry sauce   Tame Goose stuffed with apples
Roast Beef.

Sweetbreads larded with Mushrooms.
Salmi of Quail with Truffles.

Roast Partridge, bread sauce.

Chicken Salad.   Smoked Buffalo Tongue.   Paté of Snipe in Jelly

Celery.   Olives.

Baked Sweet Potatoes.   Pickled Beets.   Mashed Potatoes
French Peas.   Asparagus.   Marrow Squash.

Steamed Fruit Pudding, Cognac sauce.

Apple Pie.   Mince Pie.   Strawberry Ice Cream.   Roman Punch
Macaroons.   Confectionery   Assorted Cake.

Florida Oranges.   Apples.   Malaga Grapes.
Bent's Water Crackers.   Roquefort.   Edam.
Coffee.   Tea.

MEALS, ONE DOLLAR.

WHEN THE PERIOD which is the purview of the present volume opens, in general terms from 1890 to the 1941 war, although in some cases already established name trains have been followed beyond the latter terminal date, the Pennsylvania Railroad's crack *Pennsylvania Limited* on the New York-Chicago run was already seven years old. The menus from the company archives reproduced on the page opposite establish its existence at the Christmas season of 1883-84 and the same yellowing files indicate that it was not yet the candy train of matched Pullmans that it was shortly to become, but shared the miscellaneous passenger equipment then available to the *New York & Chicago Limited* and other overnight long run trains. By 1891, however, *The Pennsylvania Limited* was basking in the most benevolent regard of the frock coats and mutton chop whiskers that ordered the Pennsylvania's affairs from Broad Street, Philadelphia. Company literature for that year depicts *The Limited* in terms as glowing as the new electrical illuminating system which was one of its most advanced features. It was all-Pullman with a barber shop, bath and valet for gentlemen, lady's maid for feminine travelers, a superb wine list, while a young gentleman in cutaway coat and boutonniere is depicted seated at an L. C. Smith patent typewriter ready to take dictation from a gentleman in quilted smoking jacket and important cigar. By 1905, as suggested by the list of Chicago trains at the left, *The Pennsylvania Limited* had yielded the fast scheduling to *The Pennsylvania Special*. Below, opposite, *The Limited* at speed in 1890 from a rare photo in the files of Everett De Golyer, Jr. *(Other Photos: Pennsylvania Railroad.)*

PENNSYLVANIA RAILROAD.

SMOKING-ROOM CAR.

" NEW YORK & CHICAGO LIMITED."

SOMETHING OF the pastoral simplicities evoked by the white-fenced section house garden of the late sixties at Horseshoe curve as shown above survived into the nineties when *The Pennsylvania Limited* began hitting its stride as the carrier's candy train on the Chicago run, although the diamond stacked helper engine would have been a curiosity. At the right *The Limited* is shown with its Pullman consist posed on the drawbar of two dazzlingly varnished Railroad Post Offices testifying to the train's reputation for speed and dependability at a time when great store was set upon getting business paper between New York-Philadelphia and Chicago on the fastest possible timing. The operations of *The Pennsylvania Limited* have been accorded liberal space in these pages because it represented the emergence and fullest flowering of the continental de luxe name train in the early years of the *belle epoque* of Palace Car travel. Aboard it the owning carrier explored the dimension and potential of luxury travel and its findings were to have great impact on the vast and various fleet of name trains that followed its markers. *(Five Photos: Pennsylvania Railroad.)*

526

"En Suite"

Observation Car

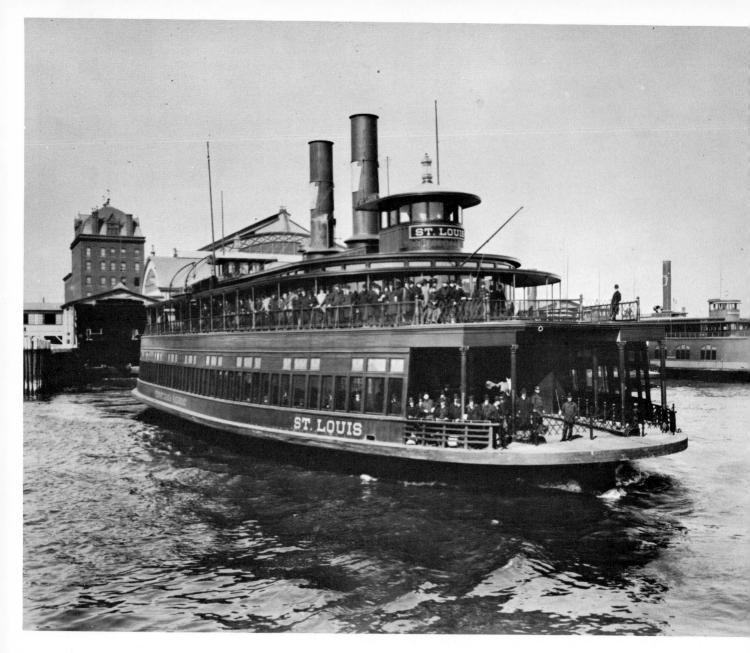

THE TRAFFIC situation in New York's West Street in 1890 as portrayed in the below drawing for *Harper's Weekly* that year would seem of a magnitude and complexity to equal anything evoked by the later and universal automobile. Here the Pennsylvania's passengers embarked aboard its considerable fleet of ferry boats, largely named for cities served by the railroad, *Washington, St. Louis, New Brunswick, Orange,* for the brief trip across the North River to the carrier's Jersey City terminal to board the cars. *Harper's* editorially applauded the construction of the covered footbridge across West Street, shown here, as well as the commodious double decked ferry boat *New Brunswick,* where horse drawn vehicles monopolized the lower deck and passengers rode the upper. On the opposite page a wintery photograph, to judge by the attire of its passengers, taken at a somewhat later date shows the Pennsylvania ferry *St. Louis,* the keystone emblem on its funnels, as it leaves the railroad's Jersey City terminal with its sister ship, *Washington* in the background. Notable in *St. Louis'* construction is the continuity of the Pullman theme, as exemplified in the photograph underneath, of the square window gothic of colored glass in both the varnish cars and ferry boats. The arched window gothic in the older vessel, *Washington* dates from a time when similarly curved window frames were in vogue in the car shops at Pullman, Illinois. *(Page Opposite, Above: The Mariner's Museum; Below: Alfred W. Johnson.)*

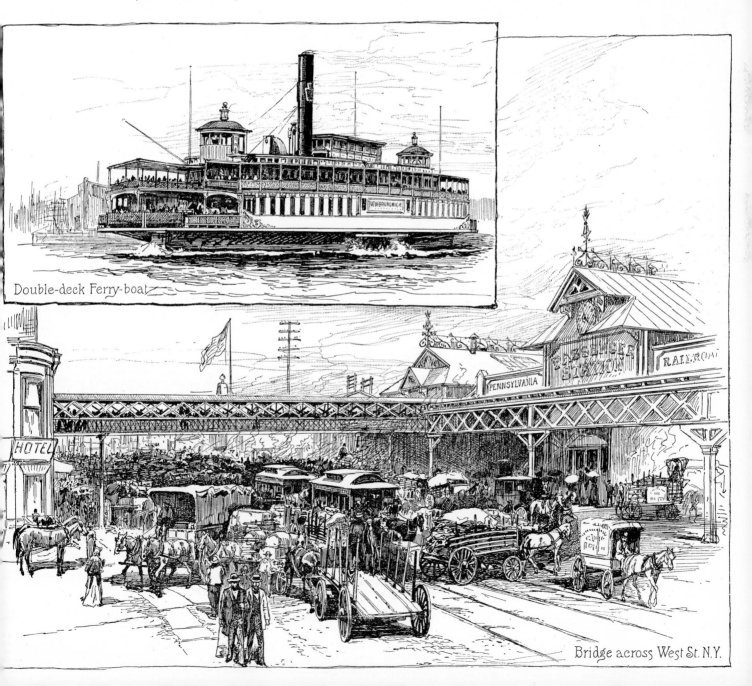

Double-deck Ferry-boat

Bridge across West St. N.Y.

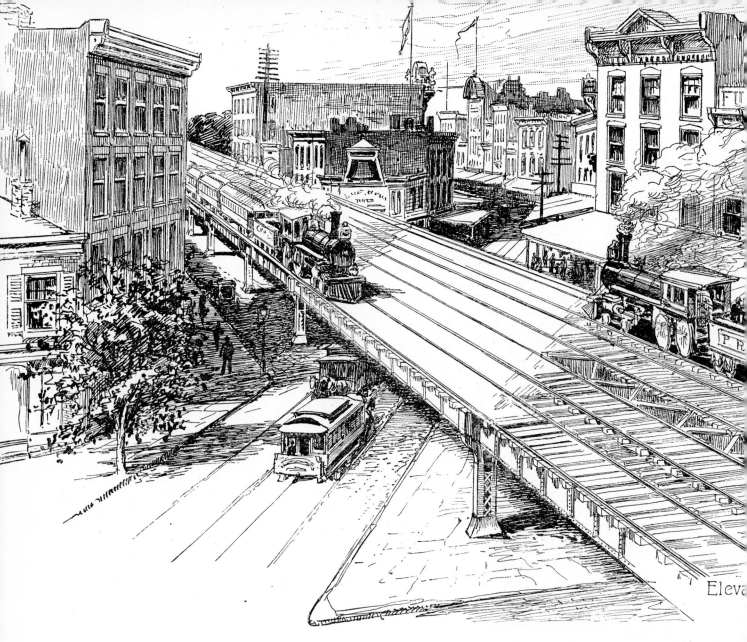

Eleva

TWENTY YEARS BEFORE the completion of Penn Station in Manhattan and its connecting tunnels under the East and North Rivers, patrons achieved the railroad's terminal in Jersey City by ferry from the West Street pier. In August 1890 *Harper's Weekly* commented that "The Pennsylvania Co., has notably moved in the right direction . . . the list of casualties at grade crossings about to be abolished is a long one." This referred to the construction at West Street of an overpass, shown on an adjacent page, and at Jersey City terminal the erection of "a four track iron structure 3/5 of a mile long, similar to but more substantial than the elevated roadways in New York City." The Jersey City viaduct is shown above. In 1890 the North and East River tunnels were unforeseen and speculation concerned a possible high bridge across the Hudson above Manhattan Island with connections to both New England and the Lower City. The woodcut at the right with its side-wheel tugboats dates from a much earlier period, perhaps 1875, but that the Pennsylvania already had a beachhead at Jersey City is indicated by the dock at the right of the engraving.

530

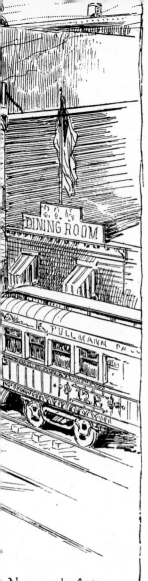

Newark Ave.,
Jersey City.

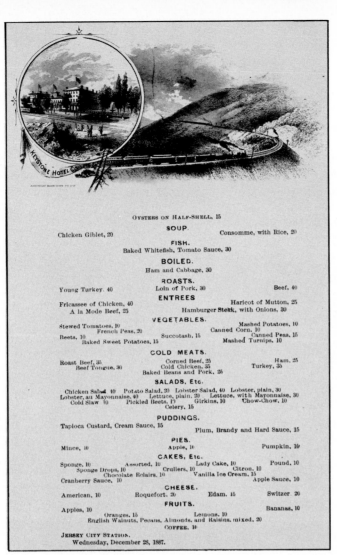

OYSTERS ON HALF-SHELL, 15

SOUP.
Chicken Giblet, 20   Consomme, with Rice, 20

FISH.
Baked Whitefish, Tomato Sauce, 30

BOILED.
Ham and Cabbage, 30

ROASTS.
Young Turkey, 40   Loin of Pork, 30   Beef, 40

ENTREES
Fricassee of Chicken, 40   Haricot of Mutton, 25
A la Mode Beef, 25   Hamburger Steak, with Onions, 30

VEGETABLES.
Stewed Tomatoes, 10   Mashed Potatoes, 10
French Peas, 20   Canned Corn, 10
Beets, 10   Succotash, 15   Canned Peas, 15
Baked Sweet Potatoes, 15   Mashed Turnips, 10

COLD MEATS.
Roast Beef, 35   Corned Beef, 25   Ham, 25
Beef Tongue, 30   Cold Chicken, 35   Turkey, 35
Baked Beans and Pork, 25

SALADS, Etc.
Chicken Salad, 40   Potato Salad, 20   Lobster Salad, 40   Lobster, plain, 30
Lobster, au Mayonnaise, 40   Lettuce, plain, 20   Lettuce, with Mayonnaise, 30
Cold Slaw, 10   Pickled Beets, 10   Girkins, 10   Chow-Chow, 10
Celery, 15

PUDDINGS.
Tapioca Custard, Cream Sauce, 15
Plum, Brandy and Hard Sauce, 15

PIES.
Mince, 10   Apple, 10   Pumpkin, 10

CAKES, Etc.
Sponge, 10   Assorted, 10   Lady Cake, 10   Pound, 10
Sponge Drops, 10   Crullers, 10   Citron, 10
Chocolate Eclairs, 10   Vanilla Ice Cream, 15
Cranberry Sauce, 10   Apple Sauce, 10

CHEESE.
American, 10   Roquefort, 20   Edam, 15   Switzer, 20

FRUITS.
Apples, 10   Bananas, 10
Oranges, 15   Lemons, 10
English Walnuts, Pecans, Almonds, and Raisins, mixed, 20
COFFEE, 10

JERSEY CITY STATION,
Wednesday, December 28, 1887.

THE INTERIOR decor of the Pennsylvania's North River ferry boats as long as they lasted on the run was ornate in the extreme and enlisted the talents of many types of artisans in their building and furnishing. Rare woods in great abundance were employed by skilled joiners for the grand salon of *New Brunswick* (below) while its stained glass windows were fashioned by no less a firm than Tiffany in Fifth Avenue. Prices on the 1887 Jersey City depot restaurant menu are reassuring compared to the inflated prices of today. *(Pennsylvania RR.)*

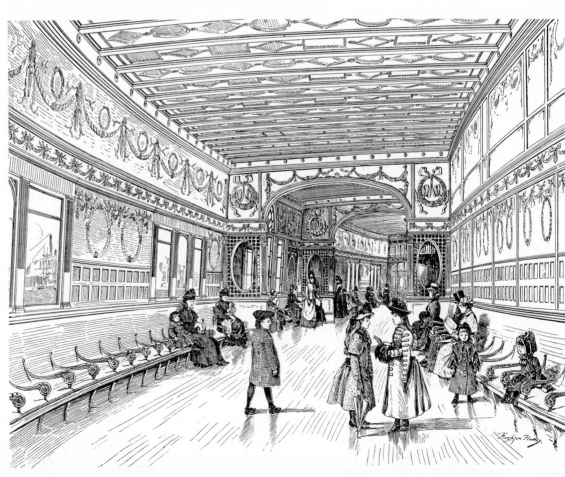

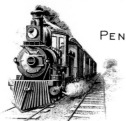

PENNSYLVANIA RAILROAD DINING CARS.

Dinner.

LITTLE NECK CLAM CHOWDER   CONSOMME

SLICED CUCUMBERS

BAKED WEAKFISH, SAUCE HOLLANDAISE
POTATOES DUCHESSE

JOWL, WITH SPINAGE

ROAST BEEF   SPRING LAMB, MINT SAUCE
RIB ENDS OF BEEF, BROWNED POTATOES

BEEF A LA MODE, WITH MACARONI
FARINA CAKE, CREAM SAUCE

MASHED POTATOES   POTATOES, CREAMED
SQUASH   NEW BEETS   ASPARAGUS

LETTUCE, FRENCH DRESSING

RICE CUSTARD

FRUIT

FRENCH ICE CREAM   CAKE   CANTON GINGER
PRESERVED FRUITS

ROQUEFORT AND EDAM CHEESE   BENT'S WATER CRACKERS

CAFE NOIR

MEALS, ONE DOLLAR.

SUNDAY JUNE 3, 1894.

WINE LIST

Champagnes.

	Pts.	Qts.
Pommery Sec	$1 75	$3 50
G. H. Mumm's Extra Dry	1 75	3 50
Duminy Extra Sec	1 75	3 50
L. Roederer, Carte Blanche	1 75	3 50
Moet and Chandon White Seal	1 75	3 50

Claret and White Wines.

Imported expressly for the "New York & Chicago Limited" from the Houses of BRANDENBURG FRERES and JOURNU FRERES.

	Pts.	Qts.
Sauternes	$0 75	$1 25
Chateau Latour Blanche	1 50	
Chateau Yquem	2 00	4 00
St. Julien	50	1 00
Chateau Belgrave	75	1 50
Pontet Canet	1 00	2 00
Chateau Leoville	1 00	2 00
Chateau Larose	1 75	3 50
Grand Vin Chateau Margaux, 1869, Brandenburg	2 25	4 00

Burgundy—R. Bruinghaus.

	Pts.	Qts.
Pommard	$1 00	$2 00
Chambertin	1 50	3 00

Hock Wines—C. Lauteren Sohn.

	Pts.	Qts.
Niersteiner	$0 75	1 50
Ruedesheimer	1 00	2 00

Wines, Liquors, &c.

	Pts.	
Ambassador Cognac, 1835		$6 00
Vieux, Old 1842		4 00
Sour Mash Whiskey, 1867		2 50
Amontillado Sherry		2 00
Bass' Pale Ale and Guinness' Dublin Porter	$0 25	
Smith's Philadelphia Ale		20
Bass' Ale, White Label	30	
Belfast Ginger Ale	20	
Champagne Cider	25	
Milwaukee Lager Beer	15	
Ballantine & Co.'s Export Beer	15	
Everard's Canada Malt Lager Beer	15	
New York Lager Beer	10	
Club Soda	25	
Lemon Soda	10	
Sarsaparilla Soda	10	
Congress and Hathorn Water	25	
Apollinaris Water	20	
Sparkling Hygeia Water	20	
" " Ginger Ale	10	
" " Plain Soda	10	
	Glass.	
" " Seltzer	10	
" " Vichy	10	
Amontillado Sherry	15	
Old Sour Mash Whiskey	15	
Cognac, very old	Pony, 25	40
Old Holland Gin	15	
Old Tom Gin	15	

Cordials.

	Glass.
Absinthe	25
Vermouth	25
Chartreuse	25
Benedictine	25
Kirschwasser	25

Cigars—Imported and Domestic.
SPARKLING HYGEIA WATER A SPECIALTY.

A THIRD OF A CENTURY after the date of the menus on the page opposite, Henry L. Mencken was to write in *The Divine Afflatus* that, "No man within twenty-four hours after eating a meal aboard a Pennsylvania Railroad dining car could conceivably write anything worth reading." Such, however, was not the verdict of passengers aboard the railroad's dining cars in the nineties or patrons at the several on-line hotels and restaurants under the company's management, and some of the available reports on the cuisine of *The Pennsylvania Limited* verge on the ecstatic. Today's epicures may raise an eyebrow at "Jowl With Spinage" on the dollar dinner of 1894, but Louis Roederer's Carte Blanche Champagne and Mumm's Extra Dry at $2.50 each the full bottle will arouse gasps of envy. *The Limited* is shown opposite in 1897 at Ardmore, Pennsylvania. Above is one of its diners in the ornate Spanish style so much admired in the Pullman Palace Car Exhibit at the Chicago Fair of 1893. *(Opposite, Three Pictures: Pennsylvania Railroad; Above: Pullman Standard.)*

533

BY THE turn of the century, the curious old sheet iron sheathed beacons used as depot signals such as that at Sharpsburg on the Conemaugh branch had largely disappeared but whiskers survived and the derby hat was, of course, occupational headgear among railroaders. *The Chicago Special, (below)* double shotted out of Paoli behind two fine Atlantics comprised a period piece. *(Two Photos: Everett L. De Golyer Collection.)*

ALTHOUGH lacking the inferential grandeur of The Paoli Local or even the Wilmington run out of Broad Street, Philadelphia, locals, as shown opposite, out of the gloomy old trainshed at Pittsburgh did their share of sooting up the Golden Triangle along with Jones & Laughlin, Youngstown Sheet & Tube and the great J. Edgar Thompson works of U. S. Steel. *(John Barriger Collection*

THE PHOTOGRAPH reproduced below
of *The Pennsylvania Limited* rounding
Horseshoe Curve in 1910 is remarkable for
its helper engine deriving from the
stable of the Pittsburgh, Fort Wayne &
Chicago whose runs usually came to an end
at Pittsburgh. The road engine is a
Class D American type 4-4-0 and more
at home on the Altoona run.
The Pullman drawing room suites on
The Limited of the period show only
vestigial traces of the ornate taste in decor
which reached its zenith at the Chicago
Fair of 1893. On the opposite page
The Limited rounds Horseshoe Curve
in its "Yellow Kid" livery of an earlier date
while in the lower frame the self-exiled
Duke of Windsor and his duchess
suggest that even in the mid-thirties *The
Limited* was still a train of enough
éclat to lend itself to the occasions of
royalty. *(Below and Top Opposite:
Gerald Best Collection;
Otherwise: Pennsylvania Railroad.)*

537

WITH THE ADVENT of the 1941 war, traffic between Chicago and the East achieved such dimensions that, as a companion train at least in name to *The General*, the Pennsylvania management added to its mainline schedules *The Admiral* which originated in Philadelphia. Leaving Thirtieth Street at nine in the evening, *The Admiral* arrived in Chicago just in time for lunch with through sleepers and a Washington sleeper it picked up at Harrisburg. *The Admiral* is shown below westbound at Valparaiso in 1942 when, even in wartime, it still carried an identifying nameplate on the smokebox of its scrupulously maintained K4s Pacific. As wartime and postwar traffic continued to tax the carrier's facilities and necessitated ever longer sleeping trains *The Admiral* was powered by assigned 4-4-4-4 duplexes identifiable as Raymond Loewy products by the sharknose profile and ornate portholes in their shrouding. The stately classic vistas of Chicago's Union Depot where *The Admiral's* passengers alighted were a fitting backdrop for the Pennsylvania's grand manner even in wartime. *(Opposite: Graham, Anderson, Probst & White, Inc.; Left: Pennsylvania Railroad; Below: Richard J. Cook.)*

WITH THE RISING sun of eight o'clock on its smokebox and side rods, Train No. 42, *The Rainbow* hastens on its eastbound occasions near Lewistown, Pennsylvania, under a flat trail of exhaust and with a liberal head-end tonnage to pay its way. *(John P. Ahrens.)*

ALTHOUGH its resplendent name closely approximated that of the Missouri-Pacific's *Rainbow Special* and it was accorded the panache of the carrier's keystone insigne on its observation railing, the Pennsylvania's New York-Chicago *Rainbow* wasn't especially notable for its character or distinction in the roster of Pennsy name trains. Christened in honor of the Rainbow Division of World War I celebrity, its almost only claim to attention was a handsome verandah observation car with its name in white against identifying red glass as it rolled on an unhurried carding. *(Right: Pennsylvania Railroad.)*

NEVER A TOTAL CASUALTY of technological progress, the car tonk found his duties measurably abated with the coming of high speed trucks and roller bearings. Once the sound of slamming journal boxes in the night at inspection points reassured uncounted Pullman passengers that their train was under the watchful eye of a benevolent management, and here a member of a venerable priesthood performs his ritual duties of inspection of the car *Tomhicken*. (Pennsylvania Railroad.)

THE STORY of the Pennsylvania's *Liberty Limited* on the Washington-Chicago run is remarkable because, in addition to being in its all-too-brief lifetime, a fine name train operation between major metropolitan terminals, it was brought into being at the apex of competition for passenger patronage between mainline carriers and because its final demise was encompassed through the agency of an intrigue that would have been suited to a ducal court in medieval Florence. Its legend has the dimension of a feud between Montagues and Capulets. For many years the cream of the Washington-Chicago traffic as well as that to Detroit, had been a near monopoly of the Baltimore & Ohio whose *Capitol Limited, Ambassador* and *Fort Pitt Limited* were celebrated for their cuisine, expeditious scheduling and courtly crews which combined to attract an enviable clientele of men of large affairs whose occasions took them between the Federal City, Pittsburgh and Lake Michigan. The management of the Pennsy viewed this traffic and the prestige accruing from it with unabashed envy. Its answer for many years was a Washington section of the *Broadway Limited* which in the beginning had been integrated to the New York section at Harrisburg and later, when traffic justified, ran as an extra section of the flagship of the Pennsylvania fleet. This was a successful operation, but failed to attract the anticipated business away from the B & O's name trains on the parallel run whose Chesapeake Bay seafood, Southern mammy type cooking and general urbanity caused it to be regarded by many regulars as a family institution. At length, in 1925 the Pennsylvania abolished the Washington section of *The Broadway,* largely because of the confusion arising from the similarity of names, and in its place inaugurated a new and entirely independent all-Pullman name train, *The Liberty,* leaving Washington in the late afternoon and arriving, as a well-conducted businessman's train should, shortly after breakfast at Chicago. *The Liberty Limited* remained all-Pullman until the late thirties, the peer in its amenities of long distance travel of other Pennsylvania headliners such as *The Spirit of St. Louis* and *The Broadway* itself. For two decades, until 1957, *The Liberty Limited* enjoyed an almost unquestioned supremacy on the Washington-Chicago run, deriving from its time advantage over the competing *Capitol Limited* which was sufficient to offset the B & O's hushpuppies and Jefferson Davis overtones of flawless service. In that year, however, *The Liberty Limited* was factually assassinated in an imbroglio that would have been acclaimed by members of the Borgia family. The Pittsburgh & Lake Erie, a subsidiary of the bitterly competitive New York Central, accorded trackage rights over its high speed right of way west of Pittsburgh to the Baltimore & Ohio, thus reversing the existing status of the two trains and giving the *Capitol Limited* a pronounced time advantage over *The Liberty Limited.* The combination of a faster schedule and a menu that included terrapin Maryland and Southern fried chicken recalled the B & O's vagrant patrons in droves and, in a matter of months, *The Liberty Limited* disappeared from the Pennsylvania timecards, its taking off as deliberately contrived a murder as any effected by the Medici. Opposite, in its splendid years, *The Liberty Limited* is portrayed in a spirited oil portrait double heading east of Harrisburg by Howard Fogg, dean of painters of the railroad scene.

BECAUSE of the scrupulously maintained competition of the Baltimore & Ohio trains on the Chicago-Washington run, *The Liberty Limited* received the best of everything at the hands of the Pennsylvania management. The handsome Fiesta type dining cars that were assigned to it late in the train's career, a profusion of cut flowers in public apartments and the top ranking personnel from the dining car pool all testified to the regard in which this classic long haul varnish was held by its owning carrier. Oceans of clean linen for its all-Pullman consist, as suggested by the servicing operation at Chicago depicted here were taken for granted. (*Two Photos: Pennsylvania Railroad.*)

THE GENERALITY to the effect that when you had seen one of the Pennsylvania name trains you had seen them all was possessed of a certain validity, but traces of identifying personality could be discerned, not only in the conduct of the carrier's pride and showpiece *The Broadway Limited* but in a number of other varnish runs where specially imprinted stationery, menus and other train literature, uniforms of the staff and the train name on the smokebox of assigned locomotives lent individuality and character to the operation. This was abundantly true in the case of *The Liberty Limited* as is suggested by this idealized official photograph of it at speed in the glory times of steam. *(Pennsylvania Railroad.)*

545

IN ITS SPLENDID years *The Liberty Limited* awaits a green light in Chicago's Union Station while a Burlington local lurks in the background. *(John Barriger Collection.)*

SOME SUGGESTION of the regard in which the Pennsylvania's management held *The Liberty Limited* in the years of its prideful going between Chicago and Washington may be implicit in the names assigned two of its built-to-order Pullman observation-lounges, *Thomas Alexander Scott* and *Alexander Johnston Cassatt*, two of the railroad's most swaggering presidents and architects of its destinies. After the advent of airflow design in the late thirties both rounded-end solariums and those with a squared-off bulkhead carried *The Liberty's* Keystone insigne as shown below in the car named for Tom Scott and in *Federal View*. (Two Photos: Rail Photo Service, W. G. Fancher.)

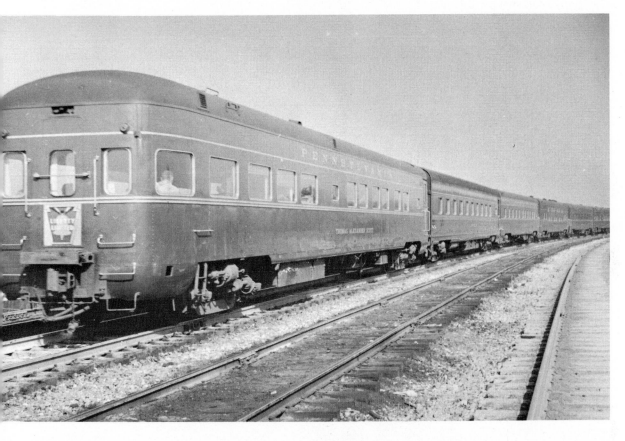

547

54

IN THE UNMISTAKABLY Chicago setting portrayed on the page above, *The Liberty Limited* and *The Golden Arrow* are shown eastbound as a single section behind two equally identifying and immaculately shopped K-4s Pacifics. The year is 1934 and the Depression suggested combining the two runs as far as Pittsburgh. Below the same train is shown in another view leaving Chicago with the conventional coach-smoker combine on the drawbar of the road engine. At the left *The Liberty Limited* is being christened in the presence of appropriate military brass and survivors of the nation's wars. To connoisseurs of Pennsy train launchings, none was authentic that didn't combine the best features of war and peace. There was always a military band in attendance and a ranking general, while Veterans of Foreign Wars rallied round The Flag and the champagne. (*Left and Opposite: Alfred W. Johnson; Above: Pennsylvania Railroad.*)

ON THE SEVENTEEN HOUR RUN between Chicago and New York, *The General,* shown at the top of the opposite page at speed through Valparaiso, Indiana, westbound and double headed with wartime traffic in 1942, was held in regard by the management second only to *The Broadway* on this important haul. House ads in company literature advertised it as "Every Inch a Leader" and it had its own menus and train stationery as long as these amenities of limited train status survived. The difficulties inherent in servicing the streamlined, articulated locomotives of experimental classes such as No. 6100 are also depicted as part of the routine of preparing the engine assigned to *The General* for its run between Chicago and Crestline. Running parts and essential lubrication points were so inaccessible that even before the demise of steam, streamlining was largely in the discard. *The New Yorker,* shown here eastbound at Valparaiso, with a single K-4s on the head end, was a full day and night haul between Manhattan and Lake Michigan and largely a train-of-all-work with a massive volume of mail and express. It was predominantly a daylight run to Pittsburgh eastbound with diner and parlor cars to that point and only a single Pullman sleeper regularly on the through assigned run to New York where it arrived before breakfast next morning. *(Above and Opposite: Richard J. Cook.)*

550

ONLY A MATTER OF WEEKS before the stock market debacle of 1929 was to set off a long period of depression and economic stagnation, the Pennsylvania on September 29 added *The Golden Arrow* to its already impressive fleet of New York-Chicago varnish flyers on the then conventional twenty-hour running time. "I anticipate that this will be the first of several more fine trains on this run in the near future," said Vice President George Le Boutillier, somewhat mistakenly as the train was christened at the Pennsylvania Station before its maiden run. At the Chicago train bay in Union Station a casting agency Indian maiden posed with a bow and arrow symbolizing the train's swift passage over the Pennsy right of way. *The Golden Arrow*, at its inception as is suggested on the opposite page was a classic Pennsylvania varnish run with coaches, Pullmans, an open observation lounge car and the train's name on the steambox of a sleek, assigned K-42 between Chicago and Fort Wayne. *The Arrow* theme in train names was continued on the Pennsy timecards in the form of *The Detroit Arrow*, *The Red Arrow* and *The Florida Arrow*. (Page Opposite, Two Photos: Alfred W. Johnson; Left and Above: Pennsylvania Railroad.)

553

NOTORIOUS for the less than clement aspects of its winters, Chicago weather is at its most infamous when the northeast wind blows in from Lake Michigan with cold and snow from the vast reaches of arctic Canada. Below is shown Train No. 22, *The Manhattan Limited* eastbound train-of-all-work with head end, Pullmans and coaches on a relaxed schedule, paused in the clutches of Chaos and Old Night at the deserted platform at Englewood depot in suburban Chicago. At the right a yard worker undertakes to prevent the switches from freezing with a long snouted flame thrower. *(Two Photos: Owen Davies Collection.)*

HERE the archetypal eagle eye, god of the right hand cushions, the brave engineer of poetry and legend oils around the motive power for one of the Pennsylvania's vast fleet of name trains in the age of steam. The company caption says it is *The Duquesne*, but it might as well be *The Broadway, The Rainbow* or the *Red Bird*. The properties of his calling were identical to all. (*Pennsylvania Railroad.*)

555

TO ADD VARIETY to the already well represented points of the compass which were identified with the Boston & Maine's *East Wind*, the Louisville & Nashville-Seaboard Air Line's *Gulf Wind* on the overnight run between New Orleans and Jacksonville and the Burlington's several *Zephyrs* apostrophising the West Wind, the Pennsylvania added *The South Wind* as a seasonal coach train between Chicago and Florida. Designed to match the company's other bids for non-Pullman patronage represented by the *Trail Blazer* and *Jeffersonian, The South Wind* operated out of Nashville over the Louisville & Nashville and its construction and overall conduct couldn't have been further removed from such early attempts at attracting coach passengers as the New York Central's improvised *Pacemaker*. Smartly uniformed attendants staffed custom-built coaches. There was a conventional dining car of *moderne* decor and an eighty-five foot buffet-lounge-observation car with a completely appointed buffet kitchen from which light meals could be served in the late evening. Its shot-welded consist and specially assigned streamlined K-4s Pacific type engine made a brave showing on its maiden sailing from Chicago. *(Kaufmann & Fabry.)*

ALL THE ALLURE of tropic skies and fronded palms that had first been invoked when Steve Hannagan placed Florida on the map as a vacationland for the masses as Palm Beach had been created by Henry M. Flagler for the well-to-do, went into the promotion by its owning carrier of the *South Wind*. Diaphonously clad damsels swam in the lazy surf of idyllic lagoons in the pages of brochures that made the sybaritic resources of sea, sand and sun available to the thrift-conscious. Never were champagne tastes more dexterously reconciled to beer pocket-books. Beholders knew that forty-eight hours after passing the handsome train gate designation shown at the left in Chicago's Union Station, travelers would be sending home postcards inscribed: "Having wonderful time; wish you were here." *(Two Photos: Pennsylvania Railroad.)*

557

THE UNION, Train No. 72, was in effect the southbound section of Train No. 71, *The Red Bird* between Chicago and Norfolk, Virginia, with Pullmans set out and picked up at Cincinnati *en route*. On the page opposite, it is photographed behind a freshly shopped K-4s as it pauses at Richmond, Indiana, in 1938, while in the lower frame *The Union's* engineer keeps a rendezvous with celluloid immortality, resting his hand of authority on the rod assembly of his locomotive. On this page, in an officially approved photograph retouched to permit just sufficient stack exhaust to suggest, at the same time, speed and economical combustion, *The Union* races southward under a picturebook sky. (*Above, Opposite: Rail Photo Service, Glenn Grabille, Jr.; Two Photos: Pennsylvania Railroad.*)

AS LATE AS THE YEAR DEPICTED opposite a few veteran Pullman sleepers were still equipped with atmospheric Pintsch lamps as well as electricity. A decade later, *The Manhattan Limited (below)* in its train-of-all-work role with much head-end business pulls into Crestline, Ohio, behind two K-4s. *(Above: Pennsylvania Railroad; Below: Rail Photo Service.)*

IN KEEPING with his innate Republican conservatism which
rejected the extra-fare splendors of *The Broadway* for a candidate for
public office, Herbert Hoover in 1928 started his first tour of the
country as Presidential nominee by visiting Vice-President
Charles G. Dawes at the summer White House in Wisconsin aboard
the down-to-earth and no-nonsense *Manhattan Limited*.
Here in the double breasted suits of the financial great of the period
they pose with Mrs. Hoover on the iron-railed open observation
platform on the train's arrival at Chicago. Dawes, who was
an established regular on *The Twentieth Century Limited*, must have
felt the gesture was a sacrifice to political expediency.   *(Wide World.)*

JEFFERSONIAN patrons were served their Martinis and Daiquiris in a sunken cocktail lounge in the recreation car or in the full dress club car shown here amidst *moderne* lighting and quilted bulkheads that would have been approved on the *Île de France*. Unusually heavy consists sometimes required double-heading *The Jeffersonian*, as is suggested below with the westbound section doing eighty near Caseyville, Illinois, in July 1940. *(Right: Kaufmann & Fabry; Below: William Barham.)*

CUT FLOWERS, expensive carpets, solicitous attendants, all combined to give the patrons of *The Jeffersonian's* spacious observation lounge a taste of the good life advocated by the third President and endorsed by the management of the carrier. *(Pennsylvania Railroad.)*

TRAIN No. 25, *The Jeffersonian's* companion train on the St. Louis-New York run with conventional Pullman sleepers, *The St. Louisan* followed on a slower schedule, its coming heralded by volumes of smoke exhaust from one of the road's massive T-1 duplex locomotives that were unable to turn a wheel without Burning-of-Rome smoke effects. *(John P. Ahrens.)*

THE EGALITARIAN SPIRIT in which *The Jeffersonian* was conceived and named was completely betrayed by its haughty pose and aristocratic profile in this uncommonly stylish photograph taken on its maiden sailing between New York and St. Louis by Carl H. Bowers of the *Dayton* (Ohio) *Daily News*.

THE ALL-COACH STREAMLINER *The Jeffersonian* was inaugurated in the mid-thirties to provide low fare transport on a twenty-and-a-half hour schedule between New York-Philadelphia and St. Louis via Terre Haute, Richmond, Indianapolis, Dayton and Columbus. Company literature in a delightfully republican vein declared that "the name selected for the new train typified Thomas Jefferson's constant aim to see the desirable things of life become increasingly available among his countrymen." Adopting a sterner view and more patriotic stance, it went on to assert that "It also commemorates his greatest achievement as the nation's third President in the famed Louisiana Purchase, by which the entire Mississippi Valley became United States soil, and St. Louis, the new train's Western terminus, an American city." Three complete trains were required to maintain the fast daily two-way schedule; all seats were reserved, and west of Harrisburg specially assigned streamlined K-4s Pacific locomotives with the train name on the smokebox roared through the night en route to and from the Mississippi. Luncheon was .65¢ and dinner six bits in that now distant and, it seems, halcyon time, and there were pier glasses in all the washrooms. (*Three Photos: Pennsylvania Railroad.*)

What the third President of the United States would have thought of a recreation car furnished in chairs upholstered in black and white zebra fur may be left to conjecture. At least it brought luxury to the masses in a demonstrably tangible manner.

The maiden voyage of *The Jeffersonian* from its St. Louis terminal was accomplished through the agency of champagne and cut flowers in profusion and a reception to civic and business dignitaries with company police in attendance to discourage any but the invited.

UNTIL THE ADVENT of *The Spirit of St. Louis*, the candy
train on the St. Louis-New York run for many years was
The American, shown here eastbound the far side of Harrisburg
under a summer sky ominous with thunderclouds.
The American was a train of the sort that still retained its hold
on the affections of many regular patrons despite the de luxe
blandishments of *The Spirit*, and its personnel comprised
a number of veteran men of veteran status as company servants
of the Pennsylvania. One of them, Raymond Thomas,
pictured here in a study that might symbolize his honored
calling everywhere, had been on the St. Louis run
twenty-four years when the photograph was taken. *(Left: John
Barriger Collection; Above: Pennsylvania Railroad.)*

WHEN THE *Congressional Limited,* by then known simply as *The Congressional* rounded out its first half century on the Washington-New York run on December 7, 1935, it had covered 8,212,500 miles of service and carried better than 7,000,000 passengers, many of them the great, powerful and celebrated names of the world. Mere statistics, however, are a chill tally of the superlatives that attached to a train that had known every President of the United States and every figure of official distinction worth naming in the Federal City since its maiden run in 1885, had catered to the whims of cabinet ministers and had carried ambassadors and plenipotentiaries as the merest commonplace. When a head of state was carried on a ranking official mission, potted palms and an American flag at the train gate in Washington were the equivalent of *The Century's* red carpet at Grand Central. Here a business car attached to *The Congressional* carrying Prince and Princess Takamatsu of Japan en route to their official reception in Washington by President Hoover is being given godspeed from Penn Station, New York, by Stationmaster William H. Egan, a functionary in whose daily life a silk top hat and frock coat were working attire. Opposite, *The Congressional* is shown in two period poses, in each case powered by the high wheel Pennsy Atlantics which were the proudest motive power of 1912. The top view at speed is from the Smithsonian Institution while that paused at Germantown Junction, later North Philadelphia, is from the collection of Everett De Golyer. *(Above: Pennsylvania Railroad.)*

568

AS IS SUGGESTED by the appearance of *The Spirit of St. Louis* as depicted below, identification placques on the engine smokeboxes of name trains do not seem to have been operational practice east of Pittsburgh. Specially assigned locomotives out of St. Louis, Cincinnati and Chicago on the lines west alone appear in the photographic record as a panache of elegance, and positive identification of a name train had to await the passing of the observation end with its illuminated train herald in the form of the Pennsylvania keystone.

EAGER TO RIDE the wave of enthusiasm that greeted Lindbergh's epochal flight across the Atlantic, the Pennsylvania management hastily recruited the first *Spirit of St. Louis* from the available Standard equipment in its St. Louis division pool to come up with the train shown here rolling, double headed out of Harrisburg across the Rockville Bridge. In 1938 when streamlining was in vogue a Raymond Loewy sheathed K-4s was assigned to the run with the train name on its bullet nose. *(Above: John P. Ahrens; Right: Pennsylvania Railroad.)*

570

THE OBSERVATION car *Golden Hill* shortly made its appearance in the consist of *The Spirit of St. Louis* as *Colonel Lindbergh* where, for the maiden run of the new train, it attracted a peculiar type of patron seldom encountered elsewhere. The *Colonel Lindbergh* was not, as has been occasionally maintained, the only Pullman ever named for a still living celebrity. There was also *Amon G. Carter,* honoring the Fort Worth grandee-newspaper publisher, and the *Adolphus Busch* for the St. Louis beer baron, both of which were ridden by their name-sakes in their lifetimes. *(Two Photos: Pennsylvania Railroad.)*

A MAJOR event of the railroad day at St. Louis Terminal was the departure, as depicted opposite, of the Pennsylvania's candy train on the New York run, *The Spirit of St. Louis.* The date of the photograph, by Elmer L. Onstott, was February 1940, and the identifying smokebox name plate was of a size more conventional than that shown in the photograph at the immediate left.

THE SPIRIT *of St. Louis* was well identified both fore and aft in its going. In the above frame on this page it leaves St. Louis terminal with an outsize name plate fixed to its automatic train control box. Below, some years later, the observation solarium crossed the diamond at St. Louis on its way East. *(Above: W. B. Cox; Below: Rail Photo Service.)*

573

EVEN THOUGH high speed streamlined runs such as *The Senator* shown below might streak over the Pennsy's main line east of Washington and Diesels take over where the electric catenaries ended west of Harrisburg, here and there vestigial traces of an older order of things along the high iron still survived on branch lines such as the grass-grown country depot somewhere along the Wilkes-Barre-Philadelphia branch where a flag hung out front called the cars to a halt. Veteran, too, of another age was the grand old man of the conductor's calling immortalized opposite by a perceptive photographer as he paused, orders in hand, at Ragan Tower south of Wilmington while his train waited on the dispatcher's caprice in the background. *(Three Photos: Pennsylvania Railroad.)*

THE SOLARIUM-lounge of the streamlined *Senator* shown above and the parlor interior of the 1930 Pullman Standard *Senator* *(right)* illustrate the transition from the luxury tradition of rich upholstery and decor of repose to the easily cleaned decor that was one of the inevitable by-products of lightweight car construction. On the opposite page *The Senator* on its way to Boston is shown from the rear end as it passes Princeton Junction and behind a GG-1 electric motor from the lens of the master craftsman O. Winston Link. *(Above: Pennsylvania Railroad; Right: Pullman Standard; Opposite: Rail Photo Service, Wayne P. Ellis, and O. Winston Link.)*

THE GAMUT of emotions was represented in the expressions of participants and bystanders alike at the *Trail Blazer's* christening, ranging from dismay, apprehension and mistrust to determined satisfaction and gratification.

WHEN, in the summer of 1939, the Pennsylvania management matched the all-Pullman, all-room sumptuousness of the new *Broadway Limited* with an all-new, all-coach run between Chicago and New York called *The Trail Blazer* many of its amenities approximated *The Broadway* itself. They included a seventeen hour schedule, airflow, lightweight equipment, flower-filled public apartments and a train company whose kitchen crew alone included fifteen cooks, two stewards and ten waiters. Attendants *(right)* as scrupulously uniformed as those on *The Congressional* showed passengers to their reserved space and *(opposite)* served meals in a two-car diner unit built in the company shops at Altoona with porthole type windows of polarized glass reminiscent of those on the *City of Los Angeles'* first observation lounge, *Copper King*. (Three Photos: Pennsylvania Railroad.)

RARE AS A company photograph because it actually shows smoke exhaust trailing from two K-4s Pacifics on the head end, is that reproduced below of *The Trail Blazer* eastbound at seventy miles an hour at Whiting, Indiana in the summer of 1941. Only infrequently have negatives been known to survive in company files unless clean engine stacks indicated the perfect combustion admired by the operating department. *(Pennsylvania Railroad.)*

THE TREND to de luxe accommodations for coach travelers before the 1941 war which was to find its ultimate expression in the Santa Fe's extra-fare all-day coach *El Capitan* operating on *Super Chief* schedules between Chicago and California had its inception in the *Trail Blazer* concept of low-cost speed and convenience. Many of the hallmarks of a status train hitherto reserved for such prestige runs as *The Broadway, The Liberty Limited* and *The Spirit of St. Louis* were incorporated in *The Trail Blazer's* equipment and conduct: specially assigned locomotives with name markers on the smokebox, the Pennsy Keystone insigne identifying it as a name train on the observation end, waiters, porters and lounge attendants in special train livery. It all added up to a not-so-poor man's second section of *The Broadway Limited* itself. *The Trail Blazer* insigne *(left)* showed in profile a backwoodsman in coonskin cap suggestive of the days when Fort Pitt had been a trading post in the Allegheny wilds. *(Left: Pennsylvania Railroad; Below: Lucius Beebe.)*

THE UNBRIDLED REVELRY depicted here was arranged for photographers from the Pennsylvania's publicity department, a liberally financed activity in the now distant year 1939, but there is no doubting that *The Trail Blazer's* commodious public apartments opened new vistas in the field of low cost travel. *(Two Photos: Pennsylvania Railroad.)*

THE PENNSYLVANIA'S candy train on the New York-Cincinnati overnight run, *The Cincinnati Limited*, had a pedigree old enough in the pages of the *Official Guide* to extend backward in time to the golden age of brass railed open platform observation cars such as is shown on the page opposite with passengers and train crew agog for the photographer's flash. The Keystone insigne rode through the Ohio night to place *The Limited* on a footing of equality with the other great name trains of the Pennsylvania peerage, *The Broadway, The Golden Arrow* and *The Spirit of St. Louis*. In the post-1941 war years when it was photographed being served *(below)* in Cincinnati yards, its solarium lounge *(right)* was identical with that of the streamlined *Broadway Limited*. (Below: TRAINS *Magazine, Wallace W. Abbey; Right and Top Opposite: Pennsylvania Railroad.*)

RUNNING an hour off schedule in the summer months in the mid-thirties *The Cincinnati Limited* is shown here nearing its western terminal double headed in a typical Pennsylvania operation of a fast name train with perhaps sixteen cars on the drawbar of the road engine. *(John P. Ahrens.)*

Broad Street Station Was a Philadelphia Legend

BROAD STREET STATION, Philadelphia, as it was known to millions of Pennsylvania Railroad patrons over the decades of its long and useful existence was epitomized by many things. To some the massive facade of its exterior architecture symbolized the formidable presence of a great railroad of feudal and hierarchical dimensions. To some its undeniably cold and drafty precincts in winter represented a tenacious survival of nineteenth century discomforts into an age scornful of obsolescence and inconvenience. Almost nobody forgot the great sweep of staircase by which all passengers save the effete or invalid, who took a primordial sort of elevator, ascended to the train level from the grottos of Market Street. *(Pennsylvania Railroad: L. R. Brittingham.)*

IN THE eighties and in addition to the railroad's own fleet of carriages for public hire, public omnibus lines also converged on the Pennsylvania's focal landmark.

ALTHOUGH IT WASN'T EVEN on the railroad's main line and served out its years as a stub terminal with sixteen tracks at the height of its fortunes, the Pennsylvania's Broad Street Station in downtown Philadelphia achieved a world celebrity comparable to far larger and more magnificent depots such as Charing Cross in London, the Gare du Nord in Paris, Boston's South Station or New York's Grand Central. Broad Street had character of a sooty and raffish order comparable to other contemporary Pennsylvania stations such as those at Pittsburgh and Fort Wayne. It was drafty, unkempt and, except for some of its fine marble handrails and bronze ornamental trim, made no pretentions at grandeur. Yet by 1886, five years after it was opened to operation, Broad Street handled a million passengers a month and throughout its annals was celebrated not only for its traffic in cars and people but as the citadel of one of the most firmly entrenched hierarchies of wealth, power and dynastic inheritance in the world. As the stronghold of the Pennsylvania Railroad's administrative bureaucracy, the ten-story Gothic-Mooresque office building that rose behind its vaulted train shed symbolized not only the railroad but the character of Philadelphia itself, aloof, disdainfully possessive, hereditary, conservative and faintly arrogant. It was the first thing millions saw on arriving at Philadelphia and the last they saw on departing and it made a lasting impression. It suggested that it had been built in the era of silk-hatted railroad presidents with gold-headed walking sticks who ate luncheons of six courses including terrapin at the Philadelphia Club. It had.

Broad Street was planned and begun in the embattled era of Tom Scott in the Pennsylvania President's office. It was opened to traffic in 1881 when patrician George Roberts was at the helm and not completed until 1894. Its years of greatest glory were, of course, those in which the magnifico of all railroaders, the great Alexander Cassatt controlled its desti-

nies. Of all the railroads in the United States, the only one whose annals can appropriately be chronicled in terms of its presidents as English history is by the reigns of its monarchs is the Pennsylvania, and Broad Street was their palace and shabby-genteel seat of power. The power itself, of course, had nothing either shabby or genteel about it.

The Pennsylvania's main line ran nearly two miles to the west of Broad Street and to achieve the baronial brick castle next door to Philadelphia's City Hall which was the heart of the railroad system, there was built a massive stone causeway a city block wide that was known as "The Chinese Wall." Cross streets penetrated this gloomy barrier through tunnels under its tracks where water seeped at all seasons and froze solid on the cobbles and car tracks in winter. Over "The Chinese Wall" shuttle trains connected the stub tracks at Broad Street with through mainline trains at West Philadelphia and over it, too, ran the celebrated Clockers to New York and the Paoli Locals that became part of Philadelphia folk-legend.

A disastrous conflagration destroyed the vaulted train shed at Broad Street in 1925 and makeshift platform shelters protected passengers embarking on its trains after that. In 1952 Broad Street in its entirety was torn down and the last train departed amidst tears as the Philadelphia Symphony Orchestra played "Auld Lang Syne" but the glory had departed at an earlier date, both from the Pennsylvania's passenger operations and from the city they served. Christopher Morley, one of the Philadelphia Main Line's most distinguished men of letters, had immortalized Broad Street when he said that after his death the words "Paoli Local" would be found graven on his heart. It was an epitaph that might also have been written for the Pennsylvania's once spacious affluence when its presidents were selected from the ranks of Rittenhouse Square aristocrats and acted the part to the hilt.

585

WHATEVER MYSTIQUE may have elevated the Pennsylvania Railroad to a position of fantastic wealth, political power and well-bred Philadelphian arrogance had its source in the Moorish structure at Broad Street Station where the railroad's headquarters were located. The depot proper was opened in 1881, but its ten story corner tower and offices were not completed until 1894 so that, although implemented in the regime of Tom Scott, it was in fact a memorial to George Roberts. Here were plotted the great campaigns of territorial aggrandizement that were to make the Pennsylvania a massive power in state and national politics and the border warfare with the New York Central which was the major preoccupation of the successive dynasties of Scott, Roberts and Cassatt. One of the truly great railroad stations of the world, not because of either its architecture or volume of traffic, but because it personified the character of the carrier itself, Broad Street is shown about 1913 as the embodiment of solid conservatism, dynastic succession and a sense of corporate destiny. (*Pennsylvania Railroad.*)

THE ARTIST'S tracing shown here of the great Broad Street depot and its complex of offices shows the train shed as it looked in its final redaction before being destroyed by fire. In the view below the buildings of the Centennial Exposition of 1876 show beyond the bridge over the Schuylkill River. Broad Street then was only in the drawing board stage. *(Two Drawings: Pennsylvania Railroad.)*

SOMETHING OF the pastoral quality that characterized the Pennsylvania's
Main Line, both in its parochial or Philadelphia sense and further afield
where it signified "The Main Line of Public Works" between the East and
Pittsburgh, is latent in this fine engraving executed for the railroad's promotion
department in 1875. The station at Altoona was an important stop for a
variety of reasons including the railroad's ever enlarging machine shops
and erecting works there and the Logan House shown just across the platform
from the tracks, was a depot hotel of more than regional celebrity.
Here in an age before diners became universal the cars paused for the
conventional twenty minute meal stop and here drummers solicited the patronage
of railroad purchasing agents for all the vast inventory of hardware
incidental to a great railroad system. At the Logan House, so legend maintains,
Andrew Carnegie, fresh from England, convinced Tom Scott that steel rails
were the coming thing and would soon replace iron on all progressive
roads both for rails and bridges, thus laying the foundation for an immense
fortune. It was the age of Saratoga trunks, Dundreary whiskers and
skirted frock coats for travel as depicted above and also attested by the
photographic evidence seen on the opposite page.
The Logan House lasted until well after the turn of the century as a landmark
of the Pennsy, although with the inclusion of dining cars in almost
all trains, its function as a meal stop had long since become a memory.

588

BROAD STREET was conceived and its construction inaugurated in the brass-knuckles era when Tom Scott *(left)* was carving out its primal destinies in a period of ceaseless warfare with unions, Pennsylvania politicians and the embattled competition. As a result its architecture suggested a baronial stronghold from which the railroad's partisans might sally forth to give battle to the enemy, which was exactly what it was. A magnificent system map of the railroad, executed in bas-relief by the ubiquitous American Bank Note Company, was located in the main waiting room of the depot in a time when black kid gloves, bowler hats and well furled umbrellas were requisites for young men going places on the cars.   *(Pennsylvania Railroad.)*

1. Eighteenth Street crossing.—2. Hansom cab system.—3. Fireplace in ladies' waiting room.—4. The station.—5 Baggage department.—6. Grand stairway.—7. Car house.—8. Main waiting room.

THE BROAD STREET PASSENGER STATION OF THE PENNSYLVANIA RAILROAD COMPANY AT PHILADELPHIA.

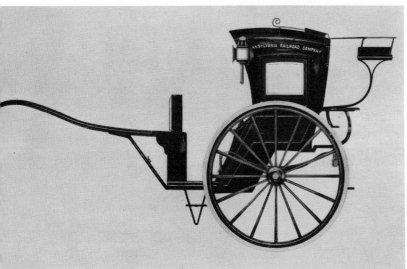

FROM the early eighties until shortly after the turn of the century when the auto-taxi made them obsolete, the Pennsylvania maintained a fleet of beautifully groomed horse cabs for its passengers and the company's officials, available at a favored cab rank and in competition with the somewhat less elegant public hackney coaches that roamed the Philadelphia streets. There were broughams, hansom carriages, as shown here, as well as victorias and even opera coaches, each painted in the company livery of maroon with a liveried driver on the box and the company name on the nameboards. No other carrier can be discovered at this remove affording such elegant service, the nearest being Parmelee Transfer in Chicago which served all the terminals in town. *(Pennsylvania Railroad.)*

IN THE YEAR 1883, two years after it had been opened for service, Broad Street Station was enough of a national institution to command the entire front page of *Scientific American.* The fact is significant because, while Philadelphians themselves considered Broad Street a parochial manifestation like Madeira at insurance company dinners, it was in actuality the front and facade Philadelphia showed to the outer world, a citadel of entrenched power and an abode of dynastic proprieties. In *Scientific American's* depiction of Broad Street Station in 1883 are many purely Gothic details of design which later and over the years became modified or disappeared altogether. Notable in this context are the grand stairway and main waiting room identified as panels No. 6 and 8, respectively, in the picture layout. Gothic, too, to a magnificent degree was the fireplace in the ladies' waiting room shown as panel 3 and the ornate baggage department in panel 5. The magazine's caption speaks of the train shed as "the car house" and specifically mentions hansom cab service to the exclusion of all other sorts of public conveyance. It is known from the company archives that the railroad's own cab ranks embraced a wide variety of other types of carriage.

Broad Street Was the Entrepot To Philadelphia's Innermost Being

IN 1895 and in what can only be described as an ill-advised if prophetic moment, management caused to be emplaced in the waiting room at Broad Street, a bas-relief by Karl Bittner entitled "The Progress of Transportation," as reproduced here. Along with symbolic likenesses of steam locomotives and ferry boats, the artist included his vision of a flying machine, an artifact which, in scarcely more than half a century, was to doom Broad Street itself and seriously menace the railroad business as a whole. When Broad Street was torn down and the ill-omened bas-relief reinstated at the main line depot at Thirtieth Street, its jinx was not felt to be abated. *(Three Photos: Pennsylvania Railroad.)*

THAT THE architects of Broad Street Station were obligated to allegory is explicit in the record of that Gothic pile. Its every vantage point bristled with classic figures representing, it may be presumed, carloadings, operating ratios and the on-time average of *The Broadway*. Details of the pediment shown on the opposite page depict the lion and the lamb in brownstone embrace, a scene whose symbolism was felt to open almost limitless vistas for its possible interpretation. Although the Market Street clock *(right)* was kept five minutes fast by the management, Clocker patrons traditionally arrived just as the guard slammed the train gates. It was a Philadelphia ritual.

NO SINGLE institution better typified Main Line Philadelphia than The Paoli Local whose train crew, in the days before the Main Line itself was electrified, are shown comparing watches. Leaving their reading glasses on The Paoli Local, according to Nathaniel Burt, to be reclaimed at the Broad Street lost and found was a hallmark of gentility in Merion, Ardmore and Haverford.

IT MAY BE DOUBTED that the personnel of Broad Street Depot felt themselves to be components and custodians of a *mystique* that was to become legendary in the annals of American travel, but the ticket taker at The Clocker gate, the brakeman taking down the markers from the arriving Paoli Local, and the train crew of The Paoli Local comparing watches, were all part of the essential personality that made Broad Street one of the great railroad terminals of the world with an individuality of its own. In the menacing grotto at the left, far beneath Market Street and dimly lit by naked bulbs, the baggage smashers of Broad Street posed for their portrait, too. The date was when the patent devisings of "innovation trunks" hadn't rendered their prudent cording for extra security obsolete. Anticipating by many years the proverbial genius of air lines for dispatching the bags of customers to the wrong continent, it may be pondered if George Baker's carefully identified possessions from Derbyshire, England, have yet arrived at their intended destination? *(Four Photos: Pennsylvania Railroad.)*

*Graven on Christopher Morley's
Heart Were the Words: "Paoli Local."*

FEW TRAINS with such humble antecedents have become part of the regional body of regional folklore on a scale comparable to The Paoli Local, Philadelphia's Main Line suburban run that originated at Broad Street and ended at Paoli at the far edge of socially acceptable real estate. "The Paoli Local has been a source of pride, convenience and affection," wrote Nathaniel Burt in "The Perennial Philadelphians," while Christopher Morley, himself a Main Line resident, followed in the footsteps of Mary Tudor of England when she said that after her death, because she had lost it to the French, the word "Calais" would be found written on her heart. Morley asserted that after his death "Paoli Local" would be found on his. In a community which cherishes the continuity of established institutions, The Paoli Local gained access, not only to letters, but to the heart of Philadelphia itself, like passing the Madeira clockwise at Insurance Dinners and keeping money in the Girard Corn Exchange Bank. On the page opposite a Paoli Local conductor assumes his responsibilities not only as a trainman, but as custodian of an article of faith. At the right is Christopher Morley, minstrel of the commuter legend. *(Opposite and Below: Pennsylvania Railroad.)*

BRYN MAWR depot, shown in this engaging view in the mid-seventies, was named for a neighboring estate of one of the Main Line landed gentry and was a byproduct of George Roberts' penchant for Welsh atmosphere wherever it could be introduced into the railroad's scheme of things. In the years of the Paoli Local, Bryn Mawr was celebrated as being the point of origin for more lady commuters to town with a genius for leaving their eyeglasses on the cars than any other mainline stop. They were retrieved from lost and found at Broad Street as a matter of course.

597

THE ORIGINAL TRAIN SHED at Broad Street, shown at the top of the page opposite, in 1882 had three arched train bays and was flanked by the offices of the Adams Express Company, then one of the several great competing express companies of the East and South although it had withdrawn from California in defeat at the hands of Wells Fargo & Co. In the lower photograph is the same scene in 1890, a date which suggests itself because the original multiple arches of 1881 had been replaced by a single huge unit but the ten-story Moorish-Gothic corner tower of the main office building, completed in 1894, is not yet visible in the background. Clearly in view, however, is the turretted campanile of City Hall topped by a heroic statue of William Penn. The historic landmark, as the train shed had by this time become, was destroyed by fire in 1925 and passengers thereafter boarded the cars under makeshift shelters until the entire structure was demolished in 1952. *(Opposite, Two Photos: Everett De Golyer Collection; Above: The Philadelphia Record.)*

ALTHOUGH NOT DISTINGUISHED by the variety of noble and imposing names which identified the Pennsylvania's fleet of varnish trains on longer runs, the Clockers between Philadelphia and New York, so called because they departed their respective terminals on the hour throughout the day and well into the evening, were at one time among the most celebrated of all the railroad's multiplicity of services. Almost without exception the Clockers carried coaches, Pullman parlor cars, a diner and a club lounge car with parlor seats and two or four tables served by a self contained grill at one end. In the days of steam motive power when a change to and from electric engines was necessary at Manhattan Transfer the run between Broad Street and Penn Station in New York took an hour and fifty minutes. When electrification was completed it was ninety minutes. Here in the twenties behind a capped stack Pacific, a Clocker awaits its highball at Broad Street before setting out along "The Chinese Wall" to join the main line at North Philadelphia. *(Pennsylvania Railroad.)*

600

REGULARLY ASSIGNED to the Clockers were the "Club" series parlor-buffet cars such as *Banker's Club* whose solarium compartment is shown above and *Union League Club (below)*. Admirers considered them among the handsomest lounge cars ever outshopped by Pullman and regulars aboard the run knew that the food from their miniature galleys, especially double English lamb chops, was remarkable. *(Two Photos: Pennsylvania Railroad.)*

Clocker leaving Broad
Street in electrified times
behind a GG1 type
motor. *(Everett De Golyer
Collection.)*

Clocker in Broad Street
Station waiting highball in
steam days behind a
K4s Pacific. *(Everett De
Golyer Collection.)*

TOM, DICK AND HARRY might and did ride aboard the crowded daycoaches of the Pennsy Clockers between Broad Street and Manhattan, "ninety miles in ninety minutes" as the company literature had it, but the clientele on the parlor cars was possessed of a social and professional *ton* comparable to that which rode the New Haven's extra fare trains out of Boston. Regular commuters found the hour and a half elapsed time between terminals useful for reading and took breakfast or tea aboard the early and late runs. Authors, editors and executives of Philadelphia publishing firms and names of distinction in science and the humanities perused learned periodicals in attitudes of fully attired decorum and there were no shirtsleeves allowed. The parlor compartment of *Engineers Club*, shown here, reflected the Clocker atmosphere of well-bred preoccupation with worldly matters of consequence.   (*Pennsylvania Railroad.*)

MANHATTAN TRANSFER, where the Pennsy trains changed from steam to electric power and patrons boarded the tube for downtown New York and Wall Street was so much an institution in the 1920s that it became the title of a novel by John Dos Passos, entering the national lexicon of belles lettres. Below, at about this time, a Clocker arrives at Manhattan Transfer to be taken over by steam for the ninety minute run over the ninety miles to Broad Street. The old time courtesy characteristic of railroads in a less urgent age radiates from the venerable company servant at the right, whose memories when this photograph was taken reached back to the days of the by now almost godlike Alexander Cassatt. *(Three Photos: Pennsylvania Railroad.)*

THE FOLKLORE of the Pennsy Clockers between Broad Street and mid-town Manhattan is a body of legend comparable to that of Broad Street itself where they originated. Excepting possibly the New Haven's *Knickerbocker* and *Yankee Clipper* no trains in the record afforded such a density of names associated with journalism, belles lettres, advertising and communications generally. Christopher Morley, although his immortality in the Pennsylvania Railroad saga is associated with the Paoli Local, was a regular commuter to Manhattan for many years when he was columnist, successively for *The New York Post* and *The Saturday Review of Literature*. Stanley Walker, the most celebrated city editor of his time, tried it briefly but found the daily strain too much. Ted Patrick, editor of *Holiday*, maintained offices in both New York and Philadelphia and read his manuscripts between them. Because of Philadelphia's handy location many Broadway triumphs tried out there and the presence on the Clockers of such luminaries as Sir Laurence Olivier, Noel Coward, Cole Porter, Moss Hart or Alfred Lunt raised no eyebrows. One of the authors of this book, assigned in the thirties to a Broadway beat, frequently interviewed notables between Manhattan Transfer and North Philadelphia, taking another Clocker back to his office with a minimum of inconvenience. Under such circumstances and with the aid of highballs on *The Poor Richard Club* Lillian Hellman, John C. Wilson and George M. Cohan told him a prudent all for the Sunday editions. The midnight departure from Broad Street after an important opening was awash with mink and tailcoats. In the John Held Jr. short-skirted twenties, a Pennsy press agent undertook to suggest the emancipated atmosphere of the Clockers and tolerant attitude of the carrier generally by setting aside a special ladies' smoking room and the above publicity photo was the result. *(Pennsylvania Railroad.)*

EXPERIENCED COMMUTERS, boarding the seven or eight o'clock Clocker at Broad Street knew that if they could get a seat in the dining space of the *Poor Richard* or *Engineer's Club,* their breakfast eggs would be cooked to order and not from the steam table which was their origin on the formal diner in the middle of the train. Even in the years of the 1941 war, everything was better on the Clocker clubcars than elsewhere in the train. Since the year 1876, when the drawing at the right was made, Pennsylvania passengers crossing the Delaware River at Trenton, especially if it were winter, made mental note that they were following (approximately) in George Washington's footsteps. *(Everett De Golyer Collection.)*

606

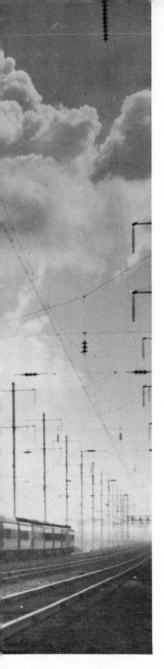

PENNSYLVANIA ticket clerks *(top)* crouched in the fastness of their grotto at Broad Street in attitudes of menace, as one critic remarked, daring anyone to attempt to negotiate a purchase. Making up the Clockers *(below)* at Broad Street was a casual chore with the better part of an hour at the disposal of switching crews and, in clement weather, as suggested here, could be a relaxed operation. *(Two Photos: Pennsylvania Railroad.)*

608

THERE HAD originally been sixteen stub tracks in the great vaulted train shed at Broad Street but one of them disappeared during the fire of the twenties. Throughout the latter years of Broad Street's life the New York Clockers for the most part left on Track 15 as is suggested opposite. Guards over the years became more or less accustomed to the ingrained habit of Clocker regulars of arriving with an irreducible margin of safety before traintime and getting through the half-closed gate by the skin of their teeth. The habit was probably entrenched in the comforting assurance that another Clocker would be along in sixty minutes and that there was a multiplicity of bars handy where one could spend the interval. Here a GG1 electric motor heads up a Clocker against the symbolic background of Philadelphia's City Hall with William Penn at its apex. The main stairway leading to the train level was much admired for its handsome marble trim and brass handrails, almost the only surviving traces of the era of George Roberts when they were conceived. *(Three Photos: L. B. Brittingham.)*

DURING THE BRIEF interregnum when the Pennsylvania's competition to the newly inaugurated *Twentieth Century Limited* was known as *The Twenty Hour Special* before it became, to everyone's confusion, *The Pennsylvania Special*, it was a train of enormous style as is suggested above and its consist, represented by the rich and massive buffet interior at the right, included the finest equipment its owning carrier could procure from Pullman. Not even *The Pennsylvania Limited* which was its contemporary in confused identity, was accorded more lavish favors in the way of luxury devisings and specially selected personnel. By the time *The Twenty Hour Special* appeared on the time cards, the Logan House, depicted twenty-five years earlier on the page opposite, was in decline as one of the notable railroad hotels of the continent. Its times of teem had been in the seventies and eighties before the universality of diners when it was celebrated as a meal stop on the Pittsburgh run as well as a legendary resort of drummers in the heyday of the traveling salesman. Here the knights of the sample case assembled in garments of voluptuous pattern and curly brimmed derby hats to exchange mendacities and cigars at the Logan Bar and buy uncounted smashes, slings and crustas for the proprietors of country stores who were their patrons. On its ample expanse of porch, as suggested here, they indulged the great American preoccupation of their time, watching the arrival and departure of the steamcars. (*Above: Everett De Golyer Collection; Opposite: Pennsylvania Railroad, Pullman Standard.*)

611

UNTIL THE YEAR 1902 the twenty-eight hour schedule of the *Pennsylvania Limited* and its opposite number the New York Central's *Lake Shore Limited* between New York and Chicago were considered adequate to the needs of the age. But in 1902 what the press was pleased to call "the great speed war" broke out between the two carriers when the Central inaugurated its epochal *Twentieth Century Limited* on a twenty hour schedule and the Pennsylvania, at the identical day and hour, countered with its equally fine and fast *Pennsylvania Special*. A great deal of confusion resulted from the similarity of names between the *Pennsylvania Special* and the long established *Limited,* but three years later *The Special* again made headlines when its schedule was reduced to eighteen hours and it was advertised as "The Fastest Long Distance Train in the World." As *The Pennsylvania Special* Trains 28 and 29 were operated until November 1912 when the confusion was resolved and the run renamed *The Broad Way Limited.* At the time of its emergence as an eighteen hour flyer *The Pennsylvania Special* was photographed arriving at Chicago with the four extra-fancy Pullman varnish cars specially assigned this favored run and the facing print was made from the original glass plate negative in the possession of The Chicago Historical Society. The eighteen hour train laid hold upon public imagination and immediately became the symbol of the fastest human travel in an age crazed with speed. Sheet music was composed in its honor and it is notable that Bandmaster Innes' two-step march was dedicated to the railroad's passenger agent, Samuel Moody, whose name appears in the company literature. *(Pennsylvania Railroad.)*

MOST ADVERTISED FEATURE of *The Pennsylvania Special* when it went into service on its eighteen hour schedule July 9, 1905 was the time it saved in transit and its extra fare was based on this advantage. But its equipment, if perhaps less ostentatious than that of *The Limited* of 1898, was the most sumptuous available as is suggested by these builder's interiors of the observation lounge. The chronologic chart *(below)* was part of the train literature given each passenger. *(Three Photos: Pennsylvania Railroad.)*

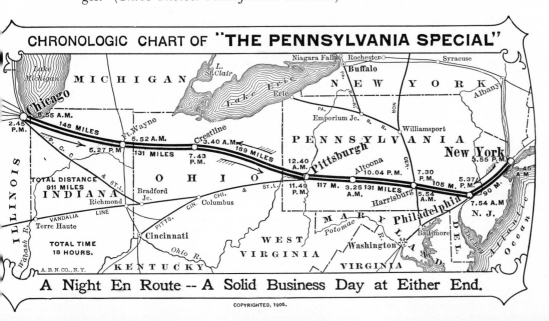

CHRONOLOGIC CHART OF "THE PENNSYLVANIA SPECIAL"

A Night En Route -- A Solid Business Day at Either End.

COPYRIGHTED, 1905.

ALTHOUGH IT LACKED the rival New York Central's transcendent genius of publicity and promotion, George Henry Daniels, the Pennsylvania in the years of the fiercest rivalry between *The Broadway Limited* and *The Twentieth Century Limited* did very well indeed in celebrating the train that was its most effulgent showpiece. To honor *The Pennsylvania Special*, which was soon to emerge as *The Broadway*, sheet music was composed, Sunday editors were induced to run formidable feature spreads, airplanes raced its progress across New Jersey (to lose of course). The delightful line drawings reproduced here together with the dust jacket are from company pamphlets of 1905. (*Pennsylvania Railroad.*)

PENNSYLVANIA
RAILROAD
THE
PENNSYLVANIA
SPECIAL

18 HOURS
BETWEEN
NEW YORK
AND
CHICAGO
ONLY A NIGHT EN ROUTE

THE FASTEST LONG DISTANCE
TRAIN IN THE WORLD·

W. W. ATTERBURY . . General Manager
J. R. WOOD . . Passenger Traffic Manager
GEO. W. BOYD . . General Passenger Agent

IN EFFECT JULY 9 TH, 1905

AMERICAN BANK NOTE CO., NEW YORK

"The Pennsylvania Special"

PIONEER 18-HOUR TRAIN

BETWEEN

Chicago = Miles 912 Miles = New York

SPEAKING GENERALLY, the original luxury equipment of *The Pennsylvania Special* when it was inaugurated in June 1902 was somewhat more elaborate in its decor and appointments than that of *The Century* which was hastily recruited from available car pools, some of it Wagner and some Pullman. Throughout its lifetime as a de luxe run *The Century* was to be more austere than its competition, even though after its first explosions of magnificence in the form of bevel edge mirrors and ball fringe curtains, *The Special* became more restrained as is suggested below. Here Pintsch illumination has been supplemented by Mazda bulbs, inlaid marquetry work by severe mahogany. The poster at the left includes in its economy the same photograph of *The Special's* stunning consist that is reproduced more faithfully on an adjacent page. *(Two Photos: Pennsylvania Railroad.)*

"CAB?" "KEB?" "COUPÉ?"

CHICAGO WAS ONLY a decade removed from The Great Fire and Mrs. O'Leary's legendary cow when the Union Station, shown opposite, was opened for occupancy in 1881. A stunning example of railroad architecture of its period with Mansard roof, Gothic windows and ornate wrought ironwork around its portes cochères and other entrances, it expressed the irrepressible optimism of the city that was even then becoming the railroad metropolis of the nation. Under its train shed arrived and departed the varnish runs of Pennsylvania, Alton, Burlington and Milwaukee as well as the Parmelee Transfer omnibuses shown ranked in their elaborately painted splendor in the photograph. The station was bounded by Canal and Adams Streets with a train shed 1,000 feet long and comprised, according to a contemporary account of "a handsome series of red brick pavilions with the larger one in the center." Telephone and telegraph wires traversed the streets in an age innocent of underground cables and gas lamps, of course, supplied illumination. It was beyond all compare a period piece. The new Union Station *(above)* which rose on the site of the old incorporated much of the Roman splendor of Caracalla that characterized Penn Station in New York and afforded stately vistas under lofty columns. The architects were Graham, Burham & Company and the engineer was William Braeger. *(Two Photos: Pennsylvania Railroad.)*

AS DETAILED and true to character as any Rembrandt portrait of a Flemish nobleman is this revealing camera study from the company files of a Pennsylvania engineer in the characteristic pose of his professional calling. The gantleted gloves, the stiff-billed cap, long snouted oil can and occupational watch chain are the hallmarks of the working stiff on the right hand cushions, while the narrowed eyes are adjusted to seeing far down the tangents of space and time in the face of the winds of hurry. On the opposite page the look and texture of Chicago's old Union Station are caught in two photographs from the recording camera of Alfred W. Johnson, venerable dean of railroad iconographers in the Chicago area. Above is a panoramic view of the great train shed with a Pennsy mainliner waiting its highball beside a Burlington suburban train. Below, *The Pennsylvania Limited* as of 1919 is ready to be off and running on the fast track to Fort Wayne behind two businesslike Pacifics.

621

DOUBLE HEADED with two K-4s Pacifics in tandem, the Pennsy's *New Yorker* emerges on a cold winter's day from the primordial catacombs of Union Station in Chicago with steam exhaust condensing for a magnificent urban portrait of double shotted steam power in varnish service. *(John Barriger Collection.)*

622

MANY of the phone numbers listed for the convenience of interested patrons on the Union Station blackboard which, in the 1920s, advertised the weekend excursion rates of the various carriers are the same as those assigned Chicago railroad offices forty years later. Below: business is only fair at the Union Depot arrival information desk where, in the early 1930s, the *Manhattan Limited* is announced as on time and later arrivals, *The Rainbow* and *The Union* are yet to be heard from. (*Left: John Barriger; Below: Pennsylvania Railroad.*)

Velvet Success Rode the Staterooms of _The Broadway_

IN ITS Pullman Standard years of prestige and splendid implications, when its motive power was one or more of the Pennsylvania's classic K-4s Pacifics and its Pullman-only consist wore the Tuscan red and gold of its owning carrier, _The Broadway Limited_ was a wonder and a glory of the railroad world.
The peer in every aspect of equipment, services, cuisine and operational technique of the direct competition in the form of the New York Central's _Twentieth Century Limited,_ it glittered from locomotive pilot beam to the brass-railed platform of its observation lounge as the showcase for its owner's wares, a paradigm of elegance and superb promotion.
Just as _The Century_ was an essentially Chicago train in the character of its patronage, so _The Broadway_ was the quintessence of Old Philadelphia and the grandeurs of the Main Line inherited from the era of Alexander Cassatt, a magnifico in whose presidency of the carrier it had been inaugurated.
Its style was that of Rittenhouse Square.

624

Aboard it on their upholstered occasions in Chicago, rode Morrises, Biddles, Reeves and Cadwaladers, Penroses and Lippincotts, and it was no error in judgment on the part of the management that there was scrapple on the breakfast menu and Chesapeake Bay oysters at dinner. If there was a smell of money about *The Broadway* it was very old money, dating back to the times of Stephen Girard and Nicholas Biddle's Bank of the United States. Passengers who boarded it in Philadelphia or Paoli carried about them the suggestion that they came directly from the Rittenhouse Club, much as those on the New Haven's *Merchants Limited* suggested arrival from the banking office of Kuhn Loeb & Co., via the bar at the Belmont Hotel. Here *The Broadway* poses briefly on a summer afternoon at Englewood south of Chicago for suburban passengers. Specially assigned K-4s Pacifics bore the train's name on their smokebox and its conductors were aristocrats. *(A. W. Johnson; Pennsylvania Railroad.)*

DRAMATIC CLIMAX of the working day at Chicago's Union Station was the afternoon sailing of *The Broadway Limited*, especially if it departed as shown here, in two or more sections. The train's partisans felt that it was the perfect expression of the *belle epoque* of surface travel and that its train services *(below)* embraced all the amenities a gentleman might require. *(Two Photos: Pennsylvania Railroad.)*

BROADWAY LIMITED

EASTWARD

Lv. CHICAGO......12.40 pm Central Time
Lv. ENGLEWOOD .12.56 pm Central Time
Ar. NEW YORK.... 9.40 am Eastern Time

WESTWARD

Lv. NEW YORK ... 2.45 pm Eastern Time
Ar. ENGLEWOOD. 9.22 am Central Time
Ar. CHICAGO...... 9.45 am Central Time

Solid train of all-steel vestibuled and electric-lighted Club Car, Drawing Room, Sleeping and Compartment-Observation Cars from Chicago through Pittsburgh to Pennsylvania Station— Only One Block from Broadway, New York City.

Also Sleeping Car arriving Washington 10.25 am, returning leaving Washington 3.10 pm.

Meals in Restaurant Car en route: Eastward—Luncheon and Dinner (a la carte) and Breakfast (a la carte). Westward—Dinner (a la carte) and Breakfast (a la carte).

ALL PASSENGERS have the freedom of the entire train. The following special features are at their command:

IN THE CLUB CAR
Shower Bath (hot and cold). Barber Shop. Writing Desk and Stationery. Magazines.

IN THE OBSERVATION CAR
Stenographer (letters and telegrams taken from dictation without charge and transmitted).
Library of Books and Magazines.
Writing Desk and Stationery.
Maid for ladies and children. Manicuring.
Valet will sponge and press gentlemen's garments over night for nominal charge.
Electric Lamps in all berths, convenient for reading after retiring.
Telephone connection in Observation Car while train is standing in Chicago Union Station and Pennsylvania Station, New York. (Calls within city free.)
Passengers may have Pullman reservations made for their return trip by applying to the Stenographer.
Passengers expecting letters or telegrams should notify the Sleeping Car Conductor.

CHARGES

Tonsorial Service

Hair Cut.......$0.50		Hair Singe.....$0.25	
Shampoo....... .50		Trimming Beard .25	
Facial Massage .50		Baths........... .75	
Shave.......... .25		Manicure....... .75	

Pressing of Clothes

Entire Suit.....$1.25   Overcoat......$1.00
Coat...$0.75   Vest...$0.25   Trousers...$0.25

THERE WERE true believers to whom *The Broadway* behind a K-4s Pacific on the carrier's New Jersey speedway in Pullman Standard and Tuscan red was the noblest handiwork of God. In 1916, however, when it was photographed on a beautifully manicured main line by Charles B. Chaney it still was to sport the characteristic keystone emblem that would, in the 1920s, identify it as a train of pedigree. *(Rail Photo Service; The Smithsonian Institution.)*

PICK OF the railroad's available personnel were regularly assigned to *The Broadway* whether they were members of the engine crew such as that shown above who changed en route or part of the train's company including waiters, porters and the train secretary. At the left the latter functionary takes dictation from a mogul of the world of finance impatient for his before-dinner Martinis. Opposite: all-Pullman and extra-fare though it was in 1919 when it is shown arriving at the old Union Station at Chicago in two atmospheric poses by Alfred W. Johnson, it didn't always end with the observation platform of certifiable elegance that later became mandatory in its consist. (*Left and Above: Pennsylvania Railroad.*)

SERVICING the club car of *The Broadway Limited* in the Chicago yards via a trap in the roof in the year 1945 differed little in its essentials from the same operation three quarters of a century earlier when, in 1870, a staff artist from *Leslie's Weekly* depicted the servicing of one of the primordial Pullmans of the Union Pacific. (*Pennsylvania Railroad.*)

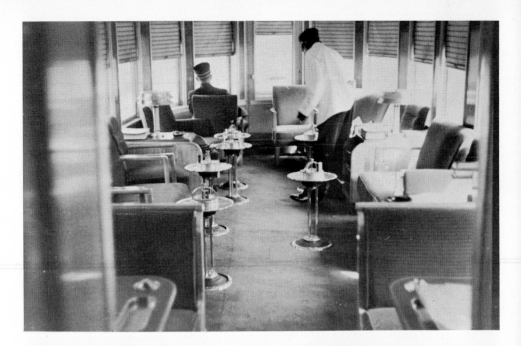

THE FINAL HOURS of *The Broadway's* run into its Chicago terminal find the scene of last evening's fraternal gathering over the Martinis deserted. In the observation end of the club car its only occupants are the rear brakeman working his train and the car attendant cleaning up. The center of population has shifted to the diner where Colonel Robert McCormick's opinionated *Chicago Tribune* is to be found at every place setting between the three minute eggs and the coffee. And finally, with the train berthed in its slip at Union Station and its passengers gone their several ways, the old time observation platform of *The Broadway* in Pullman Standard times is forlorn and abandoned until the switcher comes to take it away to the yards. *(Three Photos: John Barriger.)*

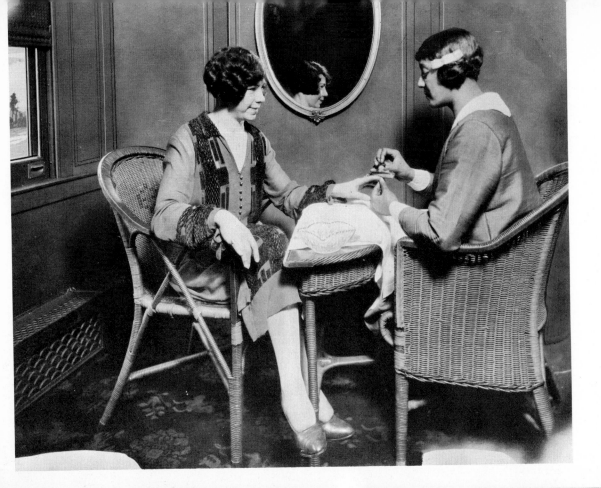

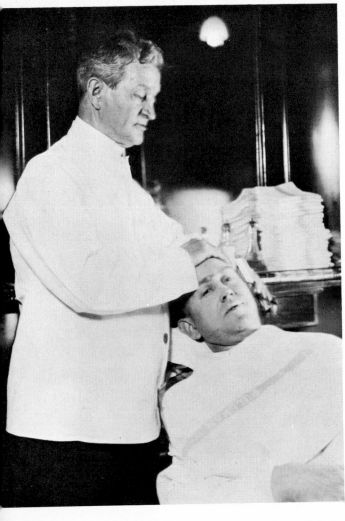

THE TRAIN BARBER on *The Broadway*, shown opposite at his professional stand, could if he wished trace his pedigree back to the ornate cars of *The Pennsylvania Limited* where, in 1898 when a singe and beard trim were in vogue, he was already an established member of the train's company. The services of a lady's maid and manicurist were also standard on the Pennsy's flagship as they were on consequential trains everywhere in the golden years of Pullman travel.

The sailing of *The Broadway* from Union Station in Chicago *(below)* while lacking the rich splendors of *The Century's* departure from Grand Central, was very much the event of the railroad day on the shores of Lake Michigan. Its tailgate insigne, visible through the grille, assured the ticket holder of a fast and very de luxe passage aboard one of the venerated name trains of the world. *(Four Photos: Pennsylvania Railroad.)*

DEPARTURE OF *The Broadway* from Chicago's Union Station, while lacking the éclat of the sailing of the rival *Century* from New York with its panache of style and red carpet elegance, was still a major event in the railroad day as is suggested by the traingate photograph at the right and the authoritative pose of the conductor as he gives the head-end its highball. Sailing of No. 28 from Chicago was protected by "Drawbridge Rule" which provided for a flexible schedule of departure if drawbridges across the Chicago River delayed access to the West Side of town. *(Three Photos: Pennsylvania Railroad.)*

AS LONG as the passenger business continued to be a major consideration in the operation of its enormous and powerful system of transport, the Pennsylvania was aware of the relentless competition of the New York Central and of the hot breath of the heirs of Commodore Vanderbilt, breathing quite literally on the back of its neck.

Every major metropolis to which its varnish ran, New York, Chicago, St. Louis, Cincinnati, Toledo, Louisville, Detroit, only excepting Baltimore, Philadelphia and Washington was accessible also to the opposition. Even Pittsburgh, a citadel of Pennsylvania power and authority, was at one time achieved by through sleepers over the Central from New York and Boston. Reversing this affront, the Pennsylvania, in the form of *The Buffalonian*, penetrated into the very heart of the Central domain in upper New York state.

When through cars came for the Pacific coast and via St. Louis to the Southwest, they ran in competing trains of the two giants of Eastern transportation. Never was the pressure relaxed, the tension abated. Most dramatic symbols of the rivalry that was once a legend of the railroad world were the line's two crack trains, *The Broadway* and *The Twentieth Century Limited,* shown here leaving Englewood on parallel tracks and identical schedules. The year was 1925 and there was no talk of mergers abroad in the land.
(Everett De Golyer Collection.)

635

IN THE YEARS before the antiseptic sterility of *moderne* decor, when railroad patrons expected from the carriers a more luxurious scheme of things than that represented by fluorescent lighting and the decorative warmth of an operating room, Pullman built for *The Broadway* such beautifully paneled mahogany diners as that shown opposite and rich fabrics were used in the upholstery. Stewards wore dinner jackets in the evening and striped morning trousers at breakfast and lunch and waiters on *The Broadway* wore distinctive tan mess jackets and wing collars. Dinner on the cars was an event and even the servicing of diners in the yards was not devoid of a certain degree of ceremony. *(Three Photos: Pennsylvania Railroad.)*

636

THICK AS autumn leaves on Vallombrosa stars of the theatrical and cinema worlds gathered aboard the lounge cars and diners of *The Broadway* in its spacious years, en route to luncheon with Ernie Byfield at The Pump Room before boarding *The Super Chief* for the ateliers of Hollywood.

On the opposite page in his years as one of the kingpins of the film world, Charlie Chaplin poses for a radiant portrait of fame still uncontaminated in a congenial setting of mobile opulence. Here *The Broadway* takes fuel on the fly at track pans just west of Paoli. At Chicago's Union Station in the apex days of railroad travel twenty-four information clerks answered 3,600 questions every day, 100,000 pouches of mail were cleared and patrons of the Harvey and other depot restaurants consumed 700 pies every twenty-four hours. *(Two Photos: Pennsylvania Railroad.)*

638

THE HANDSOME YOUTH and the pretty lady shown opposite, when they ordered *The Broadway* Dinner in 1925 paid no more than $1.75 for prime ribs with all the trimmings or perhaps a spendthrift $2.50 for Kansas City sirloin for two. In a time when the best food in America was being served on its dining cars, the carriers expected to lose money on meals and counted it money well spent. The rival *Twentieth Century Limited* expected to lose a dollar for every fifty cents it took in and *The Broadway* could hardly do less. At the top here, veteran steward C. F. Schmidt passes the Corona Corona puros, priced sixty cents and for the carriage trade only. Unlike the practice on *The Century* where no business car was ever carried until the regime of Al Perlman, *The Broadway* in 1921 if it were running in two sections might sometimes haul the varnish of high ranking brass in the second train. (*Top and Opposite: Pennsylvania Railroad; Below: Alfred W. Johnson.*)

AS FAR BACK as March 8, 1934 *The London Daily Mail* quoted the fast carding of *The Broadway Limited* in unfavorable comparison with accepted English service of the time which it claimed was lamentably slow. This was five years before the streamlined all-room, all-Pullman *Broadway* was inaugurated to give travel a dimension of luxury that would have startled Britons even more than its speed. It is shown below on its inaugural run for the press before entering service and without the buffet combine which shortly appeared in its consist in a photograph taken at Princeton by the senior author of this book.

"The Flying Scotsman" just under 7 hours from London faster than at present

In France "...
an av...

...ially high aver-
the "Côte d'Azur Pull-
Paris and Lyons, nearly 320

PERHAPS the most brilliant running in the world at present is made on the Pennsylvania Railroad.

"The Broadway Limited" is booked to run from Englewood to Fort Wayne, 141 miles, in 132 minutes. This schedule includes a very slow section at the start, so that to maintain the high inclusive speed of 64 miles an hour, the 116½ miles from Liverpool to Wayne Junction must be run in 101 minutes—an average speed of 69 miles an hour.

OVER THE YEARS and the decades the observation end of the *Broadway* and its antecedent *Pennsylvania Special* assumed many guises. For the first three decades of its life it ran with the brass railed open verandah which set the train of pedigree apart and indicated the regard in which it was held by the management. The keystone tailgate insigne was introduced in the 1920s, first as a ponderous illuminated steel herald affixed to the railing and plugged into the train electric line and finally as shown here built into the structural economy of the solarium end itself. The four track motif appeared with streamlining. *(Pennsylvania Railroad.)*

643

LACKING THE RED CARPET treatment which its owners accorde
The Century at its sailings from Grand Central in New York an
the later carnival departures from La Salle Depot in Chicago wher
floodlights, news photographers and interviews with celebriti
over loudspeakers were for a time a daily practice, the departures o
The Broadway from Union Depot, Chicago, were somewhat le
than gala. The Pennsylvania, however, making a virtue o
necessity, stressed the dignified and businesslike setting from whic
its crack train and showpiece departed and suggested, b
inference, that *The Century* was ostentatious and vulga
For many years in the field of prestige the two trains ran neck an
neck until the great and shameful downgrading of *The Centur*
when daycoaches were for the first time included in its consist in 195
After that, *The Broadway*, by default if nothing else, diverte
most of the carriage trade to its Tuscan red, still all-Pullman car
(*Pennsylvania Railroad*

644

IN 1938 the Pennsy's K-4s Pacific No. 3768, in a moment of exploratory whimsy and enthusiasm for the then universal vogue of streamlining, was given an "aerodynamic" cowl and briefly assigned to *The Broadway Limited.* The innovation lasted long enough to make the photographic record, but maintenance crews found it impossible to cope with and it went, unmourned, into oblivion. *(Left: Ivan Dimitri; Below: Pennsylvania Railroad.)*

THE SUSTAINED and bitter rivalry for supremacy on the New York-Chicago luxury run which had its beginnings when *The Twentieth Century Limited* and the first version of *The Broadway* inaugurated service on the same day and on identical schedules in June 1902 was a neck-and-neck race for fifty-five years until 1957 when the New York Central threw in the sponge and admitted defeat by carrying day coaches in what had always until then been an all-Pullman train. Largely the competition for prestige and patronage was confined to operational aspects and the amenities of luxury available to patrons, but in 1933 Ben Hecht and Charlie MacArthur wrote and George Abbott produced a sensational Broadway comedy called "Twentieth Century." Even in the depth of the depression the zany doings of Moffat Johnson, Eugenie Leontovich and Bill Frawley amongst the drawing rooms and public apartments of No. 26 eastbound were an instant hit and the play went on to become an equally successful Hollywood film. Maddened with jealousy of this more or less extra-curricular promotional coup, the Pennsylvania management negotiated with Hal Roach for participation in a screen comedy with the title "Broadway Limited." It was not a shattering success either as box office or promotion for the railroad. Shown below is Marjorie Woodworth in the starring role. Across the page, *The Broadway*, impervious to drama critics, rolls toward Manhattan near Princeton, New Jersey behind a classic GG1 electric motor in the Pullman Standard era. *(Right: Everett De Golyer Collection; Below: United Artists.)*

646

WHILE THE LOOPING catenaries and their furniture form a pleasing geometry of juice overhead, a streamlined, all-room car *Broadway Limited* heads into the last lap of its eastbound run over the Pennsylvania's main line at Monmouth Junction, New Jersey, reportedly at the period when this picture was taken, the busiest focus of railroad traffic in the world. Arriving on an earlier *Broadway* in Pullman Standard times, a genial notable was dapper and handsome Grover Whalen, official Major-Domo of New York City and greeter of celebrities in the reign of Mayor James J. Walker, shown here with morning trousers correctly hung and mustaches waxed despite the early hour. *(Left: Everett De Golyer Collection; Above: Pennsylvania Railroad.)*

649

HALF A MILLION PEOPLE every day passed through the Pennsylvania Station in New York's Seventh Avenue, making it the busiest railroad terminal in the United States, and during the record year of 1945 when all the world was on the move a staggering 109,000,000 passengers were carried in and out of the station via its two tunnels under the North River and four under the East River to Long Island. Opened to service in 1910, Penn Station was designed by the great architectural firm of McKin, Mead & White as a *coup de maître* "its interior reflorescent of the Baths of Caracalla." Penn Station as well as providing a terminal for the Long Island Rail Road and a connection for the Pennsylvania and New Haven, sheltered a multiplicity of conveniences unknown to Caracalla, the fine Savarin Restaurant, luxury shops where everything imaginable might be purchased from an opera hat to rare first editions, communications centers of all sorts and a fully staffed emergency hospital. The graceful tracery of its glass domed concourse reminded travelers of London's Crystal Palace. So vast were the distances under its roof that Penn Station provided its own messengers to run errands and retrieve forgotten parcels as a sort of intra-mural Western Union. *(Two Photos: Pennsylvania Railroad.)*

A. J. CASSATT, patrician parent of Pennsylvania Station, was the end product of a long line of Philadelphia grandees who had guided the destinies of the carrier. His spectacular affront to the Vanderbilts, alas, was fated only by a few decades to outlast the fortunes of the Vanderbilt family itself.

AN ABODE of Caracallan vistas, Penn Station abruptly reverted to the twentieth century in its newsstands where, in 1910, no fewer than eighteen competing New York newspapers were sold, as well as *Leslie's, Judge, Everybody's* and many another periodical now remembered only by historians of journalism.

THE BUILDING of Penn Station in New York represented the determination of its aristocratic, horse racing, magnifico President Alexander J. Cassatt (*opposite*) to carry the railroad's brass knuckles warfare with the New York Central into the hereditary and hitherto sacrosanct domain of the Vanderbilts. As such, it had perforce to be conceived on a scale of grandeur and spaciousness comparable to the new Grand Central Terminal which was even then building on the other side of Manhattan Island. Pennsylvania Station had the moral effect of a mortal affront to the competition and the economic impact of diverting the riches of the West into the Port of New York, thereby reducing Philadelphia to the status of a secondary seaport and a third rate entrepot of continental commerce. "But the opening of the Penn Station in 1910 was still a glory for Philadelphia," wrote historian Nathaniel Burt, "a Trojan Horse right there on the island, a massive insult to the Vanderbilts." Until it was torn down in 1965 in the most barbarous act of vandalism in New York's long record of civic atrocities, Penn Station remained one of the glories of Manhattan, a landmark which gathered to itself its own body of legend and folklore as the prototype of the railroad station as the true cathedral of the American religion of movement. The Emperor Caracalla, after whose baths it was patterned, would have approved of it. (*Pennsylvania Railroad.*)

653

IN AN AGE innocent of loudspeakers and public address systems, approximately half the 850 trains that operated daily through the Pennsylvania Station were arrivals whose docking on their appropriate tracks was proclaimed by Stentor in company livery through a megaphone. The art of train calling was shortly to be relegated to the realm of folklore, one with the link and pin coupling and hand-fired locomotives, but it was an expertise much admired in its time and connoisseurs of train calling held strong opinions about the championship of the profession. Writing a good cursive hand was also a requirement as the bulletin board will suggest. On the page opposite, Penn Station when seen from above and illuminated for the night resembled a fairy palace. In the pre-electronic age, the sale and issuance of railroad tickets, like that of train calling, was contrived through human agency by expert functionaries arrayed in alpaca jackets crouching in grottos walled with racked tickets and rate books. Telephones were upright models and *The Official Guide* in the foreground was of a nobler dimension than it was to assume in the melancholy but unforeseen future. *(Three Photos: Pennsylvania Railroad.)*

THE ENORMOUS VISTAS and majestic dimension of Penn Station as it emerged from the drawing boards of McKim, Mead & White had a fantastic impact on the imagination of travelers and even of blasé New Yorkers. It amply endorsed the Pennsylvania's claim to being "The Standard Railroad of The World." If the world of railroading was fascinated by the invasion it represented with direct access to New England and Long Island by a hitherto remote and perhaps parochial carrier, New Yorkers followed the construction of the station's seven and a half acres of structural steel and stone as it had never before followed an architectural project. No hint of the impending assault upon the Vanderbilt citadel was contained in the news in March 1900 of an increase in the Pennsylvania Railroad's capitalization by $100,000,000.00. The plan to tunnel under two rivers, acquire the Long Island and build the most majestic depot on the continent was only unveiled after sufficient real estate between Seventh and Eighth Avenue had been purchased, wiping out, incidentally, the very heart of New York's ancient Tenderloin of vice. *(Pennsylvania Railroad.)*

BUILT AT A TIME when the automobile was obviously here to stay, Penn Station was enormously more accessible to motor traffic than Grand Central whose sole covered approach for departing patrons was through the narrow defile of Vanderbilt Avenue although an obscure grotto of the existence of which many New Yorkers never learned, was intended to accommodate arriving traffic under the Biltmore Hotel. Penn Station's distances were, however, seemingly greater and its several levels were eventually made available by escalators instead of the gentle ramps of Grand Central. Steep stairs from train gates such as that shown at the top of the page achieved all tracks in Penn Station and distances were so vast and problems of personal logistics so complex that a vast intercommunication system was maintained including a private uniformed messenger service. (*Two Photos: Pennsylvania Railroad.*)

IN ITS PASTORAL YEARS, before Long Island became
one of New York City's ever multiplying bedrooms,
its long beaches and wind-blown dunes were an extension
of the South Shore of Cape Cod and its personality
was predominantly that of New England.
The trains of the Long Island Rail Road, although many
of their operations were within sight of the skyscrapers of
Manhattan on a clear day, were country trains and
their concerns were with country things:
garden truck from Mineola where now the inhabitants
of a thousand apartment developments purchase
their cabbages from a hundred market plazas, oysters from
Blue Point and Great Peconic Bay that rode to town
leaking brine from home-coopered casks, and only
secondarily in heavy carloadings of any sort. Sea and sky
met behind the tangents of the railroad that ran
through places with seafaring names: Bellport, Brookhaven,
Port Jefferson and Amagansett.
The advancing trains, like the sea and sky, merged
as in the photograph by O. Winston Link reproduced here.
Until well after the century's turn the Long Island's
station at West Islip was served by a single track pre-
cariously ballasted in sand, and, at the far end of the
platform, there was an icehouse, as there was
at every Long Island loading platform, to service the fresh
seafood that rode toward Fulton Market night and day.
(Two Photos: Everett De Golyer Collection.)

The Long Island Was A Legend of Hard Luck and Locust Years

ONE DOES NOT instinctively think of the Long Island Rail Road, sometimes unwanted poor relation of the Pennsylvania and at length wholly rejected of its parent carrier, as the setting for great name trains associated with even the comparatively short-haul New Haven just the other side of Long Island Sound. The Long Island's longer of its two main lines between New York City and Montauk is a scant 117 miles, while its secondary main line to Greenport is but ninety-six. Its Port Jefferson run, the longest of its minor branches, is sixty miles in extent. Yet in the twenties, when the carrier's affairs were so chaotic that the parent Pennsylvania was resorting to financially evasive tactics that were to lead to complete eventual disinheritance, there were listed on its summer schedules a number of name trains with luxury equipment and at least one all-Pullman, extra fare varnish haul with club cars, diners and an open platform observation lounge that was the peer in pretentions of any daylight run name train elsewhere in the land. Some of the Long Island's name trains were merely timetable parodies of the grand manner, their equipment and scheduling of museum piece dimensions that became part of the fabric of local folklore, but they still staggered down the years trailing traces of seedy grandeur in losing competition with the massive network of parallel highways. In the mid-thirties there were scheduled over the Jamaica to Greenport run *The Banker, The Shelter Island Express, The Cannon Ball* and *The Peconic Bay Express.* To Montauk there were *The Hampton Express, The South Shore Express,* each with a parlor car, *The Cannon Ball* with a parlor buffet car, and the glory of the railroad, *The Sunrise Special* and *The Shinnecock Express,* each of which was all-Pullman, extra fare with dining cars, parlor lounges, and, in the case of *The Sunrise Special,* a barbershop and fine open platform observation-parlor car. When used by the

Long Island management the word "express" was almost invariably euphemistic. *The Wading River Express,* for example, made its first stop at Westbury, just eighteen minutes out of Jamaica, and thereafter all stops until it achieved its Wading River destination. Sleeping cars appear only infrequently in the Long Island record. At one time there was a through Pullman from Pittsburgh to accommodate a small but determined group of summer commuters to East Hampton. Another short lived venture involved Pullman sleepers carried between Boston and Brooklyn over the New York & New England connection in *The Long Island & Eastern States Express,* a *rara avis* among name trains today remembered almost exclusively by collectors of such matters. This car ferry run over the Old Air Line through Connecticut lasted only four months and was terminated after a disastrous wreck. Folklore and legend cluster thickly around the Long Island, not all of it flattering, so that in its locust years it became part of the national lexicon of humorous derogation like Brooklyn, Southern fried chicken and Texas millionaires. But good humor and happy times were associated with even its darkest years. Philip Dunne, writing of his famous father, Finley Peter Dunne, creator of the immortal Mr. Dooley, remarked that a sartorial panache of which the elder Dunne was particularly disdainful was the club hatband. "Men who were entitled to a somewhat doubtful privilege used to ameliorate the harsh and unlovely headgear known, in summer months, as a skimmer, with colorful hatbands. On Friday evenings when *The Cannon Ball* rolled in from New York, the Southampton Station bloomed like a garden with the colors of the Links, the Knickerbocker, the Racquet and other famous clubs. I could always pick out my father at a distance by his Spartan black hatband, the only one in sight."

SPEONK STATION in the Long Island's salad days was a vignette of pastoral dimensions with its quota of lobster crates drying beside the single track. In the lower frame in the year 1904 a Wading River summer-time only local pulls out of Huntington Station behind a typical Long Island American type 4-4-0 while a buckboard drawn by a white horse waits at the crossing. *(Top: Everett De Golyer Collection; Below: Ron Ziel Collection.)*

INCLUDING the Great Blizzard of 1888, the Long Island was repeatedly over the years tied up by blizzards of legendary ferocity which isolated remote townships for days on end. The snow blockade at the left was at an unidentified date but bears visual witness to the elemental winters combatted by the railroad. Below: the Long Island station at Centerport in 1878 was a country thing beside two tracks whose ballast and alignment might grieve an exacting roadmaster. *(Two Photos: Everett De Golyer Collection.)*

AT THE TURN of the century and as long as steam
lasted on the Long Island, camelback motive
power such as that at Jamaica shown above in 1903
kept the carrier in good standing in the
Mother Hubbard Club along with Lackawanna,
Erie, and other eastern coal haul roads.
Not all the occupants of parlor car space aboard
The Cannon Ball derived from the social Hamptons
and the lordly summer homes of Quogue.
Some, as is suggested opposite, were descendents of
the oldest of all New England whaling families
that had settled at Montauk and Gardiner's Island in
Colonial times and viewed the Rolls-Royce set
at East Hampton as the veriest parvenus.
The Sunrise Special, shown opposite as it nears
Jamaica, brought with it a cachet of big-time railroad
operations in its all-Pullman consist and the
glittering keystone emblem on the observation rail.
*(Above: Ron Ziel Collection; Right: Everett
De Golyer Collection; The Smithsonian Institution.)*

664

PULLMAN equipment on such runs as *The Sunrise Special* was, in the later years of the Long Island's faltering fortunes, hand-me-down Pennsylvania club cars and diners so that passengers had to look out the window to be sure they were not aboard *The Congressional* or a Philadelphia Clocker. *The Peconic Bay Express (above)* in the days when it ran behind a camelback ten wheeler carried its Pullman equipment on the head end, coaches at the rear, reversing this order in one direction to save turning the train at its terminals. The depot at Babylon and Fire Island is shown at a time when the only year-round inhabitants of Fire Island were the members of a Coast Guard Station at what was later to become celebrated as Cherry Grove. Wolcott Gibbs, for many years the *New Yorker's* drama critic and the singer and minstrel of Fire Island, at one time served an apprenticeship firing on the Long Island, experience which gave him a profound insight into the conduct of this whimsical and wayward carrier. (*Above: Smithsonian Institution; Right: Pullman Standard; Opposite: Everett De Golyer Collection.*)

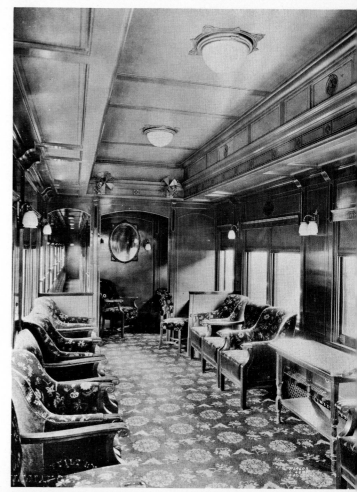

DESPITE the evidence in the foreground that much of the traffic at the Long Island Rail Road's grade crossings was of a horse-drawn character, the year 1915 saw such a rise in automobile accidents, most of them due to optimism on the part of drivers in the matter of beating the cars to the crossing, that the railroad management undertook an extensive campaign of public education combined with a widespread replacement of crossing gatemen by really formidable barriers. Where an ancient with a lantern had been ineffectual to prevent motorists from contesting the right of way, boldly painted spars such as the one shown here soon cut the incidence of accidents in gratifying degree. (*John Barriger Collection.*)

SHOWN WEARING the straw boater hat with its plain black ribbon which identified him in the club car of *The Cannon Ball,* Finley Peter Dunne was one of the Long Island's best friends and severest critics, maintaining a literary relationship with the carrier that was comparable to that of Philadelphia's Christopher Morley with the Paoli Local. Once as the result of tarrying at the bar of the Brook Club with his friend Harry Payne Whitney, Dunne missed *The Cannon Ball* when an arrogant attendant slammed the train gate in his face. Dunne, who was in wine at the time, demanded that the Long Island atone for the affront with a special train to East Hampton, but he was finally gentled by Big Bill Egan, the Pennsy stationmaster, and sent on his way in a company limousine.

DINING CARS on appropriate runs of *The Cannon Ball, Shinnecock Express* and *Sunrise Special* were, of course, hand-me-down Pennsylvania equipment and so infrequent even in the glory years of the twenties and thirties as to be an object of remark and subject of regional pride. The Long Island commissary was a subdivision of the Pennsylvania's dining car service and as such reflected Pennsylvania competence without any pretense at transcendental gastronomy. Although he was more of a regular on the Saturday afternoon *Cannon Ball,* Finley Peter Dunne occasionally rode the almost as elite *Hampton Express,* shown above pulling out of Bay Shore almost at the end of its run to Montauk. On the page opposite the creator of the immortal Mr. Dooley is shown in the skimmer with its solid black hatband which, Dunne claimed, made him a more distinguished figure of remark on the platform at East Hampton than the multicolored symbols of the Harvard, Racquet and Leash that surrounded him in the club car. (*Above: Everett De Golyer Collection; Opposite: Pennsylvania Railroad, Little Brown.*)

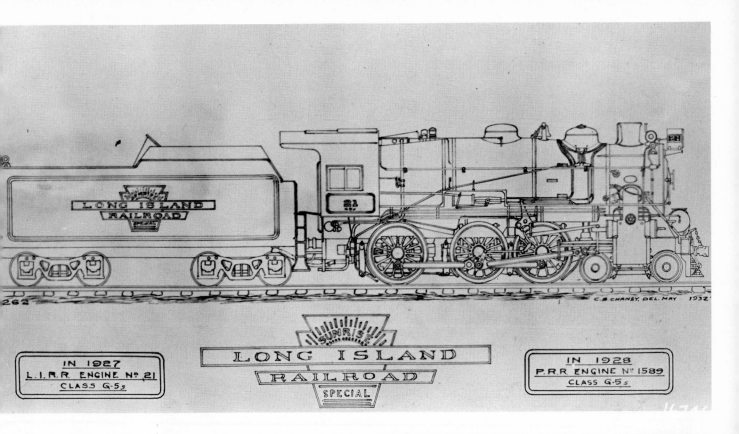

IN 1927
L. I. R. R. ENGINE Nº 21
CLASS G-5s

SUNRISE
LONG ISLAND
RAILROAD
SPECIAL

IN 1928
P. R. R. ENGINE Nº 1589
CLASS G-5s

OAKDALE Station, on the Long Island's Montauk main line as it appeared in 1880 was only a memory by the time Charles B. Chaney took the fine action photograph of the *Sunrise Special* in 1927 at the left, but once it had been one of the more important structures along the railroad's rustic right of way. Few Long Island depots of the period boasted such architectural amenities as covered platforms, whitewashed outhouses or storey-and-a-half construction. At the platform end with its vault door was the characteristic ice house where seafood was chilled until shipment was possible to Fulton Market. *The Sunrise Special* ran in all-Pullman splendor with a barber and conventional dining car and was powered by specially assigned Class G-5 ten wheelers such as that depicted above. Their tender sides were engrossed with identifying heraldry incorporating the train's name amidst the rays of a symbolic rising sun. (*Above, Opposite: Everett De Golyer Collection; Three Photos: The Smithsonian Institution.*)

671

THE OPENING in 1910 of the Pennsylvania Station in New York City
with its connecting tunnels under the East and North Rivers
was part of the long-range strategy of the Pennsylvania Railroad for
control of Long Island traffic. In the early years of its control
from Broad Street the Long Island was beneficiary
of many improvements which included a vast electrification project
radiating out of Jamaica and, of course, the disappearance of the
ferry connection or bridge route between Manhattan Island
and the Long Island's western terminal. The impress of the
Pennsylvania on the Long Island's personality continued to manifest
itself long after the romance between the two carriers
had cooled and is apparent in the two magnificent action shots of
Long Island varnish on this and the opposite page by O. Winston Link.

THE KEYSTONE INSIGNE riding the observation platform tailgate of the *The Sunrise Special,* shown here awaiting its highball at Jamaica, was, like the train it identified, a rarely encountered symbol of the grand manner with its extra fare implications in the iconography of the Long Island. Years later, a reactivated *Cannonball* (with its name a single word) was also to carry a drumhead herald but its theme was one of parody lacking the august overtones of the chaste Pennsylvania keystone. On lesser Long Island varnish runs, the rear brakeman, as at the left, merely hung out his rear markers to show that his cut of cars had an engine and had been translated into a train; on the *Sunrise* he plugged in the cord and the illuminated keystone vanishing in splendor down the right of way ennobled the string of Pullmans to the status of *The Broadway Limited* or any other train you care to name of pedigree. (*Above: W. J. Rugen; Left: Pennsylvania Railroad.*)

673

THE IMMEMORIAL functions of a car tonk inspecting the journal boxes of one of the Pullman parlor cars of *The Sunrise Special* prior to its departure from Montauk on a summer's day reassured the carrier's often important passengers that the management had their best interests at heart. *(Lucius Beebe.)*

PENN STATION, Penn side, you told the cab driver if you wanted to be set down at the depot's pillared south portal where redcaps established liason between arriving mainline patrons and the train gates.
To achieve the Long Island trains you were set down at the north entry.
Time, ubiquitous, in Penn Station, was exact on all station clocks save only those in the Savarin Restaurant bar where, as a precaution, they ran five minutes ahead.

THE BLEAK winter speed shot, probably of *The Hampton Express,* by O. Winston Link reproduced at the top of the opposite page with its backdrop of industrial skyline provides a dramatic contrast to an earlier Long Island scheme of things represented by some of the railroad's rustic depots shown on the adjacent pages of this book. When the railroad came into being in the early decades of the nineteenth century it served a community that was almost altogether pastoral from Jamaica to Montauk.
By 1950 the entire length of its right of way was industrialized and Long Island as a country residential community almost ceased to exist.

OTHER CARRIERS in the record might wheel their favored varnish runs behind museum piece motive power such as the Lackawanna's affection for camelback engines on even its well accredited *Lackawanna Limited* and the Pennsylvania's habit well into the 1920s of scheduling crack flyers behind the road's celebrated Atlantics, but few railroads of consequence maintained such extensive stables of archaism as the Long Island where all-Pullman consists were headed up by venerable camelbacks and express runs of pedigree rode behind ten wheelers. At the top of the opposite page *The Shinnecock Express*, one of the Long Island's more optimistically named varnish

hauls, is shown behind the road's ten wheeler No Below is reproduced the observation end of the cial train which in 1924 was originated on the I Island to convey the then Prince of Wales from North Shore residence of oil millionaire Joshua den to the White House to call on President Cooli Although not visible in this photograph taken as special paused for change of motive power at M hattan Transfer, it had started earlier in the behind a Long Island 4-4-0 that had been in ser since 1904. *(Above: O. Winston Link; Oppo Two Photos: The Smithsonian Institution.)*

23-TR. 12

OPERATING OVER a complex interlocking network of
New Jersey carriers whose components were the Pennsylvania-
Reading Seashore Lines and the highly involved exchange
of services over the complex formed by the Reading-Central of
New Jersey-Baltimore & Ohio, there once sped on tight
schedules a not inconsiderable fleet of name trains
connecting metropolitan New York and Philadelphia with the
watering places of the New Jersey Coast.
The most celebrated single component of these services was the
Pennsylvania-Reading Seashore Lines over a
sixty-mile-an-hour speedway over almost flawless tangents
between Philadelphia-Camden and Atlantic City.
Name trains included *The Boardwalk Flyer, The Nellie Bly*
and *Quaker City Express.* Shown here in the tule marshes
of New Jersey is *The Atlantic City Express,* while action on the
Boardwalk for which *The Flyer* was named and where
countless newlyweds promenaded on their wedding
trips is suggested in the 1905 vignette captioned
"Dolly's Go-Cart" by its photographer.   *(Library of Congress.)*

679

THE VENERABLE
Baltimore & Ohio depot at
Washington, shown on
the page opposite,
where Vice President
Hobart would be set down
at the end of the run
of *The Royal Blue* was one
of the old landmarks of
Washington in a more
tranquil time.
The tall helmet of the
policeman, the dignified
news vendor and hard
hatted loungers all
bespoke an easy-going age
in a semi-Southern
capital city. *(Smithsonian
Institution.)*

THE BEAUTIFUL all-Pullman consist pictured at the left at Jersey City on March 2, 1897, poised for a swift run to Washington, might well be taken as the paradigm of what a varnish train was felt to be at that now remote date, the most mature realization of the dreams of designers of effective motive power and the expertise of the Palace car builder. The photograph was taken by the ranking railroad photographer of the era with Central Railroad of New Jersey's proud camelback No. 457 on the head end and the train was specially assembled and run over the connecting lines of the Reading, C. of N.J. and Baltimore & Ohio for the accommodation of Vice President Hobart on what may be presumed to have been an occasion of urgency. The jacket design of the Baltimore & Ohio's house organ of the period suggests the pride of a rich and powerful carrier. *(Above: Fred Arone Collection; Left: Brown Bros.)*

THE MOST FAVORED of all American summer resorts in the mid-nineteenth
century and the summer capital of the nation in every Presidency
from that of Grant to Chester A. Arthur, Long Branch on the New Jersey
seacoast and its neighboring rival Cape May, for many decades reigned in
undisputed social supremacy as watering places until after the
Civil War when Newport achieved its ascendency. The Jersey seaside, later to be
reached aboard *The Blue Comet* and *The Nellie Bly* over the same
right of way, was originally the terminal of the old New York & Long Branch
Railroad at a time when summer cottage owners at Long Branch,
Spring Lake and Asbury Park didn't need to tip their hats in the direction of
Saratoga Springs, let alone Bar Harbor. In 1894 F. W. Blauvelt
copyrighted the fine photograph reproduced at the right with the caption
"The New York & Long Branch Express Scooping Water at 25 Miles an Hour."
The line drawing opposite shows the arrival, as depicted in
Leslie's Weekly, of the *Express* at Long Branch depot. Below on this page,
in a rite older even than calling signals with his fireman or comparing
watches with the train captain, a Central of New Jersey eagle eye oils around the
valve gear of his massive Atlantic type camelback.
Shall we say the date is 1914?   *(Opposite: Brown Bros.; Below:
Everett De Golyer Collection.)*

ALTHOUGH as essentially "Old Philadelphia" in the social and moneyed implications of the phrase as the imperial Pennsylvania, the Reading Railway System, which is an integral part of the structural economy of the Reading Company, was at one time considered socially unthinkable, a sort of negative status symbol which, in the twenties and thirties, became curiously reversed into a hallmark of prestige and snobbism. "In the old days nice young Philadelphia girls were permitted to travel unescorted on Mr. Roberts' railroad (the Pennsy) but not the Reading," wrote Nathaniel Burt in "The Perennial Philadelphians." "But nowadays connoisseurs take the Reading to New York as being far more convenient and pleasant, to Wall Streeters at least. It has acquired the same detached superior, slightly intellectual prestige as Chestnut Hill itself, and partisans of the Reading regard the Pennsylvania as distinctly middle class." Another commentator noted that Philadelphians who ride the Reading "are more inclined to be readers of *The Philadelphia Public Ledger* than of *The Bulletin,*" a subtle distinction which may be lost on outlanders but has vast validity in the precincts of Rittenhouse Square. The spirit of aloof superiority to time and change, not to mention rising real estate values, is suggested here by the depot at Hopewell, New Jersey, explicitly Victorian, mansarded and terraced with a manorial lawn on which peacocks might have paraded with complete propriety. The Reading's penchant for camelbacks is suggested by all three photographs on these pages. (*Three Photos: Everett De Golyer Collection.*)

AT THE TURN of the century, a multiplicity of ornate candlesticks on the pilot bar, usually fashioned from finely turned brass or bronze, characterized both Reading and Central of New Jersey motive power as is suggested in the two period photographs reproduced below. High speed compound Atlantic type camelbacks such as that on the commuter train at the bottom afforded a warm ride for the engineer, but opportunities for conversation with the fireman were few.

THE CONSERVATISM which retained bicycle
type locomotives and camelbacks as suggested
opposite, maintained fine fast Atlantic types
such as No. 353 shown above long after Pacifics
were fashionable. Typical, too, was the inclusion
of Philadelphia scrapple on the breakfast menus
of the Reading's diners and buffet meat breakfast menus (right). The carrier's pedigree suggested Pennsylvania conservatism deriving from
the company's founder, the aristocratic Mon-
cure Robinson who was educated at William
and Mary and married a cousin of Thomas
Jefferson. The original survey of the road, eventually to the coal regions of Mt. Carbon, was a
monument to his sagacity and Reading hard coal
maintained ample dividends for more than a
century. (Above: Everett De Golyer Collection;
Right: The Reading Co.)

686

CEREALS—Cream or Milk (Hot or Cold) Served with all Cereals
Grape Nuts, Shredded Wheat, Oatmeal, Corn Flakes, Post Toasties, All Bran,
Rice Flakes, Cream of Wheat, Wheaties, Puffed Rice or Wheat 30

FISH—Broiled or Fried Fresh Seasonable Fish with French Fried Potatoes 80
Filet of Kippered Herring 50   Creamed Finnan Haddie on Toast 60
Codfish Cakes (2) Tomato Sauce 50

EGGS & OMELETS—EGGS: Boiled, Fried, Shirred or Scrambled (2) 30; (1) 20;
Poached on Toast (2) 40; (1) 25
OMELETS: (3 Eggs) Ham, Tomato, Cheese, Jelly or Parsley 55   Plain 4
Spanish or Mushroom 65

MEATS—Single Rib Lamb Chop (1) 35; (2) 65   Small Sirloin Steak 90   Ham and Egg
Bacon and Eggs 65   Breakfast Bacon (5) 50   Bacon Rasher (2) 20
Broiled or Fried Smoked Ham 60   Reduced Portion Ham or Bacon and One Eg
Corned Beef Hash with Poached Egg (1) 55   Creamed Dried Beef on Toast
Fried Sausage (4) 50   Calf's Liver with Bacon 65   Fried Philadelphia Scrapp

POTATOES—French Fried 20   Hashed Browned 20   Lyonnaise 25

BREAD, TOAST, ETC.—Dry or Buttered Toast 15   Rolls or Bran Bre
French Toast with Jelly, Syrup or Honey 35   Individual Boston Brown Bread
Milk Toast 30   Melba Toast 15   Griddle Cakes with Syrup or Honey 35

A BIG Pennsylvania blizzard in the winter of 1905 saw this Reading camelback halted in the depot at Lebanon with the bases of its multiple candlesticks buried deep in snow on the pilot beam. *(Harper's.)*

SO CONSERVATIVE was The Reading in the matter of motive power that exotic bicycle type wheel arrangements with a single pair of drivers survived on its light, fast runs long after they had vanished elsewhere in the land.

687

THE CENTRAL Railroad of New Jersey's *Blue Comet*, inaugurated in February of the fatal year 1929 on the New York City-Atlantic City run was the first de luxe all-coach train on a daylight routing designed to give passengers Pullman comfort and style at coach travel tariff. The brain child of the carrier's President R. B. White, *The Blue Comet's* consist included a number of C. of N.J. coaches and diners rebuilt and finished throughout in a striking cream white and royal blue decor with specially assigned Pacific type locomotives which carried the train's name on a bronze insigne under the feed water heater. Regularly assigned, too, was an open end-brass railed observation coach which later received a drumhead insigne. The train was sensationally handsome and residents turned out to watch its progress as shown above, along the C. of N.J.'s own right of way from Red Bank to Winslow, whence it ran to Atlantic City over the Pennsylvania-Reading Seashore Lines. Although a fatality of the depression years, *The Blue Comet* paved the way for all-coach trains on even longer hauls, *The Trail Blazer* and *Pacemaker* and *El Capitan* in years to come. (*Above: Everett De Golyer Collection.*)

IF THE two splendid assigned Pacific locomotives with the train name riding proudly at the smokebox were in the shop, the Central of New Jersey reverted to a long standing motive power tradition and assigned a well maintained camelback to the run. (*Two Photos: Everett De Golyer Collection.*)

SMOKING SPLENDIDLY across the page in the frame above and sooting up the New Jersey landscape, a Pennsylvania Asbury Park-Seagirt local rolls down the iron of the New York & Long Branch's historic right of way at South Amboy, while on the page opposite No. 5412 with the headlight generator and solid steel pilot characteristic of the engines assigned to this run poses on the Atlantic City haul for a sunny portrait by Don Wood at Morgan, New Jersey in November 1955. Within the memory of living man some of the Pennsylvania-Reading Seashore Lines runs carried observation cars with open platforms where, in holiday mood, a family poses at the right in promotional attitudes. (*Pennsylvania Railroad.*)

THE SCENE AT THE LEFT is no
ordinary chore of oiling around
the valve gear, for the locomotive is
the Pennsy's immortal No. 460, the
great Atlantic type engine that,
on its day of glory, June 11, 1927,
averaged seventy-five miles
an hour between Washington terminal
and Manhattan Transfer with the
Lindbergh newsreel special.
No. 460 spent its final years on the
Atlantic City run.
(*Philip R. Hastings.*)

ALTHOUGH luxury equipment occupied
but little track space in the Reading's
passenger yards, over the years it ordered
from Pullman a variety of restaurant
cars and diners, of which
Cafe Car No. 1197 was a handsome
example of Pullman varnish style in the
early years of the current century.
In the 1930s Bound Brook tower *(right)*
where traffic converged over the rails
of the Lehigh Valley, the Central
of New Jersey and the jointly operated
tracks of the Reading and Baltimore & Ohio
main line from Philadelphia was the
counterpart, in its own purview, of
Monmouth Junction on the Pennsylvania,
long celebrated as the most densely
trafficked trackage in the world.
*(Right: Everett De Golyer Collection;
Below: Pullman Standard.)*

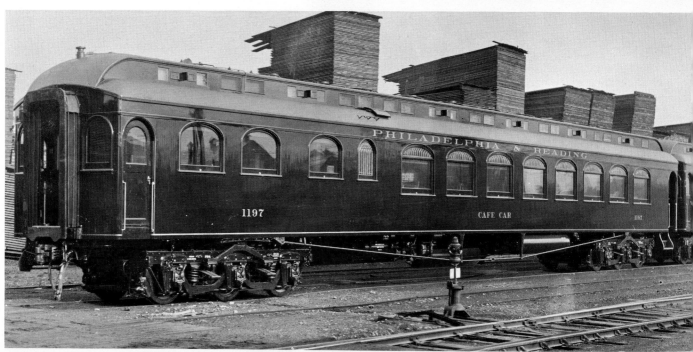

DINING CAR SERVICE

CLUB BREAKFAST SERVICE

Guests will please write on check each item desired, as our waiters are not permitted to accept oral orders. Please pay waiter only upon presentation of your check at conclusion of service.

The Price Opposite Each Selection Includes Choice of One Fruit, Fruit Juice or Cereal.
Also Choice of Bread, Rolls or Toast and Beverage

FRUITS	FRUIT JUICES	HOT or DRY CEREALS	
artlett Pear Halves	Prune Juice	Cream of Wheat	Rice Krispies
Half Grapefruit	Tomato Juice	Corn Flakes	Bran Flakes
Jumbo Prunes	Grapefruit Juice	Oatmeal	Grape Nuts
Baked Apple	Fresh Orange Juice		
Kadota Figs			

SELECTIONS:

CREAMED CHIPPED BEEF ON TOAST—1.80

FRESH COUNTRY SAUSAGE, WHEAT CAKES, WITH SYRUP —1.90

GRILLED HAM OR FRESH COUNTRY SAUSAGE WITH EGGS, "AS DESIRED"—1.90

BROWNED CORNED BEEF HASH WITH POACHED EGG—1.80

PHILADELPHIA SCRAPPLE, FRIED EGG—1.50

SUGAR CURED BACON AND EGGS—1.80

OR BUTTERED TOAST	ROLLS	HOT MUFFINS
APPLE BUTTER	JELLY	MARMALADE

Please Select from Jelly Tray Passed by Waiter

COFFEE	TEA	MILK	POSTUM	SANKA

For A LA CARTE Selections See Other Side

Four per cent sales tax applies in Commonwealth of Pennsylvania.

TWENTY YEARS after the photograph above showing The Reading's *Wall Streeter* speeding eastward down the long tangent into Elizabeth, New Jersey was taken, the breakfast menu on its successor, *The Wall Street* had kept abreast of the times. No longer could the hustling customer's man on his way to Dean Witter for a brisk day's scuffle with Minnesota Mining or General Dynamics do himself proud for six bits. Like the market itself, creamed chipped beef had soared from fifty cents to $1.80 and inflation had raised corned beef hash with poached egg in the same proportion. *(Above: Lucius Beebe; Left: Reading Railroad.)*

FOR NEARLY two decades the Reading Railroad, in direct competition on the New York-Philadelphia run with the Pennsylvania, maintained a train whose very name *The Seven O'Klocker* was an affront to the Pennsy's fleet of "Clockers" that ran every hour of the day between Broad Street and mid-town Manhattan. In 1937 *The Seven O'Klocker* was replaced by a steam powered, stainless steel streamlined luxury coach train named *The Crusader* because, as is suggested here, it was "Clad in Shining Armor." *The Crusader* served full course meat and potato breakfasts in the morning and enjoyed a brisk bar trade on its evening return to Philadelphia and twice a day gave the competing Pennsylvania a very stylish run for its money. A loyal following of conservative Philadelphia businessmen and brokers who considered the Pennsylvania trains undistinguished and lacking in exclusiveness transferred their loyalties to *The Crusader* when that streamliner was inaugurated. Usually powered by a specially assigned streamlined light Pacific, an equally well groomed locomotive in conventional livery took over when the assigned engine was being shopped. (*Lucius Beebe.*)

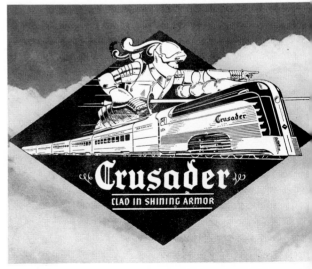

694

DEVOTIONAL reading aboard *The Crusader* was, of course, *The Wall Street Journal* and the Martinis on the Philadelphia-bound run late in the afternoon were of a dimension suitable to the demands of brokers who had spent a fatiguing day in the market place. *(Two Photos: The Reading Co.)*

Few But Choice Were the Name
Varnish Runs on the Rock Island

POWERED by a stubby Pacific with solid steel pilot and the peculiar and characteristic Rock Island adaptation of a Vanderbilt tender, the *Rocky Mountain Limited* is shown above in a consist of four cars leaving Denver of a summer's noontime in 1939 with one of the season's inevitable thunder storms forming behind it. Although the practice varied with the years, the general operational procedure sent the full dimension dining car on with the stub section to The Springs while breakfast, arriving in Denver, and luncheon departing were served on the main section in the buffet. Rock Island cuisine, like that of the Burlington, ran to country style and was nothing to excite the raptures of *bon viveurs*, but what there was was good and plentiful. In lean years after the great passenger slump of the late fifties, economies attempted on the *Rocky Mountain Rocket* ran to paper plates, no table linen and prefabricated dinners, practices of infamy which the complaints of the patrons put a stop to in short order. *(Above: Richard H. Kindig; Right: Rock Island.)*

THE COLORADO SPRINGS section of *The Limited* is shown below arriving at Limon, Colorado, with a coach, diner and Pullman where it will be integrated to the main section out of Denver for the trip east. (*Everett De Golyer Collection.*)

698

IT MAY REASONABLY be presumed that it was hot on the July morning in Horton, Kansas, in 1914 when Eugene Bourquin, a dedicated photographer of the local scene, took these views down around the Rock Island depot when the Kansas City local, shown double headed in the picture below, pulled in. The women were in white shirtwaists and sensible skirts with summer parasols and the men in shirt sleeves with their jackets over their arms. The afternoon train, shown opposite, required but a single engine. The town hack and omnibus from the Horton House stood at the platform and a single vintage motor car, parked in the rear of the depot gave pastoral Horton a touch of worldliness. The Rock Island brakeman, at the bottom across the fold, wore white cotton gloves as much to protect his hands from the heat of switch stands and grabirons as against the dirt. With a jug of drinking water carried on the catwalk where it could catch the breeze, the Rock Island's one and only camelback locomotive and its crew were an irresistible subject for Bourquin's lens. Kansas and for that matter the whole middle west of that now distant year were filled with Hortons or their facsimiles, but only Horton, Brown County, Kansas boasted the presence of Eugene Bourquin to lend it celulloid immortality. *(Everett De Golyer Collection.)*

TIPPING the depot porter at Englewood just outside Chicago in the *Golden State's* streamlined days was a matter of financial import to both parties *(right)*. Below in 1940 when clouds upon its horizon were few, *The Golden State Limited* rolls in splendor out of Tucumcari, Chicago-bound with four head-end revenue cars and a long string of Pullmans trailing behind. *(Right: Rail Photo Service; Below: Richard H. Kindig.)*

THE STUB train out of
San Diego connecting with the
Golden State at Yuma over
the San Diego & Arizona
Eastern, left the Santa Fe depot
behind a Southern Pacific
ten wheeler with a single
through Pullman on the far end.
(Rail Photo Service.)

DESPITE the Fred Harvey cuisine and the Santa Fe legend of immaculately conducted transcontinentals, there were those who felt that in its days of Pullman Standard and even later when it was modestly streamlined, there was no way to achieve Southern California comparable to the *Golden State Limited*. It was a train of solid comforts, cut flowers in the public apart-ments, heavily embossed stationery in the lounges, fingerbowls with lemon water on the diner and an over-all sense of enormous well-being. A highball with a fellow traveler in the lounge as the New Mexican night rushed past the windows was a solace for human ills. *(Southern Pacific.)*

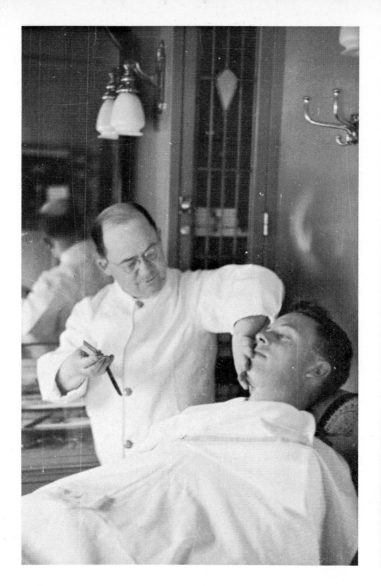

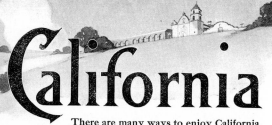

WHEN IT WENT into service on November 2, 1902 between Los Angeles and Chicago over the Southern Pacific-Rock Island connection as Trains No. 43-44, *The Golden State Limited,* even to its closely parallel name, was designed as direct competition with the Santa Fe's *California Limited* already an institution and well established in the travel habits of the Southwest. For the first five years of its life *The Golden State* was an all-Pullman consist though there is no record to show this other than a surcharge attached to its tickets. Curiously enough, because the Rock Island main line had not been consolidated to include this trackage, it ran between Kansas City and Joliet, Illinois, over the rails of the Chicago & Alton, then very much of the Kansas City-St. Louis-Chicago triangle competition. In its Pullman Standard days and in the era of later streamlining, *The Golden State* also faced the stiff competition of the Union Pacific's *Los Angeles Limited* over the Salt Lake line. Aboard it were available all the accustomed transcontinental amenities, barber and lady's maid, heavily embossed writing paper, fingerbowls and a de luxe *ambiance* generally. A noble train, it lived up to a noble name. (*Above: Richard H. Kindig; Opposite: Southern Pacific, Paul Stringham; Left: Arthur D. Dubin Collection.*)

JUST BEFORE accepting delivery from Pullman of the equipment which allowed it to place two entire new Standard trains on the run, the Rock Island's *Rocky Mountain Limited* is shown backing down to its appropriate train bay at La Salle Depot in Chicago in 1929. At the right its arrival eastbound is depicted at Englewood on a winter's day in 1930 when storm conditions have made its running in two sections prudent. The second section, snow encrusted from the Great Plains, included three head end revenue cars, a coach and two Pullmans. Company literature *(right)* suggested that a lower berth in a Standard Pullman sleeper was a snug place to be on a night when blizzards gripped the Rocky Mountain States, as indeed it was. *(Top, Two Photos: Alfred W. Johnson; Right: Rock Island.)*

704

AT VARIOUS TIMES, the secondary run over the Golden State Route to Southern California via the Rock Island and the Southern Pacific connection at Tucumcari was known as *The Californian*, sometimes as *The Apache* as shown at the right. Always it was a sort of elegant second fiddle to the candy run, *The Golden State Limited*, shown below near Beaumont in San Timoteo Canyon. But if *The Apache* and *Californian* were both very highly regarded second fiddles, their culinary resources, although at reduced prices, had about them vestiges of the grander manner of *The Golden State* and they ended with the panache of an open platform observation car and the tailgate insigne that marked them trains of pedigree no matter what their scheduling or fares.

The occupants of Pullman space on *The Apache*, shown on the facing page, couldn't have been any more comfortable on an extra fare run.   *(Below: Donald Duke; Opposite: Two Photos Southern Pacific.)*

LEAVING DENVER in a prophetic mantle of shrouded glory with the sunset behind it, the *Rocky Mountain Limited (top opposite)* made its last run on November 11, 1939 and was photographed in its going by Otto Perry. The next day saw the inaugural run in regular service of *The Rocky Mountain Rocket* and the age of streamlining was at hand. The new and gleaming *Rockets* put the carrier on competitive footing of equality with the rival Burlington and Union Pacific which already had streamliners on the Colorado run, but there were those who lamented the passing of Pullman Standard which had so long been typified by the black leather upholstered men's room, scene of pre-arrival chaos in the morning and setting for the whole long saga of traveling salesmen's tales embracing the farmer's daughter and other staples of masculine humor dear to the student of American folkways.

BEFORE construction of the present La Salle Station in Chicago which it shares with the New York Central and the Nickel Plate, the old Van Buren Street Depot saw the departure of Rock Island trains "with California excursions daily, a choice of routes to Salt Lake, Ogden, Portland, Los Angeles and San Francisco." Chicago's Victorian terminals were atmospheric if not the quintessence of convenience. (*Chicago Historical Society.*)

709

A COMPANION train in the tourist brackets to the extra fare *Golden State* on the Rock Island-Southern Pacific run between Chicago and California was *The Californian* which its owning carriers hoped might be the answer to the Union Pacific's *Challengers* in the reduced fare brackets. The Espee, then very much in the passenger business, spent money in lavish quantities on the project, advertising the run in four-color brochures and stocking its diners with out-of-season viands usually reserved for the extra fare trade. Until the construction of its magnificent Union Station, Kansas City passengers on the Rock Island got down from the cars at the venerable depot depicted at the right. *The Californian* at the top of the page is from the Collons Collection at the De Golyer Foundation, Dallas.

710

A ROUND TRIP ticket to Los Angeles on *The Californian* was an unbelievable $74 and a lower berth $8.95 each way. Breakfast was two bits; dinner with chicken pie, 35¢. Nobody could figure how the carriers did it. An additional attraction was a standup bar where prices compared favorably with those on *The Golden State*. Willing as it was to take a loss on its 35¢ dinners, the management was disinclined to invite bankruptcy with bargain Martinis. *(Two Photos: Southern Pacific.)*

IN THE CLOSING years of the 1920s when the Union Pacific's *Columbine* and the Burlington's *Aristocrat* were reeling off the Chicago-Denver miles with the finest equipment and most luxurious amenities available to long distance travel, the Rock Island's entry in the Queen City sweepstakes was *The Rocky Mountain Limited* for which all new Pullman equipment was ordered in 1929 and is shown above at Bureau, Illinois, a decade later. Barber and valet service were taken for granted and a stub train, as was the Rock Island's practice, went on from Limon to Colorado Springs while the main section headed for Denver. In 1933, with air conditioning just around the corner, it ran, as shown at the right, with a non-a.c., solarium lounge in place of the then more conventional open observation. *(Top: Paul Stringham; Right: The De Golyer Foundation, Roland Collons.)*

712

CONFRONTED BY the fine new streamliners of the competition on the Chicago-Denver run, the Burlington's *Denver Zephyr (top)* and the Union Pacific's *City of Denver*, the Rock Island, although obviously not sure that either Diesel power or airflow design was here to stay, countered weakly with a lightweight *Rocket* of its own. Reminiscent of the Rio Grande's experimental *Pioneer* except that it had no sleeping accommodations at all, *The Rocket* went into service with coach space only on summer weekends in 1937 with a conspicuous lack of success. It was shortly replaced by the *Rocky Mountain Special*, a Diesel powered run with Standard sleeping equipment which in turn yielded place to the fully staffed, streamlined excellences of *The Rocky Mountain Rocket*. *(Two Photos: Richard H. Kindig.)*

713

PLACED IN SERVICE in 1926 soon after the cresting of the wave of passenger traffic in the United States which had reached its peacetime apogee in 1922, *The Apache* was the secondary run to *The Golden State Limited* on the Rock Island-Southern Pacific joint operation between Chicago and Southern California. Although it never knew an extra fare and its sailing daily from La Salle Station in Chicago *(above)* had about it none of the red carpet overtones of *The Golden State*, *The Apache* carried its tourist class patrons in something suggesting style as is suggested by the open platform observation shown at the left. In the above frame it smokes up the Chicago skyline in 1936 in the very grand manner indeed on its westbound way to a rendezvous with the Southern Pacific at Tucumcari.
(Two Photos: De Golyer Foundation, Collons Collection; Above: William Rittase.)

715

THE SHORT LIVED *Arizona Limited* was an extra fare de luxe varnish run over the Rock Island-Southern Pacific connection at Tucumcari for winter patrons of the Arizona vacation complex centering around Tucson-Phoenix but its star came into ascendancy in evil hour in 1940 when war was already inevitable and it perished, a victim of travel restrictions, after only two seasons in service. It cost a surcharge of $6 to ride *The Arizona Limited* and when it became only a memory on the yellowing trainsheets of time, there were those who remembered it for happy hours on a run once populous with name trains and operations of splendor. *(Above: Southern Pacific.)*

ALTHOUGH the distinction of being the last custom-tailored name train
to be placed in service before the 1941 war belongs to the
Empire State Express on the New York Central, which made its maiden
run within hours of Pearl Harbor, *The Arizona Limited* was in general terms
coeval with it and shares the nostalgic overtones of things born in the
shadow of great events and soon overwhelmed by them.
It was also one of the last extra fare trains to be commissioned before
the advent of an age which would see surcharges in almost
universal abatement, so that the comparatively small group of passengers
who experienced the satisfactions of this superb but short-lived
streamliner are members of an exclusive veterans club.   (*Southern Pacific.*)

717

The Grand Hotel Concept of Railroading Flourished Luxuriously on the Southern Pacific

OTHER RAILROADS might, and indeed did achieve an imperial dimension in the world of transport and finance, at least one of them, the Santa Fe in direct competition over continental distances with the Southern Pacific. None of them, not even the New York Central & Hudson River Railroad in the years of its Vanderbilt ownership or the Pennsylvania when its writ ran with feudal overtones from Broad Street to Lake Michigan and the far bank of the Mississippi, represented such a splendidly integrated pattern of passenger accommodations, not only aboard name trains of legendary luxury, but on much-loved ferry boats and aboard ocean-going steamships that were household words.* For a time, in its Central Pacific incarnation, the Southern Pacific owned the State of California almost outright and its word was law in state capitols at Carson City, Phoenix, Salem and Baton Rouge. On its name passenger trains for three generations the Southern Pacific lavished the rich gifts of an indulgent parent. Its corporate banner rode aboard *The Sunset Limited, The Shasta Daylight, Golden State* and *Californian,* and it showed the flag, metaphorically, from smokebox and tailgate of *The Apache, Owl, Overland* and *Cascade.* Unlike the Pennsylvania, it could never be said that having seen one Espee varnish run the beholder had seen them all. Custom staled not their infinite variety and no passenger aboard *The Forty-niner* of happy memory could for a moment imagine himself enjoying the resources of *The West Coast* or the brief-lived *Arizona Limited.* While its politics and economic warfare were conducted on a scale of truculence and ferocity that would have frightened the warring barons of medieval Italy, the Southern Pacific's love affair with its passengers, as long as the management was so inclined, was on a positively idyllic scale. While it may not be possible, aboard even *The Golden State Limited,* to cite the $1,000 a month florist bills for the diners of *The Century,* the concept of a grand hotel was everywhere visible on the Espee in the form of watermarked stationery, silver fingerbowls, an encouraging assortment of fine whiskeys on the club cars, out-of-season strawberries, Eastern lobster and fresh brook trout on the menu and conductors who were very much the viceroys in an imperial scheme of things from Management at 65 Market Street, San Francisco. Marks of special favor abounded for notables on *The Overland* and *The Cascade* and no passenger who ever rode with Wild Bill Kurthy in the early days of *The City of San Francisco* forgot the gastronomic experience. In the number of its name trains, it is probable that the Southern Pacific must yield the palm to the Pennsylvania; in their amenities of comfort and expedition and the hold they exercised on the loyalties and imagination of the Western continent the Espee had few peers. On the opposite page in a day before tailgate insignes were universal, one of the Coast Route trains makes its way through flowering meadows against a backdrop of eucalyptus near Palo Alto. *(Southern Pacific.)*

*Amateurs of the Southern Pacific in search of a full scale pictorial and social history of this carrier are referred to "The Central Pacific & The Southern Pacific Railroads" by Lucius Beebe, with 121 photographs by Richard Steinheimer. Howell-North Books, 1963.

Departures of *The Sunset* from Third & Townsend were only a San Francisco memory by the time the fine snack bar shown at the right began running on a streamlined *Sunset Limited* but the picture record of the smiling porter and the two stylish women on the observation deck as it clears the yards testify to the glory it once knew. (*Three Photos: Southern Pacific.*)

NO LONGER a through train to the Golden Gate when this photograph of *The Sunset* was taken by Donald Duke in the mid-forties, it was still a many splendored thing as it surged, double headed, up San Timoteo Canyon at El Casco, California. The open platform shown at the left had by then been a casualty of the 1941 war but *The Sunset* was still a train in the grand manner with most of its amenities unimpaired. *(Left: Southern Pacific.)*

721

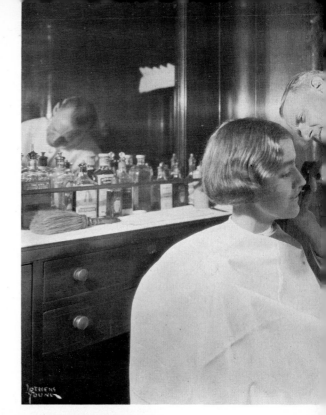

IN THE ERA of Pullman Standard when *The Sunset Limited* was flagship of the Southern Pacific's fleet of varnish trains, a barber was as requisite a part of its operation as the dining car or stock reports handed up at strategic points along the way. *(Southern Pacific.)*

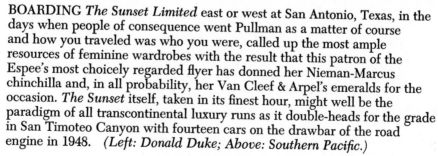

BOARDING *The Sunset Limited* east or west at San Antonio, Texas, in the days when people of consequence went Pullman as a matter of course and how you traveled was who you were, called up the most ample resources of feminine wardrobes with the result that this patron of the Espee's most choicely regarded flyer has donned her Nieman-Marcus chinchilla and, in all probability, her Van Cleef & Arpel's emeralds for the occasion. *The Sunset* itself, taken in its finest hour, might well be the paradigm of all transcontinental luxury runs as it double-heads for the grade in San Timoteo Canyon with fourteen cars on the drawbar of the road engine in 1948. *(Left: Donald Duke; Above: Southern Pacific.)*

IT WOULD SEEM unlikely that at any subsequent time in the history of overland travel in the United States, gentlemen aboard the cars ever even approximated the degree of sartorial elegance represented by pleated shirts, cummerbunds and curly-brimmed gray bowler hats depicted in this scene, identified as "a dinner stop in New Mexico" appearing on the center fold of *Harper's Weekly* supplement for February in 1891. *The Sunset Limited's* most sumptuous diners by Pullman were still four years in the future. Thirty-odd years later the Southern Pacific at its Fifth Avenue ticket office in New York *(opposite)* was suggesting that prospective patrons of *The Sunset* take through passage from the East aboard the *Piedmont Limited* or *The Crescent* over the Southern Railway-L. & N. connection at New Orleans for the 3839 miles to San Francisco. Along the way, as suggested below, the Sunset Route passed numerous reminders of mortality. The passengers paid them no mind. *(Three Photos: Southern Pacific.)*

Once
For a
Season
The
Sunset
Limited
Had
Covered
The
Longest
Continental
Run
Of All

726

IN THE YEAR 1925 when the Southern Pacific through trains
ran all the way from San Francisco to New Orleans with
direct connections to the East, Los Angeles, instead of being a
terminal was an on-line division point and *The Sunset Limited*
eastbound on its way down the Peninsula passed the
landmark shown at the left known as Palo Alto Big Pine.
The Big Pine had been there, amidst a rural setting
almost unchanged until the photograph was taken, from the time
when the first iron of the San Francisco & San Jose Railroad
had been laid in its shadow. Great name trains rolled
under it for three quarters of a century until Palo Alto's once
casually fenced meadows were engulfed in a tide of commerce
and a last link vanished between the time when the Espee
had been a country carrier and the ever crescent industrial chaos
of the twentieth century. The trainboard at Third & Townsend
depot suggested *The Sunset* as a varnish run of truly
continental dimension. *(Two Photos: Southern Pacific.)*

727

FOR TWO FULL decades previous to the coming of streamlining and through Pullmans between the East and West Coasts over a variety of routes, the Southern Pacific and the Southern Railway joined forces to stimulate and promote passenger traffic over the Sunset Route connecting at New Orleans with *The Crescent Limited* out of New York. *The Sunset Limited* and *The Argonaut* were the Espee beneficiaries of this arrangement; *The Crescent* and *The Azalean* east of the Mississippi. Schedules allowed liberal stopover time in New Orleans and passengers were encouraged to explore the culinary resources of ancestral Antoine's and the Absinthe House between trains. When the new streamlined, extra-fare *Sunset* went into service in 1950, the atmosphere of Creole New Orleans was conspicuous in its decor and a through Pullman between New York and Los Angeles was added, as is indicated at the right. Below *The Crescent* is shown leaving Atlanta in the age of the Southern Railway's splendor of green and gold motive power. *(Right: Southern Pacific; Below: Rail Photo Service.)*

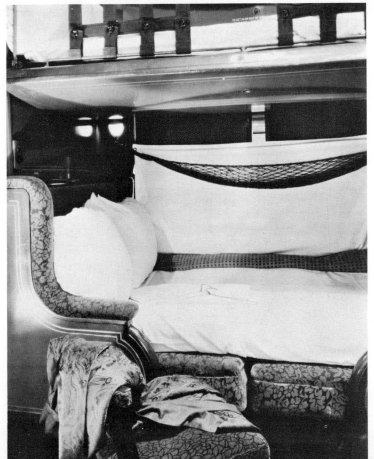

PRESUMING that the occupant of the Pullman Standard space shown here occupied a stateroom aboard both *The Crescent* and *The Sunset Limited* he would have occasion to don his Sulka watered silk bathrobe five full nights between New York and Los Angeles. Passengers aboard the *Mauretania* at this time occupied their staterooms for a similar period between New York and Southampton, but the voyage did not compare, in its duration at any rate, with that of the pre-1914 *Trans-Siberian Express* which took a full fortnight between terminals. Club cars on the Standard *Sunset (top)* showed few traces of the approach of *moderne* decor which was shortly to characterize public apartments in the name trains of the streamlined age. *(Two Photos: Southern Pacific.)*

729

IN SPACIOUS TIMES of rail travel between California and the Northwest when the Southern Pacific ran five regularly scheduled passenger trains in each direction, *The Cascade, Oregonian, Klamath, Shasta Limited* and *The West Coast, The Oregonian* shown above and at the right had taken over the fine Pullman equipment of the old *Cascade* which had been newly outfitted with all air-conditioned cars. *The Oregonian's* room observation lounge is depicted above and opposite; at the right the same train in a wintry setting at Dunsmuir when snow lies heavy on the rails. (*Two Photos: Southern Pacific.*)

730

SHOWN AT ODELL LAKE about 1930 *The Cascade* made it a summertime habit to include an open air observation car over the most spectacular portions of the Shasta route, a practice dating back to the first regular transcontinental trains on the Overland Route in 1871 when similar cars were attached at Truckee for the Sierra crossing. *The Oregonian's* observation presented a profile of enduring solidity in its conventional dimension. *(Two Photos: Southern Pacific.)*

EVERYTHING about *The Cascade Limited* in its all-Pullman days bespoke a custom built train in the great tradition, not the least detail of which was a nobly proportioned observation platform ending in a crimson and white drumhead herald so massive in its construction at the Espee's Sacramento shops that it required two men to boost it into place. Riding through the mists of Oregon uplands it was the proud identification of a train that shared alike in the regard of its owning carrier and the people who rode it. *(Southern Pacific.)*

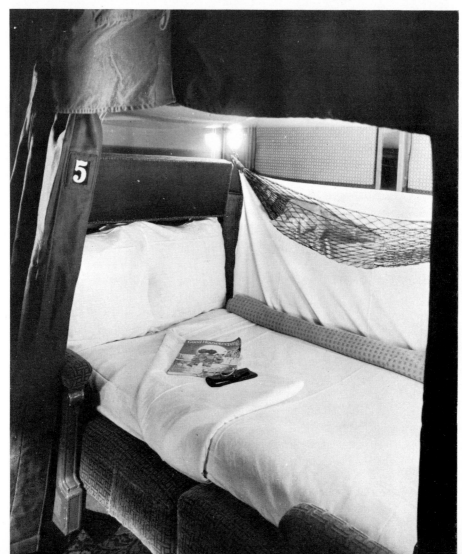

FOR THE LONG inland haul between Los Angeles and its northern terminal at Portland, the Southern Pacific maintained service aboard a train of all work called *The West Coast* which by-passed San Francisco and paid its way with vast quantities of head-end revenue. Never operated with pretentions to luxury, *The West Coast* was a service run with coaches, Pullman Standard sleepers, a diner and observation lounge whose open platform and illuminated train herald gave it its only trace of the grand manner. Below, *The West Coast* is shown against a pastoral background near Newhall, California, approaching its southern terminal. Opposite, a company photographer has invested an open section with an imaginative touch in the form of reading glasses and a copy of *Good Housekeeping*. (Below: Donald Duke; Opposite, Two Photos: Southern Pacific.)

THERE WAS PLENTY of time to catch up on one's reading or write letters on the lounge car of *The West Coast,* shown opposite on its long haul from Portland to Los Angeles over the inland route, while *The West Coast* itself *(below)* made a fine portrait of mainline passenger business as it passed through Saugus, California, doubleheaded in 1948. *(Above: Southern Pacific; Below: Donald Duke.)*

SAILING TIME for *The Argonaut* on the secondary run to New Orleans coincided closely with departure time at the old Los Angeles Station of *The Golden State* and *The Californian* for Chicago, all of them names of consequence in the transcontinental passenger traffic of another age. The density of Southern Pacific name train travel out of Los Angeles barely lasted into the lifetime of the fine new Union Station where it shared facilities in spacious Spanish Mission surroundings with the Santa Fe and Union Pacific in the years of ever diminishing passenger revenue. *(Southern Pacific.)*

SEEN through the barbershop window with the end cars of the *City of San Francisco* and *The Cascade* spotted on their appropriate tracks, the dominant character of the train shed at Oakland was one of great age and gentle decline. Knowing that its years were numbered, the railroad ignored the inroads of time until departing from its confines was as from a museum of memories and a repository of sentimental souvenirs. For San Franciscans it was just that. (*Richard Steinheimer.*)

TRANQUILITY pervades the great train shed at Oakland Mole late in the evening in 1950 between arrivals and departures. The second section, an extra run between Fresno and Oakland, of the *San Joaquin Daylight* has discharged its passengers and will shortly back into the yards while on the farther track the Pullmans of *The Klamath* await loading for a late evening departure. One of San Francisco's now vanished pleasures was the approach to Oakland Mole aboard a Southern Pacific ferry *(opposite)* at the beginning of a train trip while uncounted thousands of travelers since 1875 when the first train shed was built there and the ferries began had caught their first glimpse of the Metropolis of The West from the same vantage point. Just as Broad Street set the mood for arriving in Philadelphia, everyone agreed the water passage was the only thinkable entrance to make to San Francisco. *(Two Photos: Richard Steinheimer.)*

AT VARIOUS TIMES in its checkered career *The Imperial* ran as a sleeper hop between Calexico and Los Angeles, as a Los Angeles-Chicago through train secondary to *The Golden State Limited* via the Imperial Valley and at length as a Chicago haul routed directly between Niland-Yuma instead of the Valley Route. Usually *The Imperial* in its Valley days as shown here in 1952 made its run both ways through the Imperial Valley in darkness, but when the camera of Richard Steinheimer caught it as shown opposite it was running twelve hours off schedule and hence as Extra 4436. A tropical morning sun shines on *The Imperial* amidst the irrigational properties of modern agriculture. At the left the conductor and head-end crew of *The Imperial* compare watches at Yuma. (*Southern Pacific.*)

AS LATE as the early 1950s when *The Imperial* was only a memory in the valley of its name, perhaps the last Southern Pacific passenger run to be powered in steam by a ten wheeler was the night passenger run from Calexico on the Mexican border to Los Angeles shown here at El Centro in the midnight hours. (*Richard Steinheimer*)

JUST TO SHOW the executive brass back at Fourth & Townsend that they were operating at concert pitch, the depot staff at Grants Pass, Oregon, in 1893 had itself photographed in this atmospheric group surrounded by every available property of the passenger agent's calling including an L. C. Smith writing machine, high speed telegrapher's bug, rate books and an alarm clock to show they were on their toes. It was an impressive documentary. *(Southern Pacific.)*

IN THE YEAR 1911 when this 2300 series 4-6-0 was photographed with *The Shasta Limited* near Woodburn, Oregon, by D. S. Warnock, the Oregon-Washington Railroad & Navigation Company observation car *(below)* carried the train name in a diminutive herald hung from the platform rail instead of the imposing drumhead of the years to come. *(Southern Pacific.)*

ALTHOUGH it was later to be shamefully downgraded as a train of all work without a name, *The Klamath* in 1929 when it was inaugurated on the San Francisco-Portland run became the fifth daily train between the two terminals, a roster which included *The Cascade, The Shasta, The Beaver* and *The California-Oregon Express* and to which in a few years *The Shasta Daylight* was to be added. It is shown opposite, in a photograph by Herb H. Arey, paused at Ashland for the accustomed head-end business of a mainliner of long haul importance. At the top, opposite, its provisioning at the southern end of its run was accomplished at the Espee's all-embracing commissary at Oakland. Lounges (*left*) on long runs in those halcyon times were gentleman's clubs where a member of the Lambs or Players, far from home, could expect to find *Variety* in the reading rack along with the regional papers and *The Official Guide.* (Three Photos: Southern Pacific.)

744

IN A LESS DEMANDING age of railroad travel and before a more fastidious public became accustomed to all-room Pullmans, entire families traveled across the continent in open sections and in complete contentment. It was an age when staterooms and compartments were only for the aged and infirm or grandees of importance. Most of No. 10's passengers considered a lower berth to be luxurious. Below are depicted the celebrated snowsheds in the High Sierra at Cisco and the marvelous covered turntable where helper engines were turned for the return descent to Truckee. *(Right: Southern Pacific; Below: Fred Jukes.)*

THE SOUTHERN PACIFIC'S Train No. 10, *The San Francisco Limited* in 1915 was regularly scheduled out of Oakland Pier on a twenty-seven hour run to Ogden in two sections, the first with ten cars and an all-Standard Pullman consist through to Chicago including a ten-section observation sleeper, while the second section carried chair cars and tourist sleepers including one for St. Louis via Denver over the Rock Island. More exotic and a far heavier train was No. 6, *The Atlantic Express* which sailed five hours later with Standard sleepers for Truckee and Susanville, another for Minneapolis over the Chicago, St. Paul, Minneapolis & Omaha (North Western) and an observation car running only between Montello, Nevada, and Ogden. *(Fred Jukes.)*

IN THE YEAR 1915 when pioneer photographer Fred
Jukes, took this magnificent action shot at
Elko, Nevada, while snow was on the sagebrush
and steam exhaust condensed above the engine stack,
the Southern Pacific's Train No. 10 was
The San Francisco Limited running between
Oakland and Chicago via The Overland Route and
the connecting Union Pacific and North Western
railroads. Second in status to the all-Pullman
Overland Limited, No. 10 was still a train of style to
provide an immortal photographic vignette from
the camera of an old master in the iconography of an
as yet unspoiled West. Pullman equipment on
The San Francisco Limited included club cars in which
the smoking lounge was separated from the through
corridor by a partition with leaded glass windows.
(*Above: Southern Pacific; Right: Fred Jukes.*)

748

749

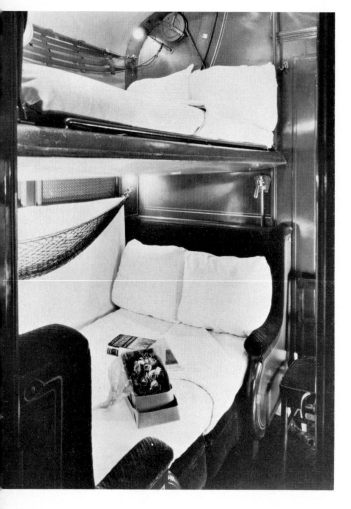

ELKO, Nevada, had changed but little since 1875 when the below sketch was made until 1916 when the photograph opposite of *The Pacific Limited* was made there. Until the coming of the motor car Nevada was still a frontier.

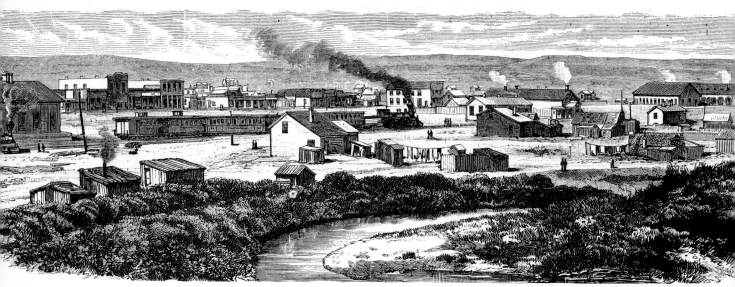

LIKE THE MORE STATELY likeness on an adjacent page, Train No. 20, *The Pacific Limited*, vignetted at the top of the page, was photographed coming out of Elko, Nevada, circa 1916 by Fred Jukes and was a favorite picture subject with the great pioneer photographer. It cleared Elko yards in the morning and hence achieved immortality in a number of Juke exposures. It is shown again below against the Nevada vastness of the Ruby Mountains in a panorama of desolation unchanged from that time until today. On the opposite page the lounge car of *The Limited* is comfortably filled with button boots and yawning young ladies while, to give a stateroom berth character a company photographer has spotted an orchid corsage on the Pullman sheets and a novel for the long jornada to Chicago. *(Opposite and Above: Southern Pacific; Top: Fred Jukes.)*

751

THREE VIGNETTES of traintime activity are characteristic of the depot at Ogden, Utah, where the Southern Pacific and Union Pacific interchanged at a period twenty years later than the portrait of No. 20 on the page opposite. *(Three Photos: Southern Pacific.)*

WHILE, IN THE NATURAL course of events the newest and finest equipment on the Ogden route to Chicago was assigned to the all-Pullman, extra fare *Overland Limited,* Trains No. 19 and 20, *The Pacific Limited* made up in fascinating variety of rolling stock what they lacked in de luxe panache of elegance. As of November 1915, the regularly assigned cars of the eastbound section of the *Pacific Limited* included a baggage car with a dynamo and complete electric plant for illuminating the train, two mail storage cars, two tourist sleepers for Chicago, one out of Omaha via the North Western and the other over the Milwaukee, a Standard diner, five Pullman Standard sleepers, one of them for Salt Lake over the Oregon Short Line out of Ogden and four for Chicago, one by way of Denver over the Rio Grande and Rock Island, one over the Rio Grande and Burlington, one through Omaha and the North Western and one via Omaha and the Milwaukee, and an observation sleeper via the U.P. to Omaha and the rest of the way by the Milwaukee. This complicated scheduling provided either tourist or first class accommodations from San Francisco to almost any imaginable point of importance in the trans-Mississippi West and divided its interchange with five mainline carriers. Even in a day of complex scheduling and involved interchange, *The Official Guide* could show few name trains of such diversification and versatility. No. 20 is shown here in a stylish action portrait taken at Elko, Nevada, in 1916 by Fred Jukes, the grand old man of Western railroad photography.

DEPARTURE OF TRAINS

No.	TO	
	AMERICAN CANYON ROUTE Via OGDEN	
24	Reno·Hazen·Mina·Tonopah·Goldfield via Stockton	
2	"OVERLAND LIMITED" All Eastern Points.	
22	"ST. LOUIS EXPRESS" Ogden Kansas City & St Louis	
20	"PACIFIC LIMITED" All Eastern Points.	
6	NEVADA EXPRESS Sacramento · Colfax · Reno · Goldfield · Susanville·	7
10	ATLANTIC EXPRESS—Reno Ogden Salt Lake City Denver.	9
	SHASTA ROUTE	
14	PORTLAND EXPRESS—Ashland Portland Tacoma Seattle.	8
12	"THE SHASTA" Portland Tacoma Seattle	4
16	OREGON EXPRESS—Klamath Falls Ashland Portland Tacoma Seattle.	8
54	"OREGONIAN" Portland Tacoma Seattle & Puget Sound.	10
	LOS ANGELES AND SAN JOAQUIN VALLEY	
36	Richmond. Martinez. Tracy. Newman. Los Banos. Kerman. Fresno.	6
32	"SACRAMENTO LOCAL" Sacramento via Niles · Stockton · Lodi · Galt · Ione.	7
84	"VALLEY FLYER" Richmond Port Costa Martinez Tracy Modesto Turlock Merced Yosemite Madera Fresno	9
82	Niles · Pleasanton · Livermore·Tracy · Newman · Los Banos · Patterson · Stockton · Oakdale · Sonora	9
8	Richmond Pt. Costa Martinez Byron Hot Springs Tracy Modesto Fresno Bakersfield Los Angeles	6
50	"TEHACHAPI" Fresno Bakersfield Los Angeles	8
26	"OWL" Fresno Bakersfield Los Angeles	6
86	"Oil Fields Express" Martinez. Yosemite Fresno. Visalia. Porterville. Tulare. Bakersfield. Los Angeles.	11
	SACRAMENTO AND SACRAMENTO VALLEY	
24	Niles Tracy Stockton Lodi Galt Sacramento Colfax	6
28	Richmond Vallejo Pt. Costa Benicia Suisun-Fairfield Vacaville Davis Sacramento.	6
32	"SACRAMENTO LOCAL" Sacramento via Niles Tracy Stockton Lodi	7
18	"THE STATESMAN" Richmond Port Costa Benicia Suisun-Fairfield Davis Sacramento	8
18	Red Bluff Redding Dunsmuir Via Woodland Williams Willows Corning	8
14	Dunsmuir via Richmond Sacramento Marysville Red Bluff.	8
22	"St. LOUIS EXPRESS" Truckee via Port Costa Benicia Sacramento Colfax.	9
22	Roseville Marysville Chico	
46	Richmond· Port Costa·Benicia · Suisun·Elmira·Dixon·Davis·Sacramento.	5
38	Niles Pleasanton Livermore Tracy Lathrop Stockton Lodi Galt & Way to Sacramento.	4
48	Richmond·Port Costa·Benicia·Suisun·Davis·Sacramento	5
48	Gerber via Davis Williams Willows Orland Corning.	5
80	"STOCKTON FLYER" Tracy Stockton Lodi	6
20	"PACIFIC LIMITED" Colfax Grass Valley Truckee.	6
6	Truckee Colfax via Benicia Davis Sacramento.	7
16	Dunsmuir via Richmond Sacramento Marysville Red Bluff.	8
	VIA VALLEJO OR MARTINEZ	
124	Ship Yard Train. (Daily except Sunday)	
122	Richmond Oleum Selby Vallejo Jct. Crockett Port Costa (Daily except Sunday)	
42	Richmond Vallejo Napa St.Helena Calistoga Crockett Port Costa Martinez Concord San Ramon	
22	Vallejo. Port Costa.	
50	Richmond Port Costa Martinez Pittsburg Brentwood Byron Hot Springs Tracy	4
44	Richmond Pinole Vallejo Napa Santa Rosa Crockett Port Costa Martinez Bay Point	5
130	Richmond Rodeo Oleum Pinole Crockett Martinez, Except Sunday	7
132	Richmond Pinole Vallejo Crockett Port Costa Martinez, (Sunday Only)	8
	LIVERMORE AND SAN JOSE VIA NILES OR NEWARK	
90	San Leandro Lorenzo Hayward Decoto Niles Irvington Warm Springs Milpitas San Jose	7
32	Stockton via Niles Livermore.	7
502	Way Stations to Santa Cruz & San Luis Obispo via Newark & San Jose .	8
82	San Jose via Niles · Irvington · Warm Springs	9
92	San Leandro Hayward Niles Irvington San Jose	9
902	Stonehurst Local	3
96	San Leandro. Hayward Niles. Irvington. Milpitas. San Jose.	5

A ROLL CALL of the names of the great departed which in the noontide of their going had been the good familiar things of California life made up the list of train departures from Oakland Mole in 1922, which as is suggested below, was the high water mark of passengers on American railroads. Here were rare birds in the lexicon of train amateurs: Train No. 24 for Tonopah and Goldfield a wistful souvenir of the time, more than a decade gone, when the Southern Mines of Nevada and the California border were the talk of every mining exchange in the world, the *St. Louis Express*, depicted opposite, and the old *Portland Express* which took the better part of two days time to achieve Multnomah. Oil was a new thing in Bakersfield and there was an *Oil Fields Express* on the inland run to Los Angeles. There was the *Tehachapi*, too, on the southland run, a name long since forgotten by all but aging students of the legend of Southern Pacific. Wonder, at this remove, rode them all and wonder, of course, rode in steam.

IN THE YEAR 1920 and for six years thereafter there were carried on the Southern Pacific trainsheets Trains No. 21-22, *The St. Louis Express*, an authentic *rara avis* to connoisseurs of such matters, almost as elusive in the pictorial record as the short lived *Arizona Limited* of 1940-41. *The St. Louis Express* ran to the Union Pacific connection at Ogden over the Espee, to Kansas City via the U.P. and into St. Louis by way of the Wabash. It carried a conventional consist of Pullmans, tourist sleepers and chair cars with an open platform observation lounge and tailgate insigne (*vide* "The Central Pacific & The Southern Pacific Railroads.") and its life span bracketed the all-time high in railroad passenger travel which is generally accepted as being reached in 1922. In 1926 it was merged with *The Pacific Limited* and a vestigial trace of this vanished run survives until now in the through St. Louis sleeper that leaves Oakland in *The City of San Francisco*. (*Three Photos: Southern Pacific.*)

754

PERHAPS the noblest name in all the lexicon of Western railroading, *The Overland Limited* between San Francisco and Chicago for more than half a century set a standard of excellence widely imitated but seldom achieved on other transcontinental runs. Opposite in a magnificent portrait taken at Elko, Nevada, in the winter of 1916 by Fred Jukes, *The Overland* heads east through the snowy sage. Jukes, a celebrated pioneer action photographer believes this to be his best of many action views of *The Overland* and himself processed the print from which the reproduction was made. At the left is *The Overland* train gate at Oakland Mole in an atmospheric double exposure while below is its club car circa 1919 from the internal evidence of attire and manners. (*Opposite: Fred Jukes; Two Photos: Southern Pacific.*)

THE GOLDEN SPIKE Hotel at Promontory, Utah, a dodger or handbill for which, reproduced on the opposite page, was handed out aboard all Central Pacific trains without diners as late as 1905, was a relic of primeval times on the transcontinental run and dated from boom days at Promontory in 1869 when the rails were joined there. The inclusion of through diners on all first class runs and the completion of the Lucin cutoff across Great Salt Lake spelled the end for Promontory's foremost eating house as it did for the long haul around the north end of the Lake through the desolate Utah uplands. Above is shown *The Overland Limited* in the days when it was the most compelling name in Western travel taking off at sunset across the Lucin trestle that spelled the doom of Promontory. It is depicted from the head end in a portrait taken in 1916 at Elko, Nevada, by the pioneer railroad cameraman, Fred Jukes. *The Overland's* buffet *(right)*, in the days of hot filament Edison bulbs supplemented by Pintsch gas in case of power failure, was the finest thing on wheels west of Chicago. *(Opposite: Fred Jukes; Three Photos: Southern Pacific.)*

758

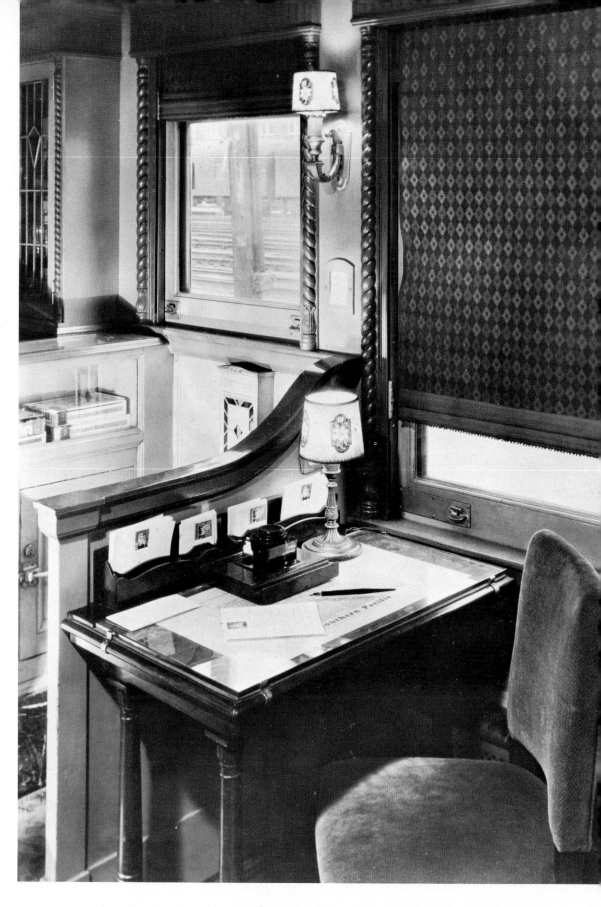

PEOPLE WROTE LETTERS and addressed postcards in the spacious days of *The Overland's* supremacy between Chicago and San Francisco. Such pleasant occupations were accomplished aboard the Southern Pacific's Pullman-Standard lounge cars such as that shown here where abundant resources of heavily embossed stationery and company blotters were available and there was a handy postbox which the car attendant emptied at Omaha, Cheyenne, Green River or Ogden as might be required. It was all part of the pleasant way of travel. *(Southern Pacific.)*

PRETENTIONS to transcendent gastronomy were, in the last years of *The Overland*, more or less abated, but steaks and chops were, until the shortages of the 1941 war, of splendid dimensions and breakfasts were always superb. The Southern Pacific Salad Bowl was institutional wherever the carrier's writ might run and not indigenous to *The Overland* but it was a favorite with passengers and so much in request that its formula was included on the menu. In summer months, as is suggested below, slip covers appeared on the diners and iced tea was in universal demand at meals. *(Two Photos: Southern Pacific.)*

AT WELLS, Nevada, in a series of sweeping curves mounting the only grades of importance between Truckee water and Great Salt Lake, *The Overland* eastbound as shown in the center of the page surged up the Ruby Mountains where to this day elk and antelope are a commonplace outside the car windows. Immediately above, in a view from about 1910, *The Overland* rides the Straits of Carquinez aboard the vast car ferry *Solano*.

At the cartop of the observation rides one of the first illuminated heralds proclaiming the train's name, predecessor of the later tailgate insignes that were the identification of trains of name and breeding everywhere. (*Above: Fred Jukes; Right: Southern Pacific.*)

762

FOR SIX full decades, *The Overland* breasted the
High Sierra, sometimes at dawn, other times at
dusk as a changed carding might indicate.
The abrupt ascent west of Truckee often demanded
helper engines, while double heading was less
frequent on the gentler approaches to the western
foothills out of Sacramento. But whatever
the scheduling or motive power a constant was the
forest solitude and the towering conifers of the
Sierra passes, muffled with snowfall in winter,
mysterious still in the clement seasons and, as is
suggested here a stately frame for the passing
of a great name train of an older West.
(Southern Pacific.)

WHEN THE second streamlined *City of San Francisco* on a bi-weekly schedule was the fastest thing on wheels between Chicago and the Golden Gate its Diesel units required a steam helper out of Roseville if its tight schedule was to be maintained over the Sierra, and it is shown so running as the shadows deepen on a summer's evening somewhere above Auburn. Its standup bar in the Pullman lounge did a land-office business at cocktail time and, during the war years, even its coach space *(opposite)* was sold out to travelers on urgent occasions who could have afforded better had it been available. *(Below: Jim Morley; Opposite, Two Photos: Southern Pacific.)*

FOR EIGHTY full years the Virginia & Truckee cars met the mainline transcontinentals of the Southern Pacific at the depot they shared at Reno. The train board shown here was photographed in the last year of the long and useful partnership of two carriers with their roots in the legendary old West. *(Southern Pacific.)*

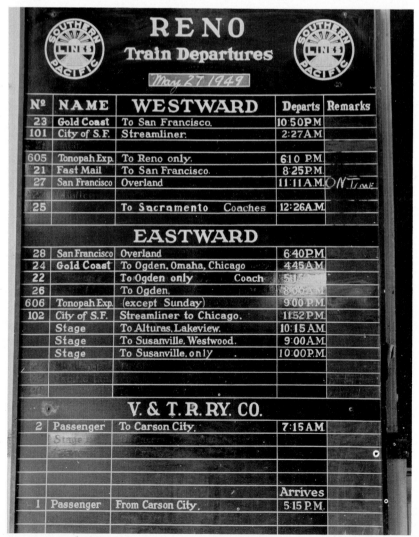

RENO
Train Departures
May 27 1949

Nº	NAME	WESTWARD	Departs	Remarks
23	Gold Coast	To San Francisco.	10:50 P.M.	
101	City of S.F.	Streamliner.	2:27 A.M.	
605	Tonopah Exp.	To Reno only.	6:10 P.M.	
21	Fast Mail	To San Francisco.	8:25 P.M.	
27	San Francisco	Overland	11:11 A.M.	ON TIME
25		To Sacramento Coaches	12:26 A.M.	

EASTWARD

28	San Francisco	Overland	6:40 P.M.	
24	Gold Coast	To Ogden, Omaha, Chicago	4:45 A.M.	
22		To Ogden only Coach	5:11	
26		To Ogden.	8:00 A.M.	
606	Tonopah Exp.	(except Sunday)	9:00 P.M.	
102	City of S.F.	Streamliner to Chicago.	11:52 P.M.	
	Stage	To Alturas, Lakeview.	10:15 A.M.	
	Stage	To Susanville, Westwood.	9:00 A.M.	
	Stage	To Susanville, only	10:00 P.M.	

V. & T. R. RY. CO.

2	Passenger	To Carson City.	7:15 A.M.	
	Stage			

			Arrives	
1	Passenger	From Carson City.	5:15 P.M.	

OF ALL THE once populous and profitable short lines serving the Nevada bonanzas and connecting with the Central Pacific transcontinental main line in the nineteenth century, none was more celebrated or enjoyed as refulgent a longevity as the Virginia & Truckee built in 1870 to serve the Comstock Lode at Virginia City. Wealthy argosies of gold and silver rolled over the V & T's immaculately maintained operations as long as the bonanzas themselves lasted and the end only came in 1950 when the V & T had been an institution of the Old West for eighty glamorous years. In its final days it was a still functioning anachronism, its yellow wooden coaches and beautiful motive power reminders of a way of life that was gone forever. Below, the down train for Carson City rolls smokily through Washoe Canyon while opposite the wooden Kimball coaches appear against a background of the High Sierra near Washoe City. *(Two Photos: Lucius Beebe.)*

LONG A FAMILIAR PROPERTY of California travel, the *Lark* was placed in service on the Coast Route between Los Angeles and San Francisco in May 1910, traversing in the night hours the most spectacular seashore route in the world covered between breakfast and dinner on *The Daylight*. On the opposite page, the all-Pullman *Lark* approaches its Los Angeles terminal in a time when grade crossings were commonplace before construction of the present Union Station. Above, the breakfast time lounge of the *Lark*. (*Two Photos: Southern Pacific.*)

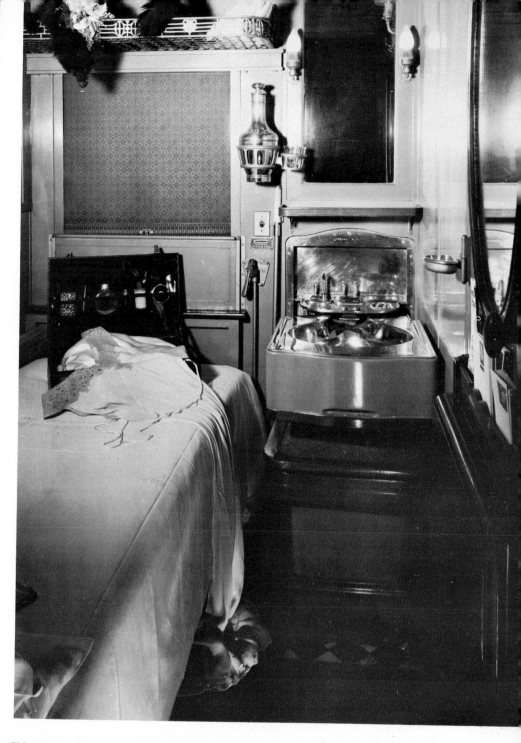

IN THE GREAT DAYS of passenger travel, the Southern Pacific maintained downtown ticket offices at strategic points in both San Francisco and Los Angeles, as shown on the page opposite, as well as in suburban Oakland and other population centers. There a derby hatted generation of travelers could book passage anywhere in the United States, much of it actually over company iron and, as an alternate, take space on the fine fleet of Espee steamers in service between California and New York. The northbound *Lark* is shown opposite passing through South San Francisco in a time when second sections were commonplace. Here the company photographer lent realism to a Pullman Standard single stateroom with a silk nightgown, silver-fitted dressing case and furs and orchids in the familiar Pullman rack above the window. *(Four Photos: Southern Pacific.)*

THE ESPEE station at Third and Townsend was one of the carrier's two entrepots in urban San Francisco, the other being the famed Ferry Building at the foot of Market Street where the ferries connected with Oakland Mole. Built in appropriate Spanish mission style, Third and Townsend was terminal for a large fleet of commute trains as well as Los Angeles and transcontinental runs in happier times. *(Southern Pacific.)*

SOMETIMES in its days of Pullman Standard equipment double-headed as
it appears on the opposite page, the *Lark* often ran in two sections
and is shown southbound at Glendale as it neared its southern terminus in
1935. The new streamlined equipment which was placed in service
after the 1941 war was actually liberally populated with the social
and worldly types depicted in the wash drawing shown here and the train
on its northbound run stopped not only at Palo Alto but also at
Burlingame to accommodate the convenience of San Francisco residents in
that exclusive suburb. *(Two Photos: Southern Pacific.)*

FEW NAME trains in the history of transport occasioned more elaborate promotional literature than the Espee's several *Daylights* when they were placed in service variously over the Coast Route between San Francisco and Los Angeles and the Valley Route between Sacramento-Oakland and Los Angeles. The card reproduced immediately below is evidence of the column of traffic the *Coast Daylight* enjoyed in its years as "The Most Beautiful Train in The World." *(Three Photos: Southern Pacific.)*

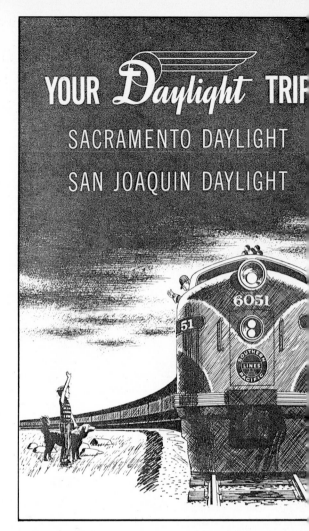

YOUR *Daylight* TRIF

SACRAMENTO DAYLIGHT

SAN JOAQUIN DAYLIGHT

To Our Patrons on the Second Section of the "Daylight":

Because all accommodations on the regular streamlined "Daylight" were sold out we are operating this second section. We regret that all could not be accommodated on the regular train but we are trying to do everything we can to make your trip on this section a pleasant one. On the other side of this card we give the schedule of the second section, believing you will want it for convenient reference, and call attention to the fact that the schedule is only 19 minutes slower than the first "Daylight" and is the fastest train schedule between Los Angeles and San Francisco with the exception of the "Daylight" itself. All available streamlined chair cars (like those on the "Daylight") are used on this train. When necessary other air-conditioned chair cars or coaches are used. In addition this train carries a diner, also a unique Tavern and Coffee Shop car which we feel sure you will be interested in seeing.

F. S. McGINNIS
Vice President, System Passenger Traffic.

SOUTHERN PACIFIC COMPANY

LA

BECAUSE OF its spectacular routing
through the Tehachapi Mountains
in the California southland, the
San Joaquin Daylight at one time in its
career was assigned a vista dome
lounge car as an added attraction.
The Valley Daylight itself is shown
above, double-headed on its westbound
run in Soledad Canyon in 1941
for a stately portrait of mountain railroading by Donald Duke.

775

TAKING A LEAF from the book of the Santa Fe's famous *de Luxe* (see Volume I) which boasted the only other luggage sticker of any name train in the American record, the Espee designed the cachet reproduced below with which passengers on *The Daylight* were urged to identify their bags and at the same time acquire a status symbol.

Southern Pacific

Daylight

LOS ANGELES - SAN FRANCISCO

Daylight

AME

DDRESS

TY   STATE

I'm just as good as *he* is!

It's terrible to have an older brother get all the breaks when he's really no better than you are. Take me. I'm just as good as the Morning Daylight - got baggage elevators, coffee shop, diner, tavern, foam rubber cushions, passenger agent and everything. But because the Morning Daylight was born first, all the boys are selling him instead of me. I'm doing fairly well, but I could do a lot better. Please don't forget me when people ask about the Daylight.

Thanks,

Your NOON DAYLIGHT

THE DEPARTURE of *The Daylight* from Third & Townsend Depot at San Francisco was the event of the day *(opposite)*. Well tended flowering shrubs blossomed at the track bumpers, station personnel stood at attention as one of the great name trains of the West made its departure in glory. *(Southern Pacific.)*

777

IN ITS Standard equipment years, *The Daylight* was still a train of noble dimensions and institutional amidst the tropical palms that lined the Southern Pacific right of way in the vicinity of Santa Barbara. The white faced locomotives assigned to the run even then were semi-streamlined with what was known as a "skyline casing" along their boiler tops. *(Donald Duke.)*

ALTHOUGH in the years when it was advertised by the Southern Pacific as "The Most Beautiful Train in the World" the *Coast Daylight* in its red, orange and black streamlined livery was also perhaps the most photographed train in the world, its connecting stub run, *The Sacramento Daylight,* shown here at Lathrop with a rare Atlantic type locomotive, was one of the least frequently pictured. Although the magnificent equipment which ran in the *Daylight* when it was first placed in service was the most modern that could be had from any carbuilder, icing its cars through a trap in the roof differed but little from the same process which had been in vogue when the first Pullmans started rolling west after Promontory back in 1869. *(Left: Southern Pacific; Below: Donald Duke.)*

IN WINTER months during its glory years *The Daylight* arrived, as shown below, at its terminals by dusk or in total darkness. Here at Glendale in 1951 there still were train-watchers on hand for the arrival of "The Most Beautiful Train In The World" before it whistled off for the brief run to downtown Los Angeles. Its departure then *(right)* was a crowded hour for station personnel. *(Right: Southern Pacific; Below: Richard Steinheimer.)*

BORN UNDER ADVERSE stars despite its lovely name, *The Starlight*, a night companion coach train to *The Daylight* via the Coast Route between Los Angeles and San Francisco, was inaugurated just in time to be cut down by the ever crescent competition from highways and planes and lived a brief life. Here the northbound *Starlight* gets its highball out of Glendale station in the early fifties that will send it on its way through the perfumed California darkness over one of the most spectacular railroad routes in the world. *(Richard Steinheimer.)*

THE SAILING from Los Angeles of *The Daylight* in the years before the 1941 war was, as is suggested on these two pages, an event comparable in its own diminished way to the departure of *The Lurline* from the San Francisco Embarcadero or *The Queen Mary* in the North River. Often, in those happy times, the train was sold out and the management undertook to steer the overflow to *The Coast Passenger,* an accommodation run which left five minutes later. It was, however, a poor substitute for space aboard "The Most Beautiful Train in the World." *(Four Photos: Southern Pacific.)*

783

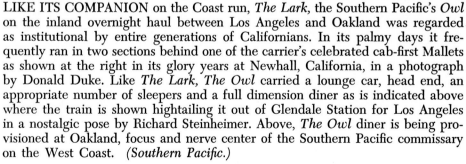

LIKE ITS COMPANION on the Coast run, *The Lark*, the Southern Pacific's *Owl* on the inland overnight haul between Los Angeles and Oakland was regarded as institutional by entire generations of Californians. In its palmy days it frequently ran in two sections behind one of the carrier's celebrated cab-first Mallets as shown at the right in its glory years at Newhall, California, in a photograph by Donald Duke. Like *The Lark, The Owl* carried a lounge car, head end, an appropriate number of sleepers and a full dimension diner as is indicated above where the train is shown hightailing it out of Glendale Station for Los Angeles in a nostalgic pose by Richard Steinheimer. Above, *The Owl* diner is being provisioned at Oakland, focus and nerve center of the Southern Pacific commissary on the West Coast. *(Southern Pacific.)*

CELEBRATED AS perhaps the most convivial of all Southern Pacific name
trains, *The Del Monte's* stand-up bar was a well recognized and
approved rendezvous for thirsty patrons who found it inconvenient to
wait for their first Martini of the evening in the butlered precincts of the
Lodge at Pebble Beach or the stylishly maintained residences of
Carmel. Here foregathered, often before the cars had cleared
South San Francisco, entire generations of Tevises, Morses, Crockers and
other feudal grandees of Monterey. The fashionable Stuyvesant Fish
of Carmel was a regular and the two formidable brothers Lloyd and Gordon
Tevis, descendents of the first president of Wells Fargo and swaggering
magnificoes in their own right, laid down Tevis' Law to the effect that
"Three House of Lords on the rocks before San Jose means straight to bed
on arrival at Pacific Grove." Here a pair of less
exalted patrons are cautiously sampling *The Del Monte's* liquid assets
in a vignette by Richard Steinheimer.

786

NOT ALONE were the passenger accommodations on *The Del Monte* perfumed with privilege and an abode of the polite amenities. Up in the baggage car ahead rode elegant Towser in style to be delivered at Monterey to the chauffeured Bentley of his owner. Below, in the 1880s, *The Del Monte* was pictured in a pastoral setting of open meadows and rail fences at a time when its speed was as sensational as the exalted names on its passenger list. *(Left: Richard Steinheimer; Below: Southern Pacific.)*

ABOVE and at right are two views of
San Francisco's Third and Townsend station
from whence *The Del Monte* departed laden
with clientele on pleasure bent.
The porter's wide smile undoubtedly reflects
the generous tip he anticipates pocketing from
the golf bag's owner, just returned from a
weekend on the greens of Del Monte Lodge.
(Three photos: Southern Pacific.)

LOCALLY KNOWN, in its latter years as "The Rattler," *The Del Monte* as it neared its southern terminal at Pacific Grove traversed manicured vistas in a landscape largely owned by Samuel F. B. Morse, also locally known as The Duke of Del Monte.

Romance Rode The Mopac Out Of St. Louis Into The Old Southwest

NO RAILROAD terminal in the American record ever saw the recurrent arrival and departure of such a rich multiplicity of eye-filling name trains under the corporate banners of so many carriers over so long a period of time as the Union Station in St. Louis. None ever will again. Built in 1894 in the mid-morning of railroad travel, St. Louis Terminal reached its apotheosis in the national folklore a decade later when the Louisiana Purchase Exposition brought hundreds of thousands through its train gates to "Meet Me at St. Louis, Louis, Meet Me at The Fair." No carrier was more entitled to think of the St. Louis Terminal as home than the Missouri Pacific, the greatest of the Gould railroads reaching south and west with connections for California and a purview that regarded the entire Southwest as its feudal domain. From its train bays there departed under the Mopac banner, *The Scenic Limited, The Kay-See Flyer, The Sunshine Special,* in many sections *The Southerner, The Missourian,* and *The Texan.* The last of these is shown here storming up from the river bottom toward St. Louis yards on a winter's day in the long ago of steam and Pullman Standard. (*Two Photos: Everett De Golyer Collection.*)

THE EARLY MORNING ARRIVAL *(top)* of *The Sunshine Special* from Texas
at the peak of the rush hour at St. Louis finds it waiting green from the
tower in company with overnight varnish of the Wabash, Illinois Central and
Gulf-Mobile & Ohio. Below is the interior of the stunning mission-style
observation-lounge car *Xochimilco,* one of the several similar public
luxury cars assigned *The Sunshine* which gave it luster in the highly competitive
traffic between St. Louis and East Texas. It was also a sample of
the carriers' passion for unpronounceable car names.
(Above: Rail Photo Service, Harold E. Williams; Below: Missouri Pacific.)

EAST TEXAS sections of *The Sunshine Special* running over the Texas & Pacific between Fort Worth-Dallas and Texarkana almost invariably rode behind specially assigned motive power with the train name and company heraldry on the smokebox or feedwater heater, and a sufficient pool of engines was maintained for second sections. Below, *The East Texas Sunshine* rolls out of Dallas in 1938 on its overnight run to St. Louis. *(Two Photos: Lucius Beebe.)*

LAST LANDMARKS outbound from the picture windows of *The Sunshine Special*, West Texas section, were the Texas & Pacific's turretted offices at Fort Worth and the vast water tank in the yards advertising the company's stock in trade of travel and transport. The beautiful Spanish Mission styled club-lounge-observation cars in use in the thirties on the El Paso run were numbered 10230-10237 and recapitulated the theme which dominated the public car decor of the St. Louis sections of *The Sunshine*. *(Right: Lucius Beebe; Below: Missouri Pacific.)*

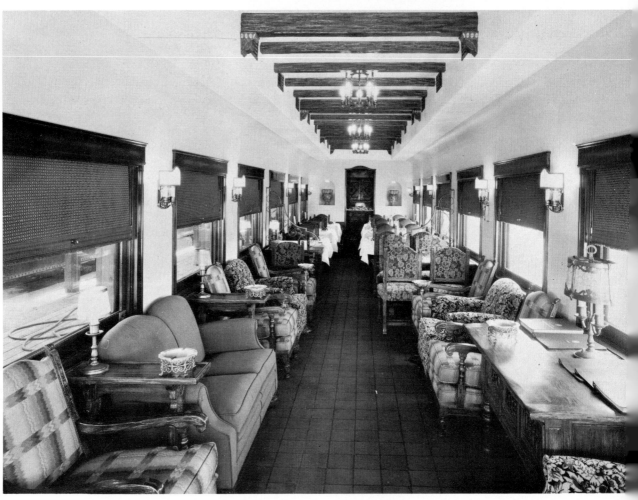

THE WEST TEXAS section of *The Sunshine Special (opposite)* headed for the Great Plains in 1944 behind unmistakable Texas & Pacific motive power and often ran in fourteen car trains with heavy head end to pay the way on the long Lone Star haul to El Paso. *(Lucius Beebe.)*

ALTHOUGH, when the photograph at the right of *The Scenic Limited* was taken by Roland Collons, air conditioning and the general retreat from open observation platforms was still in the future, the Missouri Pacific provided an enclosed solarium observation car in the consist, a forerunner of a type of lounge that was to see far wider use once air conditioning became universal. Breakfast on *The Scenic's* diner and coffee over a copy of *The Post Dispatch* or *The Kansas City Star* could be an event of tranquil satisfactions. *(Above: Everett De Golyer Collection; Right: The De Golyer Foundation.)*

"I WASN'T fortunate enough to be on the initial run of *The Scenic Limited* (above) in the spring of 1915," wrote John Barriger of this important event, "but I stood on the platform at St. Louis in envy of a young schoolmate, Cecil Whitmarsh, who was a passenger. His father was a local lumber man who was a representative of the Business Man's League of St. Louis (as the Chamber of Commerce was then called) to the opening of the Panama Pacific Exposition at San Francisco. This picture, enlarged to a five or six foot dimension and done in sepia tones was widely distributed by the Missouri Pacific throughout the country and was for many years almost a company trademark." Mr. Barriger recalled the event a full half century after *The Scenic's* first run as a high point in the railroading of the period. (*Missouri Pacific.*)

797

THE DUST SCREEN portrayed below was neither a devising of Rube Goldberg nor a property of "Believe It Or Not," but a devising at least in operation long enough to take the photograph on which this drawing is based. "Patrons of the Missouri Pacific," read the caption in a house organ for the year 1930, "may now enjoy the pleasure of lounging on the observation platform of the modern new cars with a minimum of dust due to the placing of newly designed dust screens on the rear of that type of car. The screen is simplicity itself and its operation will contribute greatly to the comfort and convenience of passengers. It serves to prevent dust and dirt from being thrown in the air as the train speeds onward. At present these devices have been installed on many of the fast through trains and others will be installed in the immediate future." The lounge shown at the right rode in *The Scenic* at this time all the way to the coast via its Rio Grande connection out of Colorado. (*Right: Missouri Pacific; Below: Howard Fogg.*)

ROLLING THROUGH THE MISSOURI meadowlands behind a nicely maintained Pacific No. 1151, *The Scenic Limited* was a classic train in its true operational sense, with head-end revenue cars, coaches, diner, lounge and through Pullmans, all the components of a first class train just short of the limited of *grande luxe.* (Charles Clegg.)

799

THE SCENIC Limited after it left the rails of the originating Missouri Pacific at Pueblo became a Colorado institution as the brightest jewel in the diadem of the Denver & Rio Grande Western. Here it is shown pounding up the westbound grade toward Tennessee Pass with coaches and through Pullmans for the Western Pacific connection next day at Salt Lake. *(Richard H. Kindig.)*

THE BOMBAZINE lady crouching over the L. C. Smith Patent typewriter in the year 1907 is secretary to the Missouri Pacific's chief dispatcher at Pueblo. The chief dispatcher himself is the hard looking character in the foreground with the hard hat and hard jaw. The photograph was taken with a wide-angle lens by pioneer cameraman of the time, Fred Jukes.

AWASH with the handsome Gothic bay windows beloved of the period, the Missouri Pacific-Rio Grande uptown ticket office in Denver, also in 1907, was, in a manner, a crossroads of the Gould railroad empire midway between the Mopac and Texas Pacific to the east and the Rio Grande and Western Pacific to the west. (*Western Collection, Denver Public Library.*)

WHILE THE TRAFFIC of the other Nevada short lines, the Virginia & Truckee, Nevada Central and the Eureka & Palisade, connecting in each case to the north of their originating terminals with the Central Pacific main line, had been in precious metals, the commerce of the Nevada Northern which outlived them was in copper. When, in 1906, Mark Requa's Nevada Consolidated Copper Company, later to become the Kenecott Copper of today, brought the Nevada Northern Railroad into being, it was strictly a company carrier most of whose through or continental traffic derived from the Southern Pacific at Cobre and to a lesser degree from the Western Pacific at Shafter, where, at the left, one of its trains is shown silhouetted against the Ruby Mountains. First president of the Nevada Northern was incredibly rich Colonel Daniel C. Jackling, founder of Utah Copper and in its passenger carrying days it rode company officials in a rococo coach that met the *Overland* and other transcontinentals at Cobre. Half this car was a conventional coach, the other half was more elaborately decorated as a parlor-buffet for the benefit of the copper grandees who rode it in great numbers. The Western Pacific's exchange of passengers with the Nevada Northern, effected at Shafter, was largely in the time of the *Scenic Limited* and *The Exposition Flyer*, shown below double headed out of Salt Lake in war time. By the time of the *California Zephyr* it was negligible although the *Zephyr* still paused on demand at Shafter. No W.P. trains in recent years, however, stopped at nearby Tobar, a post office address which, in construction days had been indicated by a sign in the desert reading "To Bar." The name remained. *(Left: Robert Le Massena; Below: Lucius Beebe.)*

THE WESTERN PACIFIC's secondary run from Oakland to Salt Lake City, optimistically known as *The Feather River Express*, was very secondary indeed since it required just under twenty-nine hours to cover the 928 miles between its terminals. This was cut to a breathless twenty-four and a half hours when a railcar known as *The Zephyrette* replaced it but there was still time on its schedule to eat a full steak dinner at the Stockman's Hotel at Elko. Here *The Express* in its days of steam prepares to depart from Oakland Mole with a combine and coach which will lurch over the High Sierra and across the Nevada wastelands in a reasonable facsimile of second class travel in the Old West before the turn of the century. Only the conductor and a single fare share the venerable combine *(right)* as it sets out for Stockton and Marysville over the route followed long ago by the Wells Fargo stages. *(Two Photos: Richard Steinheimer.)*

ALL THE PANOPLY of a mainline sailing of *The City of San Francisco* was invoked in the ritual of departure for *The Feather River Express:* Mars light, air pressure gauges, full train crew and a meticulously lettered train gate board. There was no abridgment of protocol even for a milk run. *(Richard Steinheimer.)*

THE MISSOURI PACIFIC
was not, truth to tell, an
abode of transcendental
gastronomy. To be sure, its
diners in no way reflected the
dyspepsia that was one
of the several ills to afflict
Jay Gould, architect of
its original destinies; quite
the opposite; Mopac fare was
notoriously for heroes at
table and its plentitude
legendary, reflecting the outsize tastes of its Texas
clientele and the bounty of
the Ozarks through which it
ran. At the left a chef
aboard *The Kay-See Flyer*
prepares order of roast
Vermont turkey. Taken with
a bowl of the carrier's
navy bean soup this was
calculated to last a passenger
until he arrived. *(Two
Photos: Missouri Pacific.)*

806

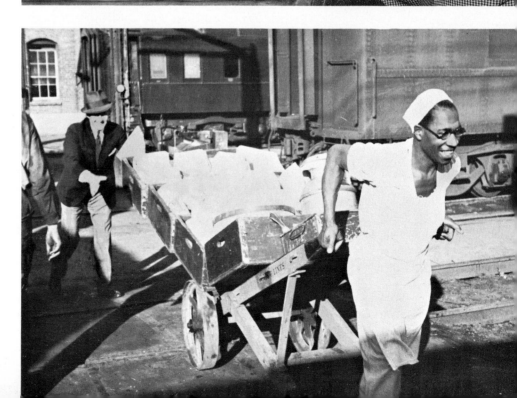

THE GREYHOUND straining-at-the-leash look of the Missouri Pacific's massive No. 5339 shown below characterizes the carrier's *Texan* about to get its highball at St. Louis Terminal for its run westbound through the Ozark night. The unseen length of its consist may be imagined from the vast distance its motive power extends beyond the train shed. Below, the same train is shown from the rear end at Poplar Bluff, Missouri, in 1936, its seven head-end revenue cars suggesting the business it carried in mail and express as well as in passengers. (*Top: William Barham; Below: Everett De Golyer Collection, Roland Collons.*)

AS BEFITTED the most affluent of the great Gould network of carriers whose owning family was among the most conspicuous of the gold table service era, the Missouri Pacific's crack name trains were distinguished for the handsome service plates on their diners. The one of these reproduced at the far left bore the likeness of the *Sunshine Special* in steam, but by 1949 the management evidently felt that internal combustion was here to stay and replaced it by an image of *The Texas Eagle*. The plate at the immediate left, fabricated in 1951, was designed to be sold as a collector's item and was never placed in service. Dieselization was only months away when A. E. Brown took the spirited action shot of *The Louisiana Sunshine* on the page opposite epitomizing the ultimate of steam and Pullman Standard in the blue and white colors of *The Eagle*. *The Sunshine* is depicted at Tioga, Louisiana, en route from Lake Charles to Little Rock. The solarium-lounge was of the familiar *Puebla* and *Xochimilco* decor. *(Four Photos: Missouri Pacific.)*

ALTHOUGH DOUBLE HEADING on the Missouri Pacific's lines running through the steeply graded Ozarks was far more frequent than on the almost gradeless tangents of the connecting Texas & Pacific, it was rare enough to secure the interested attention of A. E. Brown of Shreveport when *The Fast Mail* came into view with tandem motive power out of Texarkana in 1944 as shown in the panoramic view above. The main signal tower *(right)* governing traffic in and out of St. Louis Terminal was burned on July 22, 1940 when traffic was mounting to an all-time peak on the eve of the 1941 war. A period of near chaos followed in which trains were guided in and out of their slips by lanterns and manual signals, and it was not until November of the same year that the first train was guided through the new interlocking by the senior collaborator in this book, acting in an honorary capacity and as the guest of the Terminal Association.   *(Lucius Beebe.)*

810

EQUALLY as atmospheric as the Spanish Mission style lounge-buffet-observation cars on *The Sunshine* were the all-purpose cars listed by the management as dining-sunroom-lounges on such trains as *The Southerner* in whose consist it is listed on the page opposite. An exterior and interior of these versatile and opulent cars are shown below on this page. *(Two Photos: Missouri Pacific.)*

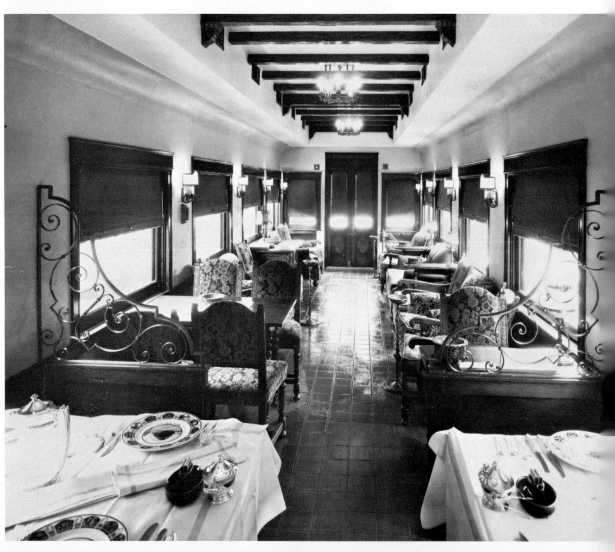

AS IS SUGGESTED by the full dress court portrait of *The Texan* in the opening layout of the Texas & Pacific-Missouri Pacific section of this book, the arrival of heavy Mopac varnish runs in St. Louis during the winter months was accomplished in a spectacular chaos of steam and smoke exhausts. The long grade up from the river bottoms to St. Louis yards was made with the engineer working steam to the limit of his engine's capacity and the effect is recorded here in *The Sunshine Special* with seventeen cars on the drawbar in the now distant year 1937. Carrying green to indicate an extra section, the big 4-8-2 puts on a show worthy of the varied assortment of cars it carries as recorded in the train's consist reproduced on the page opposite. *(Lucius Beebe.)*

813

ON ITS COMPARATIVELY gradeless runs, double heading was
almost unknown on the Texas & Pacific in its years of steam
save for the purpose of moving motive power to different points on the
system without recourse to a caboose hop and special train
movement. Here on the outskirts of Shreveport two 400 series
ten wheelers hurry *The Louisiana Limited* in June 1939. The extra
engine was in request at Marshall, Texas, for a football special and
The Limited afforded the handiest way to get there.
On the page opposite is shown the maiden run over the Pennsylvania
of a New York section of *The Sunshine Special* which was inaugurated
in the first flush of passenger optimism that followed
the 1941 war. The through Pullman sleeper for Mexico City
made one of the longest through runs anywhere in the United States
and informed travelers paused to look twice in Pennsylvania Station at
a name made famous on the Missouri Pacific.   *(Below: A. E. Brown.)*

MARY Hoegberg, a wartime train gate guard at Penn Station in New York charged with seeing *The Sunshine* off on its maiden run out of Manhattan, was so diminutive she had to look up to arriving patrons. (*Three Photos: Pennsylvania Railroad.*)

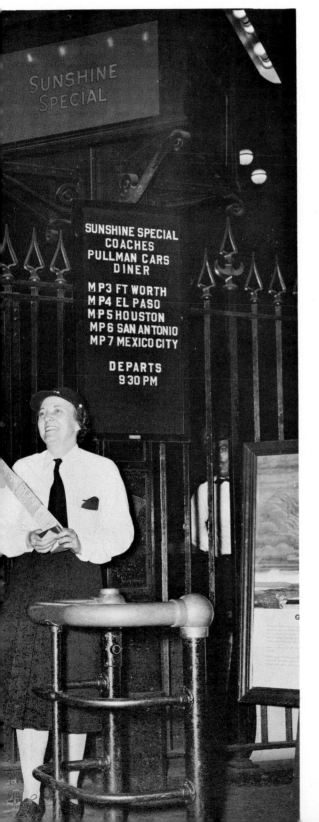

SUNSHINE SPECIAL
COACHES
PULLMAN CARS
DINER

MP 3 FT WORTH
MP 4 EL PASO
MP 5 HOUSTON
MP 6 SAN ANTONIO
MP 7 MEXICO CITY

DEPARTS
9 30 PM

Union Pacific and The Old West
Were the Extension of One Another

The Pony Express, Adams, Colorado, 1939

MOTHER OF WESTERN MAIN LINES and a railroad whose name itself is forever part of the lexicon of the Old West, Union Pacific has been at various times the pioneer transcontinental, a synonym for political corruption, a component of the ambitious transport empire of Jay Gould, a gilt edge investment under Edward H. Harriman and at all times the strong bond and connecting link that joined America west of the Missouri River with The States in post-Civil War times. Like the Santa Fe and Burlington, one of the most influential architects of its maturity was a Boston Brahmin in the person of Charles Francis Adams, and in later years the Harriman heirs maintained continuity in its affairs to give Union Pacific the identity it still has with this powerful family. The first of the great luxury name trains to roll in the splendor of Palace Cars beyond the Mississippi, *The Golden Gate Special* between Omaha and San Francisco was a Union Pacific innovation. The romantic *Overland Limited* was a U.P. varnish run for ten full years before its name was recognized west of Ogden. Originally no more than an indispensible bridge carrier from Omaha to the edge of Great Salt Lake, the eventual absorption of Senator William Andrews Clark's Salt Lake Line to Los Angeles and The Oregon Short Line to Portland gave it access to Pacific entrepots and strategic continental importance. Perhaps because its long haul luxury trains shared trackage rights and prestige with its connections east and west, Union Pacific in recent years originated few name trains of its own, among them the *Portland Rose, Los Angeles Limited, Columbine, Mountain Bluebird, Utah, Pony Express, Idahoan* and *Yellowstone Special.* But with the coming of the age of streamlined Diesel its *City* runs to Portland, Denver, San Francisco, Los Angeles and St. Louis became a hallmark of operational excellence. Its affairs on a truly imperial dimension have always been administered out of Omaha but the seat of executive authority and financial operation has been in downtown New York and in the shadow of Wall Street. For many years its connection with Chicago was divided between the Chicago & North Western and the Milwaukee, but in the fifties its entire passenger traffic was routed over the Milwaukee and the left hand operation over the North Western became a memory. Always there is the long continuity between today's Union Pacific and the heroic past where its roots are, one in the American awareness of a continental destiny with the Concord Coach, Wells Fargo and the Winchester repeater, with the Seventh Cavalry band playing "Garry Owen" and the days of the cattle trade on the Great Plains. It was no accident of chance that saw Buffalo Bill Cody as a professional hunter in construction days on the Kansas Pacific which was in the fullness of time to be the U.P. It has been a name at whose mention the American imagination has always stood at attention.

ONE OF THE HIGHLY REGARDED varnish runs over the iron of the Oregon Railway & Navigation Company before it was completely absorbed by the Union Pacific as a by-product of the Harriman regime was *The Chicago Express* shown below in a spirited action pose dating from 1902 from the collection of George Abdill, ranking Boswell of steam and steel in the Northwest. Like its opposite number, *The Oregon Express,* the eastbound train rolled out of Multnomah with coaches, Pullmans and a brass railed observation car. Denver and St. Louis cars were cut in and out at Cheyenne in a day before the Borie cutoff and may well be part of the photograph of Denver Union Depot at roughly the same period shown at the right. (*Below: George Abdill Collection; Right: Denver Public Library, Western Collection.*)

THE CLOTH traveling cap was de rigueur aboard the lounge cars of *The Chicago Express* soon after the turn of the century and the train's consist as it appeared on the Union Pacific main line near Rawlins is shown in the lower frame in a rare action pose by Fred Jukes and dated 1902 in his own handwriting. *(Library of Congress; Fred Jukes.)*

THE RAILROAD WEST of Fred Jukes, pioneer cameraman of 1906 along the Union Pacific, as depicted on these two pages was not too much removed from the original West of the U.P.'s contriving when it opened up the Great Plains and the route to California in 1869. True, coal had supplanted wood for locomotive fuel, block signals were universal and electric light had replaced the earlier coal oil, but the distances between towns was still immeasurably greater than they were to be in the motor car age, the elements were more hostile and population along the Overland Route was still minimal. Something of the Old West, vast, menacing and primordial, invests the photograph reproduced here of *The Pacific Limited* in 1906 westbound through the deep cut that marked the yard limit at Rawlins. Below, at the eastern approach to the same wide open town, Jukes captioned the lower action shot "A Cold Day at Rawlins, 1906." The above vignette of the Union Pacific's third depot structure at Julesburg, Colorado, conveys much of the flavor of the time and place, the vast coal oil storm lanterns, the shirt-sleeved loungers and the tarpaulin-covered baggage truck all bespeak the lonely Great Plains with the Denver cutoff unseen at the left. *(Western Collection, Denver Public Library.)*

820

THE OVERLAND LIMITED operating as a through train to San Francisco was six years old and a resounding success from every angle in 1905 when the Union Pacific management placed in service an opposite number on the Southern California run named *The Los Angeles Limited*. The new train was fully as handsomely turned out as its transcontinental prototype with luxury equipment, such as the observation-lounge car shown opposite built to specifications by Pullman with the train's name on its nameboards and in a primeval illuminated insigne built into the observation platform roof. Here *The Los Angeles Limited* is shown westbound out of Rawlins from the camera of Fred Jukes. On the opposite page in a rare cracked glass plate from the Wyoming State Archives it is shown on its maiden run a few miles out of Ogden where it would commence the last leg of its routing over the rails of Senator William A. Clark's Los Angeles & Salt Lake Line. The crowded platform of the Union Pacific depot at Los Angeles represented a normal sailing of *The Los Angeles Limited* in the 1920s. (*Above: Fred Jukes; Opposite: Wyoming State Archives; Everett De Golyer Collection.*)

822

LIKE ITS INSPIRATION, *The Overland Limited*, running with fifteen or sixteen cars and often in two and three sections, *The Los Angeles Limited*, shown here in a massive consist in the thirties out of Ogden, Utah, en route to Salt Lake was a train of ample amenities if not actually de luxe dimensions. With the disappearance of open observation platforms and the introduction of the enclosed solarium lounge as shown opposite, something of the dusty charm of viewing the passing countryside disappeared from train travel. So, however, did painful cinders in the eye and the minstrel show appearance of determined platform riders who had spent protracted periods on the verandah riding over indifferently ballasted roadbeds. *(Above: Everett De Golyer Collection; Opposite, Top: Alfred W. Johnson; Below: Union Pacific.)*

A SPECTACULAR interlude in *The Limited's* history was when, on October 17, 1917, it pulled into Laramie to find the depot burning briskly. Danger from falling walls halted the cars until the roof had fallen in. *(Wyoming State Historical Society.)*

THE INAUGURATION in 1906 of *The Los Angeles Limited* on the Overland Route west of Omaha and from Salt Lake to Southern California over Senator Clark's Salt Lake Line was a direct result of the success of *The Overland Limited* on the San Francisco run and the train itself was, in large measure, an opposite number to *The Overland* in conduct and equipment. It was scheduled in direct competition with the Santa Fe's long established *California Limited* and in a few years attracted to itself a following of loyal partisans who felt that Union Pacific was tops in transportation west of the Missouri River. Contrary to general belief and a legend which the Santa Fe was happy to help perpetuate, *The Los Angeles Limited,* not to mention the Rock Island's magnificent *Golden State Limited,* enjoyed a brisk trade in film celebrities of whom Alice Brady, photographed in 1916 at Chicago was one. Opposite, *The Limited* smokes up The Cajon for a portrait of double-headed action by Richard Kindig. Below, its observation end in pre-air-conditioned times was occupied by car No. 1551. *(Left: Chicago Historical Society; Below: The De Golyer Foundation.)*

A TRAIN OF GOLDEN memories in the Western continent, *The Overland Limited*, later known as *The San Francisco Overland* was as much a part of legend as the cable cars and Lotta's Fountain. Generations of San Franciscans took passage on *The Overland* with the same assurance of familiarity as Bostonians rode *The Merchants* on the New Haven and their grandchildren rode the same train when they in turn went east to St. Paul's or Groton and later to Yale or Harvard. Songs were written about *The Overland;* at least one full length book* was devoted to it and countless saloons, restaurants and hotels along its right of way from Nebraska to California bore its name and emplaced its likeness behind the back bar. Its life span lasted from a time when gentlemen took passage on the cars at Oakland Mole or Chicago's old Union Station in silk top hats carrying Gladstone valises until at long last the air age dimmed its marker lights forever. Here *The Overland* seventeen car consist is powered as it topped Sherman Summit double headed by a brace of what many amateurs considered the most beautiful of all locomotives, the Union Pacific's Northern type running under a flawless summer sky in 1953. Relaxed attitudes in open sections and in the diner made a trip from Chicago to the Pacific a lyric experience. *(Opposite: Richard H. Kindig; Two Photos: Southern Pacific.)*

*"The Overland Limited" by Lucius Beebe; Howell-North Books, 1963

OVER ITS trackage through the Blue Mountains of Oregon, the Union Pacific mainline to Portland and the Northwest traversed in the years of steam some of the last truly untamed wilderness areas of the continent, little changed in its essential components of the big sky and the big woods since it was first explored by Lewis and Clark a century and a half before. Here, double headed for the two and a half percent grade, the eastbound *Idahoan* passes a westbound freight that has taken siding for it at Kamola, Oregon, for a notable study of big motive power to match the landscape and the elements with which it contends. *(Henry W. Griffiths, Jr.)*

WHEN THE Union Pacific's rails during the seventies and eighties ran across
the windy summit of Sherman Hill along the original survey, the
transcontinental mainliners all paused to allow passengers to descend from
the cars and admire the Ames Monument, a practice followed by other carriers in
a generation that wanted to see all the sights: notably the Southern Pacific
at Cape Horn in the Sierra and the Rio Grande in the Canyon of the Arkansas.
The Ames Brothers, Oakes and Oliver of Boston had supplied most of the
tools and earth moving machinery used in U.P. construction times when
an Ames shovel was a standard of quality in its field comparable to jewels from
Tiffany or dinner at Delmonico's. Subsequently the Ames Brothers
figured in the Credit Mobilier revelations, a circumstance which in no way
abated the esteem in which they were held either by the railroad or the general
public. The Ames Monument, shown in a contemporary drawing at the
right was at the highest point of Sherman Hill, 8,500 feet above sea level and
was built of pink granite at a cost of $80,000. Likenesses of the
Commonwealth Avenue nabobs adorned the faces of the pyramid. Successive
relocations of the railroad right of way across Sherman Summit removed
them from proximity to the monument and today it stands almost forgotten on a
windy upland, a memorial at once to the men who helped build the
railroad and to the odds against immortality in an unheedful generation.

AS LONG AS STEAM LASTED Sherman Hill on the Union Pacific's main line west of Cheyenne, Wyoming, was a continuous parade of noble motive power and great name trains, usually double headed westbound, and even after the advent of Diesel *The City of San Francisco, The City of Los Angeles* and *The Overland Limited* left Cheyenne depot, shown at the bottom of the page, with steam helpers to the top of the long grade. At the left, toward the end of its glory years, a second section of *The Overland* is running as an extra at the very summit of wind-swept Sherman. Below is depicted the rear end of the *City of Cheyenne,* the most abbreviated of all the U.P.'s *City* trains both in its consist and territory covered. It performed shuttle service between overland mainline trains at Cheyenne and Denver and passengers who made the short but fast two-hour ride aboard the all-aluminum Pullman lounge car *City of Cheyenne* complained bitterly of its rough riding qualities. *(Left and Below: Richard H. Kindig; Bottom: Western Collection, Denver Public Library.)*

THE NAME OF the Union Pacific-Southern Pacific, all-Pullman, extra fare, super de luxe *Forty-niner* that ran from Chicago over the North Western connection to Oakland during the two summers of the San Francisco World's Fair of 1939-40 is marked with a star in the lexicon of Western railroading. Few trains were ever inaugurated with a happier objective, none was ever planned by its owning carriers on a more lavish scale of tangible and operational excellence. Painted grey with white finelining, it ran in steam all the way with specially assigned engines of its several carriers, terminating with a unique two-unit sleeping observation-lounge originally named *Advance* and *Progress* but, in the second year of its operation, more happily renamed *Bear Flag* and *California Republic*. *The Forty-niner* is shown below at Roseville in the Sierra foothills behind one of the Southern Pacific's legendary cab-first Mallets. *(Three photos: Southern Pacific.)*

NO FORMAL restaurant in New York or San Francisco boasted finer kitchen premises with more modern facilities for the service and preparation of luxury food than did *The Forty-niner* as is suggested by the view of its galley reproduced opposite. Every appointment of flowers, wine, cutlery, linen and personnel would have done credit to the Pump Room in Chicago or The Palace in San Francisco, whence many of its patrons derived at either end of its transcontinental run. *Forty-niner* staterooms actually afforded all the room suggested by its promotion photos, but its duplex singles were never intended for an occupant of more than modest size. They contained only token luggage space and use of their plumbing facilities taxed the ingenuity of tall men, but the train's public appointments were beyond reproach.

835

ROLLER BEARING trucks,
then far from universal,
mitigated the risks of shaving
aboard *The Forty-niner* even
though the hour when most
passengers arose westbound
found it on the looping curves of
the Southern Pacific's high
line above Donner Lake.
(Southern Pacific.)

THE DINING CAR *Angel's Camp* on *The Forty-niner* had originally been built to the specifications of a President of Mexico who had not survived to take delivery. Aboard it the Southern Pacific's legendary steward Wild Bill Kurthy plied his patrons with rare viands and suggested champagne for breakfast. *Angel's Camp* at cocktail time *(opposite)* had overtones of the Colony Restaurant in New York with a profusion of cut flowers, smartly uniformed attendants and a clientele of conservative affluence. The dinner hour *(left)* was an event that caused the train to linger in memory as one of the most beautiful and luxurious consists ever assigned to a continental run in the United States. *(Left and Opposite: Southern Pacific; Below: R. H. Kindig.)*

HIS NAME was George or Fred or Henry at the whim of the passenger and with only infrequent reference to the card in every car which proclaimed his proper given name, and he was an American institution. A man of infinite resource, limitless guile and the patience of Job, the Pullman porter has ridden a long way in the American legend. The first porter's name, according to Stewart Holbrook, an authority on such matters, was lost when the records of the Pullman Company were destroyed in the great Chicago fire of 1871, but his universal and generic name has to be George. All, that is except Daddy Joe, the bigger than life Pullman porter of folk-legend who is to the fraternity of Pullman attendants what Paul Bunyan is to woodsmen, a mythical character of incredible achievements. Often in critical moments he saved the day. Sometimes, when railroading was still an adventure, he lost his life doing it. This is not Daddy Joe, but Porter A. B. Jackson welcoming the occupant of Lower 6 to his car in Portland Union Station to ride all the way to Chicago on *The Portland-Chicago Special*. *(The Smithsonian Institution.)*

838

ONE OF THE FEW trains in *The Official Guide* to be named for a flower, *The Columbine, Bluebonnet, Mayflower* and *Azalean* are others—*The Portland Rose* replaced *The Chicago-Portland Special* and antedated *The City of Portland* as the Union Pacific's candy train on the prestige run between Multnomah and Lake Michigan. On it, in its *Portland Special* years, the finest devisings of Pullman craftsmen were lavished and luxury equipment, specially assigned to the run, carried its style in gold letters on the nameboards. At the left its Pullmans are being secured into train line at Portland Union Station in the era of wooden car construction. Above, No. 17 poses for an official photograph in a pose as richly regal as that of any train in the record. *(Two Photos: Everett De Golyer Collection.)*

IN 1913, the predecessor of *The Portland Rose* on the Oregon Short Line, *The Chicago-Portland Special* is shown at the right pounding up Sullivan's Gulch under the 12th Street Bridge at Portland. (*Herb H. Arey.*)

ALL THE AMENITIES of de luxe travel rode *The Portland Rose,* many of them aboard the company-built observation-club-buffet shown on the page opposite and including barber, valet service and soda fountain. With five head-end revenue cars as depicted here, it also carried set-out Pullmans from Salt Lake, Yellowstone, Denver and Green River as well as through cars from Puget Sound to Chicago. A charter member of the railroad horticultural club, along with *The Azalean* and *The Columbine, The Portland Rose* is shown here blooming smokily against the Idaho sky near Boise for its portrait by Henry W. Griffiths, Jr.

841

PERHAPS THE LAST of the long tally of name trains that rolled up to Denver in the era of overstuffed sofas, lalique glass partitions and ornate radio consoles, a list that must include the Burlington's *Aristocrat* and later the U.P.'s own *Denver Limited, The Columbine* represented a final blaze of plush and ormolu before the coming of *moderne* austerity in the decor of *The City of Denver* and, to a lesser degree, in the first *Denver Zephyr. The Columbine's* lounge-observation-buffet whose interior is vignetted above was outshopped in the U.P. car shops at Omaha and furnished by company artisans in a voluptuousness suggestive of the then vanished days of Pullman's Palace luxury. The exterior was painted in royal blue and terminated with a bulkhead herald teeming with regional symbolism. When *The Columbine* was retired in favor of the first *City of Denver* the wonderful lounge cars were reassigned as shown at the right to *The Denver Limited.* (Union Pacific; Rail Photo Service.)

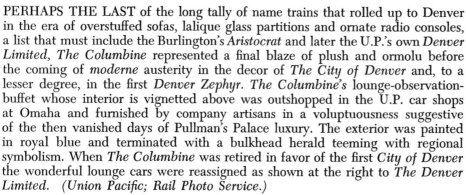

FEW TRAINS, even on the Southern Pacific where identifying train numbers were shuffled in a complexity of change to baffle company historians, were so mutable in their train numbers as *The Columbine* which, at various stages in its life span, ran as No. 11-12, No. 19-20 and finally as No. 15-16. Here it is shown making an early morning arrival in Denver yards with six cars during the interlude when it was identified on company literature as No. 11. *(Richard H. Kindig.)*

843

The COLUMBINE

Flower of Travel Comfort to Colorado

You are viewing today what we have tried to make the finest train in America, a train built especially to typify and represent the state of Colorado. Its name is that of the state flower of Colorado; its beauty is inspired by the exquisite blue Columbine.

Notice the unusual features of the Columbine as you go through it today. Mark how well it typifies the beauty of Colorado. Its interior decorations are the Columbine motif throughout, combined with the state crest of Colorado. Even the china of the dining car is in Columbine design. Each of its new matched Pullmans is named for a flower or tree in the Colorado Rockies, each carries the picture of the flower or tree for which it is named. Dining car and observation car walls are hung with original paintings of Colorado scenes. While you are viewing the interior of the beautiful club observation, stop for a moment to try the luxurious easy chairs and divans in its lounge-rooms, and listen to its radio. Notice also the exterior of the observation car, painted in the colors of Colorado's state flag. Even the coaches are models of luxury, with deep-cushioned individual seats and porcelain-fitted smoking rooms, and decorated with Colorado pictures.

The Chicago & North Western-Union Pacific appreciate the interest you have shown in coming to view this new train, and hope that you will use this train on your trip to Colorado and will recommend it to your friends.

"Flower of Travel Comfort"

RIDE the Columbine this summer on a vacation to the cool Colorado Rockies. You can leave Chicago on the Columbine today and be in the shadow of Long's Peak tomorrow afternoon. It isn't far, and it costs no more than an ordinary vacation. For full information, call or write

H. G. VAN WINKLE   GEO. R. LEMMER
Chicago & North Western Ry.   Union Pacific System
148 South Clark St., Chicago   6 South La Salle St., Chicago

A RANKING member of the horticultural club which included such blooms as *The Azalean* and *Bluebonnet*, *The Columbine*, named for the state flower of Colorado, went into service between Denver and Chicago over the U.P.-North Western rails in 1927 to replace the older *Colorado Special*. Its twenty-eight and a half hour schedule would not have been breathless in comparison with *The City of Denver*, but in 1927 it was considered commendable. (*Top: Union Pacific; Below: Richard H. Kindig.*)

EVERYTHING about *The Columbine* bespoke the varnish run of pedigree basking in the regard of its owning carrier, nothing more than the limousine design, as the company's promotional literature was pleased to describe it, of the solarium lounge car *The Colorado Club* with its intricate blue and gold heraldry symbolic of The Centennial State. Although it antedated the age of air conditioning, the limousine lounge foreshadowed the time when the open observation platform with its aloof implications would be a casualty of air conditioning and vastly greater operational speeds than had hitherto characterized the timecards of even the fastest runs. (*Union Pacific.*)

THE CONSIST of *The Columbine* which had been elaborately designed and built at the Union Pacific Omaha shops was on a scale of luxury to furnish explicit competition to the Burlington's *Denver Special* and later *The Aristocrat* (see Volume I of this book). Although antedating the actual advent of air conditioning, the lighter hues of its decor forecast a day when the abatement of soot in the cars would usher in a vogue for pastel shades and cheerier fabrics. (*Two Photos: Union Pacific.*)

845

THE CHALLENGERS, which served both San Francisco and Los Angeles and ran during the 1941 war in as many as three sections to a train each way, were designed to carry coach passengers and tourist sleepers together with dining car service where breakfast was two bits and dinner an unbelievable thirty-five cents. *Challenger* coaches, as shown opposite, were outshopped specially for the run by Pullman. Sleepers were rebuilt Standard equipment lacking the drawing rooms of conventional usage. Above the *San Francisco Challenger* is shown at Archer, Wyoming, the week before Pearl Harbor. Lacking the panache of an observation, *The Challengers* carried their insigne on the tailgate of the last sleeping car. (*Above: R. H. Kindig; Right: Jim Ady.*)

846

The Chicago & North Western's contribution to *The Challenger* pool was in the form of some of the handsomest and most luxurious streamlined coaches ever built by Pullman. In 1959 the Los Angeles section, as shown at the top of the page where it is being serviced at Cheyenne, carried a vista-dome coach No. 7010 which was cut out of the eastbound section at North Platte and cut into the next day's westbound when it came through. (*Above: Douglas Craig Wornom; Below: Pullman Standard.*)

RUNNING WITHOUT numbers on the Southern Pacific and as Nos. 47 and 48 on the U.P., *The Treasure Island Special* was the companion run on alternate dates to *The Forty-niner* between Chicago and the coast during the two summers of the World's Fair at Treasure Island in San Francisco. It was all-Pullman, extra fare, with the best of everything, lacking only the splendors of the diner *Angel's Camp* which made riding *The Forty-niner* an experience with Delmonico overtones. Here *The Special's* patrons are doing themselves proud in the steaks and chops department. At the right it pulls into Cheyenne in August 1939. (*Above: Southern Pacific; Right: Richard H. Kindig.*)

848

AT THE LEFT, President A. T. Mercier of the Southern Pacific inspects the solarium lounge of *The Treasure Island Special* for the photographers. Company literature promoted *The Special's* fortunes in almost the degree *The Forty-niner* was advertised. *(Two Photos: Southern Pacific.)*

IN THE BELLE EPOQUE OF RAILROAD travel the fastest ride on many a railroad was not aboard the crack flyer or its most highly regarded varnish run but on *The Fast Mail* which carried the government's business and achieved higher speeds than the management would have cared to think about on the timecard of *The Limited*. *The Mail* always carried a rider coach for the accommodation of the crew where passengers who were in a hurry and could do without Pullman accommodations could ride for a first class fare. One of the great sights of riding the old *Chief* in the thirties was to watch the Santa Fe's pride take siding just west of Glorieta and see *The Fast Mail* roll up in thunder on the horizon behind it and pass in smoke and glory at a hundred miles an hour. Here is the Union Pacific's Train No. 26, *The Fast Mail & Express* in Snake River Canyon nearing Glenn's Ferry, Idaho. Opposite is the mail and merchandise it set down at Baker, Oregon, to be carried into the Blue Mountains by the narrow gauge Sumpter Valley Railway from its connection there. (*Above: Henry R. Griffiths, Jr.; Opposite: Owen Davies Collection.*)

851

A TRAIN OF ALL WORK with Standard Pullman sleepers from everywhere to everywhere from Kansas City to Puget Sound was the Union Pacific's *Pony Express*. As the *Pony Express* it existed in proper fact only between Denver and Salt Lake in competition to the more direct scenic route of the Denver & Rio Grande Western's several trains on the run, but it carried a through sleeper from Denver to Portland which was picked up by *The Portland Rose* at Green River, one from Denver to Los Angeles which went on from Salt Lake in No. 7, *The Los Angeles Limited* and another from St. Louis to San Francisco which joined *The Overland Limited* at Ogden. There was also a tourist sleeper from Kansas City to San Francisco which, together with a club-observation car, diner, chair cars and head end often made a twenty-car consist in and out of mile high Denver. To maintain its schedule on May 5, 1946, *The Pony Express* was assigned one of the U.P.'s fast, heavy duty Challenger type articulated engines shown passing Brighton, Colorado, at seventy miles an hour in the below photograph by Otto C. Perry.

AT BORIE TOWER where the Borie cutoff diverges from Union Pacific main line to route traffic south to Denver and by Cheyenne, the tower operator hands up orders to the rear brake of *The Pony Express* on the last Pullman. No. 38 will take the to the left through Greeley on its way to the Queen City of Plains. Like *The Pony Express* itself, Borie is now only a men *(Lucius Beebe.)*

THE ADVENT of the first primeval intimations of Diesel motive power in the West often found it integrated to established Pullman Standard steel name trains for which no lightweight equipment had yet been procured with two conspicuous results: the individuality of the consists so achieved made them acceptable as curiosities to die-hard enemies of internal combustion, and it resulted in frequent power failures and late trains because the Diesels couldn't handle the assigned tonnage. Here the Union Pacific's E-6 type Diesel-electric unit No. 8-M-2 rolls eastbound out of Denver in 1940 with seven Standard cars of the *Portland Rose-Pony Express* bound for Kansas City. Although its departure from the Queen City of the Plains was on schedule, nobody, least of all the management would make book on the hour of its arrival at Kansas City. (*Lucius Beebe.*)

WHEN, in the late 1930s, the long established *Los Angeles Limited* was replaced by the streamlined, Diesel-powered *City of Los Angeles*, the equipment assigned to the run changed with such rapidity that confusion was excusable among the desert sourdoughs along the Utah and Nevada right of way of Senator Clark's original Los Angeles & Salt Lake Line. Within a decade no fewer than five different types of solarium-lounge cars terminated *The City's* consists, three of which are reproduced on these pages, together with the Electromotive power unit that hauled them. Most spectacular of the several innovations in car design was the portholed lounge car *Copper King* whose circular windows were individually adjustable to the desert sunlight. Other blind end cars, some with the train herald, others without identification for interchange with other trains, were sometimes assigned to the run. *(Opposite Two Photos: Everett de Golyer Collection; Below and Left: Union Pacific.)*

IT MAY BE difficult at this remove to imagine the impact on the general awareness of the new streamlined, Diesel-powered *City of Denver* when it was placed in service on the Chicago run in 1936. Diesel was something new and wonderful and not a threat to the entire structure and legend of conventional railroading. So were 100 miles an hour speeds as the veriest incidental to the carding of name trains, and so were the refinements of comfort which manifested themselves in air conditioning, rubber draft gear and unit trains. Nothing possessed greater customer appeal than The Frontier Shack bar car. Repeal was still a novelty and, for many, drinking was still a full time occupation and any departure from conventional decor and train appointments a source of delight. The vogue for Victorian atmosphere and the Old West was at its zenith and the Frontier Shack was so successful that imitations sprang up on every hand. Within the limitations of car construction, it was a decorator's dream and comprised all the atmospheric components that, elsewhere at *The City's* western terminal, could be encountered in the Victorian bar at the Cosmopolitan Hotel, the Teller House in Central City and, somewhat later, in the Strater Hotel at Durango. Here were "Wanted" posters from Wells Fargo, the bloodhounds on the ice from Civil War road companies of "Uncle Tom," the pugilistic profile of Jim Jeffries and the voluptuous likeness of Lillian Russell. Long forgotten race horses peered from ornate frames and playbills heralded the arrival nearly a century later, of Adah Isaacs Menken in "Mazeppa." There were crying towels at the bar and the barkeep wore roached hair and satin sleeve suspenders. The Frontier Shack had everything and, in time, the U.P. imitated its own success and emplaced a Little Nugget bar car on *The City of Los Angeles*. (*Three Photos: Union Pacific.*)

856

*The Old West
Lived Once More
Aboard
The Frontier Shack*

DINNER on the dining car has been, in the American awareness, possessed of a special significance as a sort of participation in a ritual or sacrament of travel. Its service on *The City of Denver*, where the tufted red leather upholstery was a hallmark of Union Pacific gastronomy, was an occasion at once for the lady passenger shown in silhouette as she lifts the first Martini of the evening and for the camera of Richard Steinheimer which was ready to hand for this moment. That *The City* afforded a variety of rear-end insignes is suggested below and opposite. *(Richard H. Kindig.)*

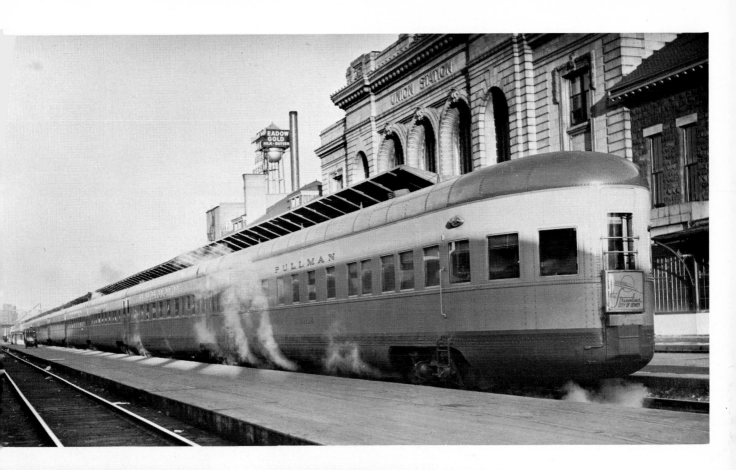

RAISING the window blinds of his midnight stateroom, the wakeful passenger on *The City of Denver* at Lincoln or Omaha beheld one of the ancient rituals of railroading, the icing of reefer cars laden with perishables from the rich farmlands of the West, some of which would almost certainly appear on the dining car breakfast table next morning. (*Above: Richard H. Kindig; Left: Richard Steinheimer.*)

THE VERITABLY Spartan simplicity of decor that characterized the public apartments of *The City of Denver* as shown on this page was in dramatic contrast to the wildly ornate decorative scheme of the train's Frontier Shack bar, shown on an adjacent page and to the profligate elegance of The Little Nugget that shortly appeared on *The City of Los Angeles.* With these splendid exceptions, the era of plush and ormolu had ended on the Union Pacific. The fact called attention to the still modestly voluptuous equipment of the Burlington's *Denver Zephyr* on the competing run where matched woodwork and rich appointments still maintained continuity with an older tradition of railroad luxury. *(Three Photos: Richard H. Kindig.)*

The Bird in The Gilded Cage Sang
Again in The Little Nugget Bar

THE SHOW STOPPER of *The City of Los Angeles* was not so much the *Copper King* observation lounge with its $175 Polaroid lenses in porthole windows as it was The Little Nugget bar car which, if possible, transcended the atmospheric success of The Frontier Shack on *The City of Denver*. The Little Nugget was a decorator's dream of Victorian love seats, rich velvet portières, bevel-edged mirrors and gas lighting fixtures. The bartenders wore gay nineties attire with horseshoe tie pins and button boots, and late tarriers were sometimes moved to song which invariably turned out to be an approximation of "A Bicycle Built For Two." For a brief interlude before the advent of the 1941 war curtailed all non-revenue equipment, the Frontier Shack and Little Nugget were the sensations of Western railroading. (*Union Pacific.*)

THE NOW distant year of 1905 found Fred Jukes, boomer railroadman and the great pioneer of modern railroad photography, working the Union Pacific on its transcontinental main line between Cheyenne and Green River, a time and place where not all transport was aboard the steamcars as is suggested by the busy scene at Rawlins (right) as photographed by Jukes a decade later. The Saratoga & Encampment Valley Railroad, a U.P. feeder joining the main line at Walcott, Wyoming, had not yet been built and if you wanted to get to Encampment, a smelting town on the Wyoming-Colorado boundary, or fish the North Platte in the mountains to the south, you took the stage coach depicted above. "I was a passenger on that particular stage," recalled Jukes nearly six decades later, "having to take the train from Rawlins to Walcott which is a few miles east of the U.P. bridge across the North Platte River. It was beautiful country and the Saratoga & Encampment Valley line didn't then exist. The passengers on the stage when I took the picture were a couple of traveling men (salesmen) in hard derby hats, the others were ranchers for Saratoga, a small ranch town about two-thirds of the way to Encampment. The driver, a real old timer, wore engineer's goggles. It was something right out of the Old West you read about." Still another conveyance that Jukes rode and photographed in 1905 was Union Pacific motor coach No. 1 above and opposite. This experimental vehicle was assigned to local runs out of Rawlins where it is shown with C. M. Beard, its motorman, later U.P. Superintendent of Motive Power, and the car's mechanic, Floyd Schultz. These are vignettes of the legendary past when the century was young. (Three Photos: Fred Jukes.)

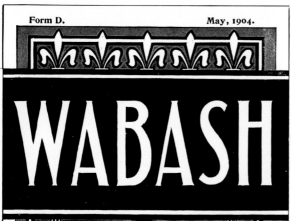

WABASH

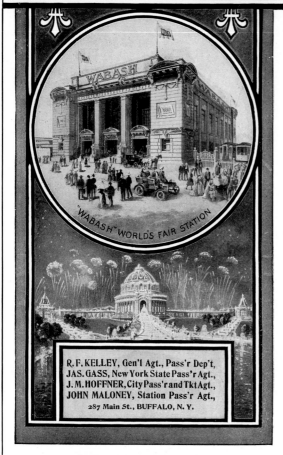

"WABASH" WORLD'S FAIR STATION

R. F. KELLEY, Gen'l Agt., Pass'r Dep't,
JAS. GASS, New York State Pass'r Agt.,
J. M. HOFFNER, City Pass'r and Tkt Agt.,
JOHN MALONEY, Station Pass'r Agt.,
287 Main St., BUFFALO, N. Y.

HEARTS and handkerchiefs fluttered as one to greet the arrival over the trestle of the great Eads Bridge across the Father of Waters at St. Louis of the Wabash's *Centennial Limited* with sleepers out of Boston over the Boston & Maine and from New York by the then flourishing West Shore Line, all concentered on Buffalo whence they achieved St. Louis itself over the Wabash's own iron. For it was the year of the great St. Louis Fair and all the world was telling Louis to meet it there.

No motor car was visible beneath the deck of Eads Bridge where drays from the Levee were plentiful, but the Burlington Route, in competition with the Wabash west of The Gateway and for the Kansas City traffic flaunted its advertising in the background. The atmospheric photograph was taken in the now distant year of 1904 by Harry Boggs and is from the collection of Bernard Corbin.

A TRAIN which became a legend in commercial circles in its own lifetime, *The Detroit Arrow* maintained jointly by the Pennsylvania and the Wabash on the Detroit-Chicago run enjoyed such prestige as a businessman's train as almost to eclipse the rival New York Central *Twilight Limited* which was all-Pullman parlor car and provided a far more comfortable ride. *"The Detroit Arrow* of The Pennsylvania Railroad," said the company literature for 1938 rudely neglecting to mention the Wabash, "is the fastest train in America. It makes the run from Liverpool Tower (Gary, Indiana) to Junction (Fort Wayne) a distance of 116.4 miles in eighty-nine minutes—which is at a rate of 78.47 miles per hour." From Fort Wayne to Detroit over the rails of the Wabash no such spectacular carding was maintained, but sharing a pool of diners with the connecting carrier notably improved the Pennsy's indifferent cuisine. The Wabash cream chicken pie with dumplings was (and is) almost as celebrated a component of dining in motion as the lobster Newburg on *The Twentieth Century Limited*. Above, *The Detroit Arrow* with a K4s on the head end and a Wabash diner six cars back pulls out of Englewood depot in 1949. (*Rail Photo Service, Harold E. Williams.*)

866

4¾ hours
from the Heart of
CHICAGO
to the Heart of
DETROIT

The DETROIT ARROW

Chicago to Detroit

Lv. Chicago . . 5:15 P. M. (E. S. T.)
    (Union Sta.)

Ar. Detroit . . . 10:00 P. M. (E. S. T.)
    (Fort St. Sta.)

(WESTBOUND)

Lv. Detroit . . . 4:25 P. M. (E. S. T.)

Ar. Chicago . . 9:10 P. M. (E. S. T.)

2 other great trains daily

DETROIT EXPRESS

Lv. Chicago (Union Sta.) 10:30 A. M. (E. S. T.)
Ar. Detroit . . . . . . 4:30 P. M. (E. S. T.)

(WESTBOUND)
Lv. Detroit . . . . . . 12:07 P. M. (E. S. T.)
Ar. Chicago . . . . . 5:55 P. M. (E. S. T.)

MID-CITY EXPRESS

Lv. Chicago (Union Sta.) 12:30 P. M. (E. S. T.)
Ar. Detroit (Fort St. Sta.) 7:50 A. M. (E. S. T.)

(WESTBOUND)
Lv. Detroit . . . . . . 12:15 A. M. (E. S. T.)
Ar. Chicago . . . . . 7:50 A. M. (E. S. T.)

All trains air-conditioned for all-weather comfort.
Reclining chair coach service.

PENNSYLVANIA RAILROAD
WABASH RAILWAY

IN THE LONG AFTERNOON of Pullman
Standard, *The Detroit Arrow* kept the faith with
the open platform observation-parlor cars *Queen
Anne* and *Queen Mary*, shown on an adjacent
page, even though the train's speed made occupancy of the open platform a debatable pleasure.
The Arrow was making tracks in the lower photograph behind K4s Pacific No. 5492 before it
had cleared the shadow of Union Station in the
Chicago background.   (Left: Rail Photo Service;
Below: Pennsylvania Railroad.)

AS STYLISH a daylight run as the most exacting perfectionist could ask, *The Detroit Arrow* on the page opposite rolls decorously out of Detroit yards behind Wabash Pacific No. 689 before hitting its full stride on the Wabash racetrack to Fort Wayne for its rendezvous with the Pennsylvania. The Pennsy's assigned engine for the run with the train name on its smokebox was a high-wheeled Atlantic entirely capable of hauling its valuable train on one of the tightest cardings on the timetable. On this page is reproduced an idealized view of *The Arrow* storming out of Chicago behind a K4s Pacific, while below in the carrier's familiar Tuscan red livery, the Pullman-built, parlor-observation car *Queen Mary* gleaming with gold finelining and brass was a tribute to the beloved English queen. At ninety miles an hour, however, admirers either of the monarchy or the scenery didn't care to use the open observation deck. *(Opposite, Two Photos: Rail Photo Service; Left: Pennsylvania Railroad; Below: Richard J. Cook.)*

ROLLING OVER the 488 intervening miles between Detroit and St. Louis in the classic tradition of steam, the *Detroit-St. Louis Limited* was the overnight counterpart of *The Wabash Cannon Ball* on the daylight run. The Wabash delighted conservatives by retaining on both *The Cannon Ball* and *The Banner Blue* to Chicago the open platform observation car of tradition with its identifying train herald. Opposite, *The Limited* runs westbound through Sangamon, Illinois, in 1941 behind a characteristic light Pacific No. 688. The sleeper-lounge *Salt Lake City* is shown in detail at the bottom of the page and at the immediate left as it backs down past Perry Tower prior to leaving St. Louis. Below is the coach-buffet interior of *The City of Kansas City* built in 1947 by A.C.F. for the convenience of passengers desiring drinks and snacks. *(Opposite, Top: Paul Stringham, Rail Photo Service; Left: Rail Photo Service; Below: Wabash Railroad.)*

ON A COLD autumn morning in the mid-1930s when it was still a varnish run of pedigreed dimensions and the principal contender for daytime passenger traffic between St. Louis and Kansas City, The Mopac's *Kay-See Flyer* gives scant attention to grade crossings as it rolls through Webster Grove on the outskirts of St. Louis on its westbound run. For the carriage trade *The Flyer* carried a parlor car which brought up at the rear with a fine open observation platform. The carrier favored A.C.F. rather than Pullman with its patronage, a circumstance perhaps dictated by the presence of the former's shops within the St. Louis industrial complex. *(Right: Missouri Pacific; Below: Lucius Beebe.)*

AT Jefferson City, Missouri, *The Kay-See Flyer* pauses and car tonks give its journal boxes a hasty inspection to assure safety on its tight schedule. At the left it gets a wheel out of Kansas City while the Kansas City Southern's *Southern Belle* paces its departure with a business car on the track immediately to the right.   (*Howard Fogg; Rail Photo Service.*)

873

ANCIENT, AMBLING and much loved, *The Carolina Special* came into being
in 1911 as a Chicago-Charleston daily over the rails of The Big Four from
Chicago to Cincinnati where it was taken over by the Southern Railway for an
unhurried schedule through the cape jasmine (at appropriate seasons) to the
ancient citadel of the Confederacy. Frequently operated in two sections with
coaches, diner and Pullmans terminating in the brass-bound observation verandah
of tradition, *The Special* was a name train of homely destinies and folksy ways.
It made long stops to handle head end and seldom hurried between them. Five
cars, as shown in this 1912 photograph meticulously copied from an original
print by the master craftsman, Fred Jukes, were about as many as its motive
power could haul and second sections, as shown on the page opposite, frequently
carried additional coaches. The Southern's depot at Richmond in the year 1906
showed a conventional cab rank of victorias and growlers with a single high-
backed touring car of unidentified make at the *porte cochere* to symbolize the
dawning age of internal combustion. (*Cook Collection, Valentine Museum.*)

875

Competition For the Twin Cities Traffic
Was Conducted With Brass Knuckles

VERY MUCH OF a component in the Chicago-Twin Cities rivalry for passenger favor between the Big Three of the region was the Milwaukee's *Morning Hiawatha* shown here sooting up the skyline in a splendid display of ambitious firing as it clears the depot in downtown Milwaukee itself. Two other daytime *Hiawathas* not to mention the overnight pride of the line *The Pioneer Limited* with affable Dan Healy managing the diner were the road's entries in the sweepstakes whose other competitors were the North Western, the Burlington and, at one time, the Soo and Chicago Great Western. *(Lucius Beebe.)*

FULLY AS DETERMINED and almost as ruinous to the contestants as the competition for passenger traffic between Chicago and St. Louis in the great years of surface travel was the rivalry for the prestigious varnish business between Chicago and the Twin City terminals at St. Paul-Minneapolis. Here as many name trains cleared the Lake Michigan metropolis on competitive schedules at identical hours of day and night on the Big Three of the regional rivalry, the Milwaukee, the Chicago & North Western and the Burlington as cleared for the St. Louis Gateway on the Illinois Central, the Wabash, the Chicago & Alton, and the Chicago & Eastern Illinois. And on the North Woods run there was minor but still spirited competition from the Soo and the Chicago Great Western. The Burlington carried sleeper passengers west and parlor car patrons east in the Great Northern and Northern Pacific connecting runs for the *North Coast Limited* and *Empire Builder*, and in their own *New Black Hawk* and *Mississippi Riverview*. Patrons of the North Western by way of Milwaukee aboard *The North Western Limited, The Viking-Soo-Dominion, The Victory* and *The Duluth-Superior Limited* were offered an alternate routing via Madison on extra sections of the same trains with the addition of *The North Western Fast Mail, The*

Chicago Limited and *The World's Fair Special*. Partisans of the Chicago Great Western might take space, at various times, aboard *The Minnesotan, The Great Western Limited* and *The Legionnaire*, while perhaps the ranking name train of them all in Standard Pullman times was the Milwaukee's classic *Pioneer Limited*, flagship of the carrier's fleet of name trains made famous by the presence as dining car steward of venerable Dan Healy. There was also *The Day Express* and *The Olympian* which made St. Paul-Minneapolis as on-line stops on its through routing to Seattle. When the high speed runs with streamlining and airflow design arrived to stimulate competitive cardings, the North Western's *400* was briefly the wonder of the railroad world while the Milwaukee inaugurated an all-new streamlined *Pioneer Limited* and no fewer than three *Hiawathas* daily in each direction. The Burlington retained its old established *Black Hawk* and the conventional Great Northern-Northern Pacific connecting runs and laid on a *Morning Zephyr* and an *Afternoon Zephyr*. The Chicago-Twin Cities competition represented the last great brass-knuckles warfare for passenger patronage on parallel runs before the carriers began retrenching and ceased to care about revenues from their once proudly maintained varnish runs.

877

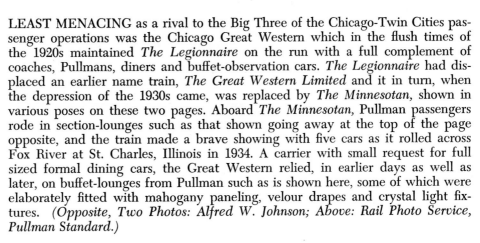

LEAST MENACING as a rival to the Big Three of the Chicago-Twin Cities passenger operations was the Chicago Great Western which in the flush times of the 1920s maintained *The Legionnaire* on the run with a full complement of coaches, Pullmans, diners and buffet-observation cars. *The Legionnaire* had displaced an earlier name train, *The Great Western Limited* and it in turn, when the depression of the 1930s came, was replaced by *The Minnesotan,* shown in various poses on these two pages. Aboard *The Minnesotan,* Pullman passengers rode in section-lounges such as that shown going away at the top of the page opposite, and the train made a brave showing with five cars as it rolled across Fox River at St. Charles, Illinois in 1934. A carrier with small request for full sized formal dining cars, the Great Western relied, in earlier days as well as later, on buffet-lounges from Pullman such as is shown here, some of which were elaborately fitted with mahogany paneling, velour drapes and crystal light fixtures. *(Opposite, Two Photos: Alfred W. Johnson; Above: Rail Photo Service, Pullman Standard.)*

879

SOME CARRIERS were fortunate, before the end of steam came to abate their photogenic qualities, in having devoted photographic admirers who made a specialty of their regional pictorial record. The Southern Pacific had, among others, Richard Steinheimer, the Union Pacific gloried in Richard Kindig and Henry R. Griffiths, Jr., the Colorado narrow gauges had their pictorial minstrel in Otto Perry and the Chicago terminals achieved immortality through the camera of Alfred W. Johnson. The jongleur of the Soo was Leslie V. Suprey several of whose photographs are reproduced in this chronicle and who here presents a study of Train No. 65, the Moose Lake local as it clears the Moose Lake yards in 1948.

SEEN FROM Roosevelt Road overbridge at Chicago in 1949, *The Soo-Dominion*, freighted with intimations of a northern continent, races double headed into the yard on the overnight run from Minneapolis against an unmistakably Chicago backdrop of railroading. Lacking the panache of an observation car, the summer-time-only *Mountaineer* approaches its Chicago terminal with its train herald affixed to the tailgate of its final sleeper. (*Rail Photo Service, Robert H. Heurman; Alfred W. Johnson.*)

SO CLOSELY intertwined, in the case of *The Wabash Cannon Ball* are fact and folklore that it is difficult to establish where legend ends and the ascertainable record begins. As with the Lackawanna's *Phoebe Snow*, however, it seems likely that the myth antedated the actual train, since before the turn of the century there was a music hall ballad about "The Wabash Cannon Ball" although no such train appears in the company literature of the time. The song had little relationship with Wabash geography of fact since it depicted the carrier's tracks as reaching from the Atlantic to the Pacific and skirting the lakes of Minnesota. In 1946 the Wabash translated folk-legend into reality when it inaugurated *The Wabash Cannon Ball* on the daylight run between Detroit and St. Louis with new streamlined coaches, a company-owned diner-lounge and a parlor-observation car with a single drawing room. To power the train, as shown in Howard Fogg's painting, the carrier rebuilt several locomotives into truly beautiful 700 series 4-6-4s. Other *Cannon Balls* have run over the Long Island and the Texas & Pacific, the latter of which once figured in a spectacular head-on collision. Legend, too, ascribes immortality to Casey Jones while driving an Illinois Central "Cannon Ball" but no such train appears in the timetables of the period. When the Wabash's fine business car *City of Wabash* rode the end of *The Cannon Ball* its tailgate insigne was fixed to its observation rail as shown here. (*Above: Wabash Railroad; Right: Paul Stringham.*)

882

Way Down East

IN THE PEACEFUL WORLD that knew the summer of 1912, the Boston & Maine Railroad's *Montreal Express* out of Boston for the Canadian metropolis was photographed by Herbert Lincoln Arey as it stopped for water at Potter Place, New Hampshire. The fireboy pulled down the spout toward the tender of No. 1366, a couple of passengers descended from the cars to take the air, and an intelligent photographer recorded a scene that might have served as backdrop for the Broadway production, decades later, of "Ah, Wilderness!"

PASSENGER OPERATIONS north and west of Boston in the period which, in general terms confines the contents of this volume to between 1890 and 1950, might categorically be divided into runs originating and confined to Northern New England and those originating elsewhere and having New England terminals or vice versa. In the first group would fall, for example, *The Kennebec Limited, The Flying Yankee* and *The Pine Tree Limited* while the much larger classification would include *The Bar Harbor Express, The Minute Man, The Gull, The Ambassador, The State of Maine, The Alouette, Redwing* and *East Wind.* Obviously the greater number of luxury name trains were on the longer hauls, to Montreal, Philadelphia, Washington, Chicago, and in the more distant past, St. Louis, Pittsburgh and Cincinnati. Whether or not their destinations were within territorial New England or farther afield, the concern of the following pages is with trains of essentially Yankee character with part or all of their mileage through the New England heartland and the Way Down East that is the subconscious home of so many Americans even though they live in Wisconsin or Arizona. Their pictures are a nosegay of remembrance for the varnish that once ran over the Boston & Maine, the Maine Central, the Central Vermont, the Rutland and the immortal Fitchburg in their long ago country yesterdays. To those who loved them, if only at second remove and in the telling, their memory is an article of faith.

AT THE TOP of the page is a fine period view of the Causeway Street depots of the Eastern Railroad and, beyond it, the Lowell, when they were two of the components of Boston's "Railroad Row," the others being the Fitchburg and the Boston & Maine.

885

Gateway To The Yankee Heartland

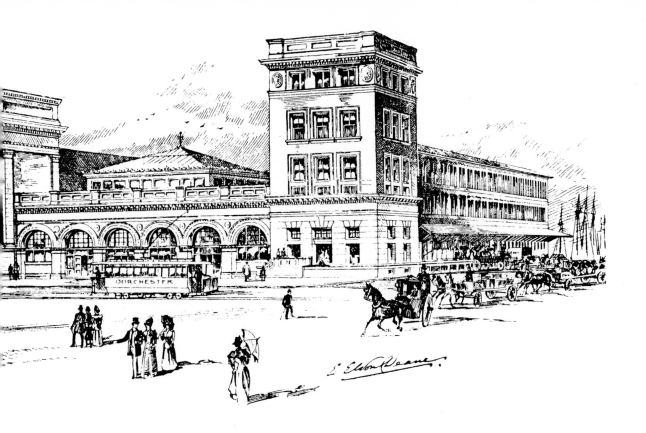

BOSTON'S UNION STATION, as it was formally known at the time of its construction in 1893, or more familiarly the North Station, was the terminal of the Boston & Maine-Maine Central complex of carriers which fanned out from its throat tracks across Charlestown Estuary to send varnish trains over the home iron as far west as Troy and by connecting carriers to Portland, Montreal and far-off St. John's, Newfoundland. Subsidiary roads, branches and short lines covered New England with a close-grained network of railroads, all of them terminating, like vines in a pot, in the train bays of North Station. No interchange existed between North Station and the New Haven-Boston & Albany terminal at South Station a mile and a half across town. Instead North Station routed its debouching passenger traffic to urban and suburban destinations over an equally complex network of public carriers via subway, elevated and surface trams and, of course, public hackney carriages and private conveyances. Few all-Pullman trains were ever scheduled out of North Station, the resoundingly named *Boston & Mt. Desert Limited Express* of 1897 being an exception to this generality, but there were sleeping cars and diners in rich profusion of vintages in

the consists of *The Montreal Express, The Gull, The Ambassador, Minute Man, Flying Yankee, Kennebec Express* and *East Wind.* New England railroads had neither the resources nor the incentive of competition for updating equipment or motive power that animated carriers elsewhere and, as a result, the traffic that flowed north of Boston as long as steam and Pullman Standard lasted was an antiquarian's dream. Wooden underframe Pullmans, colored glass transoms, ornate wrought iron observation platforms rolled under summer suns and through the Down East winters in an animated facsimile of turn of the century operations that was perpetuated until the 1941 war. No all-room sleeping cars, no enclosed solarium lounges or chromium decor marred the facade of 1910. As long as passenger traffic lasted in New England it went fanwise north of Boston as it had done last year and year before that, and when at last it vanished into the coachyards of Acheron, it was beckoned to rest by a highball hoisted to a yard on rope halyards in the same manner the first varnish run had been given green more than a century before. New England railroading, to the end, kept faith with yesterday. *(Opposite: H. W. Pontin.)*

CUSTOMS INSPECTION at Vanceboro, Maine where the St. John & Maine Railroad crossed the Canadian border, was less formal in the year 1900 than it was to become at a later date. Gladstone valises and Saratoga trunks were inspected in the informal setting of a cow pasture, which may have been acceptable enough in summer months. What it must have been like in winter and the less clement seasons of spring and fall when sub-arctic elements were in possession, may be left to the imagination. Presumably travelers were a sterner breed of men in those days. *(Brown Bros.)*

A FINE THING to see and very big time railroading in its place and era was the Boston & Maine's *Montreal Express* rolling downgrade at Gale, New Hampshire, in 1912 on its all-day *jornada* across New England.   *(Herb L. Arey.)*

A PERIOD piece, the dispatchers' office at Boston's North Station in the year 1890 guided traffic over the Eastern and Western Division and the Fitchburg in a classic atmosphere of wing collars and propriety suitable to the conduct of one of New England's greatest enterprises. *(Bradlee Collection, Essex Institute.)*

THE REMARKABLE photographs on this and the opposite page represent the Boston & Maine depot at Lynn, Massachusetts, then the shoe and leather capital of the world, as it appeared in the fullest flower of daily traffic *(right)* in 1888 and *(below)* as seen from almost the identical spot after the Great Fire of November 26, 1889. In the before view a Boston-bound local is emerging from the arched train shed that spanned the tracks between the north and southbound waiting rooms. After the conflagration only structural elements have survived the flames and even the crossing tender's shanty has lost its windows while bowler-hatted commuters stand on the unsheltered platforms. *(Two Photos: Laurence Breed Walker Collection.)*

RAILROAD CROSSING
LOOK OUT FOR THE ENGINE

BEGINNING IN THE SIXTIES as the railroads eliminated the long rough journeys in stage coaches over usually execrable roads, the White Mountains of New Hampshire suddenly flowered with prosperity as vacation spots and idyllic retreats not only for the wealthy and leisured classes from Boston and New York but for the commonality much as the jet age a century in the future would see ribbon clerks vacationing in Hawaii and small tradesmen taking the grand tour of Europe in three weeks' time. "It was in those years," wrote Alvin Harlow in *Steelways of New England*, "that famous hotels had their heyday—the Profile House, the Crawford House, the Summit House on Mt. Washington, the Pemigewasset; Littleton, Bethlehem, North Woodstock, the Conways and other villages became tourist centers." The superb photograph reproduced here depicts the Boston & Maine's gleaming No. 775 with a varnish run paused at Franconia, New Hampshire, about 1900, Franconia Notch being the scene of some of the most rugged mountain vistas in New England. *(Everett De Golyer Collection.)*

WHEN THE White Mountains were first made available to the tourist trade on a large scale toward the end of the nineteenth century, it was through the agency of the railroads that first penetrated the primeval wilderness with trains originating from Boston and Portland. The Portland & Ogdensburg Railroad, a carrier enjoying an enviable summer trade, carried open observation cars such as that shown above on all through trains.

The same car is shown at the left traversing a roadbed only recently carved from the wilderness. (*Two Photos: New Hampshire Historical Society.*)

893

THE CONCORD & MONTREAL RAILROAD, whose two fine Palace Parlor Cars *Passaconaway* and *Lafayette* are shown at Boston's North Station in 1895, was a consolidation of the earlier Boston, Concord & Montreal which connected at Fitchburg, Massachusetts, with the Fitchburg Railroad out of Boston and achieved Wells River, Vermont, via Concord, New Hampshire, which gave it an entrepot to the rich White Mountain tourist trade in competition with the Boston & Maine, the Maine Central and the Portland & Ogdensburg. It connected for Canada over the Grand Trunk and was one of the richest railroad properties in New England until the time of its lease to the B.&M. for ninety-nine years the year these photographs were taken. Its proud title of Concord & Montreal was swallowed in the corporate entity of the Boston & Maine but its slogan, "The White Mountain Line," shown on the car nameboards was retained for many years. Over it *The Montreal Express* and the cars *Lafayette* and *Passaconaway* rolled on happy traffickings that provided the largest dividends of any New England carrier for several decades.

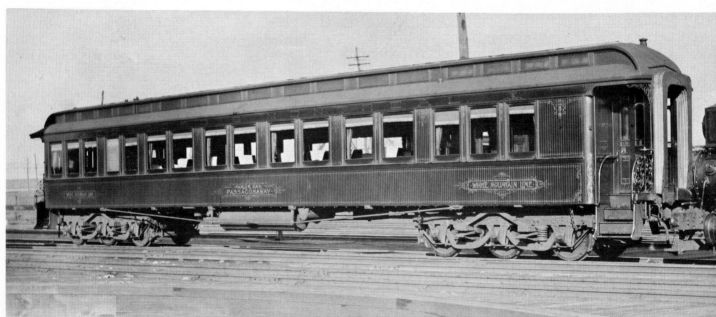

WHAT WILL attract students of railroad operations in this sketch of a Boston & Maine newspaper train from *Harper's Weekly* in 1890 is the inclusion, according to the specific testimony of the artist, of a Woodruff Parlor car as rider coach. More usual practice was the use for occupancy by the train crew of a downgraded day coach rather than a rare and exotic piece of luxury equipment. Not so exotic, perhaps, but still a rare item of varnish stock is the combination sleeper-parlor-observation car *Fernie* which for many years ran between Boston and Canada in the overnight *Red Wing,* a sleeper hop on the Boston & Maine and Canadian Pacific. *Fernie* had begun life when it was outshopped by Barney & Smith for the Soo's Chicago-Twin Cities service and rounded out its long and useful lifetime in the New England hills. *(Below: Arthur D. Dubin Collection.)*

HEAVILY patron-
ized in the summer
months, *Alouette* was
sometimes reduced
in winter to three
or four cars besides
head-end revenue,
Here, at Newport,
Vermont, in the
winter of 1947 the
management felt that
doubleheading was
indicated in the face
of a Yankee
blizzard and a 4-6-0
helper was taken
on ahead of a 4-6-2
road engine.

SHOWN below, *The Alouette* is posed beside a Concord local under the historic and ornate Boston & Maine train shed at Concord, New Hampshire in 1946. (*Two Photos: Philip Hastings.*)

IN THE TEEMING DAYS of railroad travel in New England, the Boston & Maine's day train, *The Alouette*, ran over its originating carrier from the North Station as far as Wells River, Vermont, where it was taken over by the Canadian Pacific for the remaining five hours' run to Canada. A train of leisured pace, it rolled all day through the lush New England countryside as shown above and passengers could get breakfast and lunch on the comfortable C.P. buffet-observation car, carrying one of the last brass-railed platforms with its identifying train herald north of Boston. It arrived at Montreal at 6:16 giving travelers plenty of time to check in at the Ritz or Mount Royal and tidy up for dinner. *(Two Photos: Rail Photo Service; Above: H. W. Pontin; Right: W. G. Fancher.)*

897

ALTHOUGH the terminal of the Boston & Maine's Gloucester Branch at Rockport was a scant thirty-five miles distant from North Station, the status of its patrons back in 1906 when the photograph at the bottom of the page was taken was so exalted that an all-parlor car train left Boston on Friday afternoon and returned Monday morning for the convenience of a clientele to whom coach travel would have been unthinkable. Patrons included Henry Cabot Lodge, Henry C. Frick and Searses, Lowells and Saltonstalls past all counting. When patrons of "The North Shore Dude" in a moment of hauteur changed the corporate name of their residence from Manchester to Manchester-by-the-Sea, Dr. Oliver Wendell Holmes subscribed his letters "Beverly-by-the-Boston & Maine." "The Dude" is shown below paused at East Somerville and arriving at Magnolia where it is being met by an ancestral Packard with a *Roi des Belges* tonneau. *(Rail Photo Service; Library of Congress.)*

THE LEGEND engrossed over its imposing main entrance ran for all to read "Union Station" but no Bostonian worth his salt codfish on Sunday morning knew it as anything but The North Station, to identify it from the South Station where the New Haven and Boston & Albany arrived on the other side of town. A vast preponderance of the North Station's traffic was in commuters bound for Melrose, Malden or Haverhill, Winchester or Woburn in the Boston & Maine's characteristic red and green upholstered, open platform day coaches impregnated from decades of service with a smell of valve oil and coal smoke that was all their own. The elite of these commuters, especially in the summer months, and many of them regulars on the "North Shore Dude" headed for Pride's Crossing, Beverly Farms, Magnolia and Nahant where servants were already preparing cooling drinks for them on the wide porches of massive Victorian mansions and the Eastern and Corinthian Yacht Clubs. Luxury equipment, except on a few through trains for Canada and the West was infrequent at North Station and such ostentations of splendor as private cars almost unknown. Carpet bags and chin whiskers and Yankee accents that could pronounce "cow" in four sylables, poke bonneted old ladies and shoebox lunches were a commonplace long after they had become the properties of comedy elsewhere in the land. (*Above: The Smithsonian Institution; Opposite: Rail Photos, The Library of Congress.*)

ALTHOUGH, in the Great Fire of 1872 which
flattened much of Boston's commercial district, the
Mansard roof had been much blamed as one
of the agencies in spreading the catastrophe, it
was still incorporated in the overall design
of the Boston & Maine North Station when it was
built, in part on the site of the old Eastern Railroad
depot, some twenty years later. Most prominent
feature of the truly noble brick, granite and
stone structure fronting on Causeway Street was a
massive colonnaded archway in classical style
seventy-five feet high "and said to be the largest
in the U.S." The public hack stand, which,
in order to abate the truly furious competition of
cabmen of the time, was a concession, was enclosed
against the elements, a fact noted with much
satisfaction by the Massachusetts Humane Society.
Two miles of track within the depot proper
terminated in twenty-three train gates under a
vast wire-glass canopy piped for steam
against the snows of winter. When this photograph
was taken in 1898 it is notable that the only
vehicles in sight not horse-drawn were two of the
open electric trolley cars immortalized in a
poem by Oliver Wendell Holmes as "broomstick
cars." The ark-like conveyance at the far left
was long a familiar sight in downtown Boston,
surviving well into the motor age and an era of
more sophisticated advertising. It was a
horse-drawn structure in the shape of a house
whose sides and roof were plastered with
advertising matter for Stewart's Cut Rate Railroad
Ticket Agency at 231 Washington Street.
Here frugal Bostonians were advised bargain
tickets to anywhere were sold, having been made
available by railroad patrons unable to use
transportation already purchased but unwilling to
abide the delay implicit in its redemption at
face value by the carrier. *(Library of Congress.)*

IN THE YEAR 1897 when the photograph immediately above was taken at the Fitchburg Railroad's imposing home depot at Fitchburg, Massachusetts, the *Green Mountain Flyer* on the Boston-Montreal daylight run was already a New England institution with a life expectancy of more than five decades ahead of it. Its classic 4-4-0 No. 47 had been built a few years before as Fitchburg No. 97 but renumbered in 1895 to take the *Green Mountain* through to its Rutland connection at Bellows Falls. The fine Fitchburg covered depot at Keene, New Hampshire, was also a classic of the covered shed station of the nineteenth century and the *Flyer* paused here too. The Asa Dunbar House with its handy railroad cafe at the left of the tracks had been the birthplace of the mother of Henry David Thoreau. *(Top: Essex Institute; Below: Herb H. Arey Collection.)*

IF THE FITCHBURG Railroad achieved immortality for nothing else (and it was in fact a major influence on Boston's highly solvent economy in the nineteenth century) it would have been famous for its massive Boston terminal shown here hard by the Boston & Maine's North Station in Causeway Street and for the circumstance that, running as it did past Walden Pond, it delighted Henry David Thoreau, patron and spirit of that enchanted mere. Quite unexpectedly in so anarchistic an individualist, he saw beauty in the approach of the locomotives at sunrise, marked the dedication of the track workers clearing snow in winter and discerned virtue in the flanged traffickings of commerce as readily as any Beacon Street shareholder. "What recommends commerce to me is its enterprise and bravery. . . . It seems as if the earth now had got a race worthy to inhabit it." Fitchburg Station in Boston, whence at one time through Pullmans departed via the West Shore, the Wabash and the Nickel Plate for Chicago, was in the best tradition of New England railroad architecture, which is to say it was designed to resemble something else. Built at a time when Italian villas, Egyptian temples, Roman baths and Islamic mosques enjoyed a widespread vogue, the Fitchburg took note of the already widely admired Boston & Maine station at nearby Salem and elected a Gothic castle as its paradigm. Like the structure at Salem it was built of massive masonry with crenelated and turreted towers. Unlike the Salem landmark which permitted trains to run right through it, the Fitchburg was a terminal depot ending in stub tracks. Shown at the right of the photograph are the horse cars to Charlestown where the carrier's first station had been before it moved in-town. (*Bostonian Society.*)

903

JUST three quarters of a century after the photograph reproduced below was taken in 1875 at the Boston & Maine-Rutland Railroad interchange at Bellows Falls, Vermont, the highball signal on its tall mast or a replacement thereof was still in place to govern the movements of the *Green Mountain Flyer* depicted on the opposite page with the Rutland's No. 92 on the business end. The train shown is No. 64, the southbound New York section of *The Flyer* and the River Street highball shows two globes to indicate a clear track into town. At the right the Rutland's No. 78 poses by the Bellows Falls coal dock waiting to take *The Flyer* north. (*Right and Opposite: Philip R. Hastings; Below: Everett De Golyer Collection.*)

SURROUNDED by racks of travel brochures, old fashioned letter presses, Cunard Line lithos and the other properties of his calling, William C. Hall was Boston & Maine ticket agent at Keene, New Hampshire, and for the Fitchburg before it. The photograph reproduced here was dated 1915 and the space on the *Green Mountain Flyer* sold by Mr. Hall could have been beyond all counting. *(David R. Roper Collection.)*

905

EVEN IN WHAT WERE DESTINED to be the declining years of its operations, the Rutland saw the smoke and heard the familiar sounds of railroading by day and by night in the Northern Vermont city of Burlington hard by the haunted shores of Lake Champlain. On the opposite page a series of photographs taken in the midnight hours in the year 1946 depict the pickup of the Burlington sleeper by the southbound *Mount Royal* with its early morning destination in New York City. At the top the southbound train arrives while the Pullman is still spotted on the far track while at the right a carman signals that it has been coupled into the train consist. Below, switcher No. 100 moves the darkened car with its occupants warm and secure in their berths into the trainline. *(Three Photos: Philip R. Hastings.)*

THE DAYLIGHT COUNTERPART of the midnight hours depicted opposite at the Rutland's station at Burlington, Vermont, was supplied by the arrival and departure in either direction of one of the oldest and most venerated names in New England railroading, *The Green Mountain Flyer* which had been running between Boston and Montreal since before the turn of the century. Here *The Flyer* heads west out of Burlington on its long tangent across the islands of Lake Champlain into a sun that is setting alike upon its coaches and parlor cars and on the fortunes of the railway itself. *(Philip R. Hastings.)*

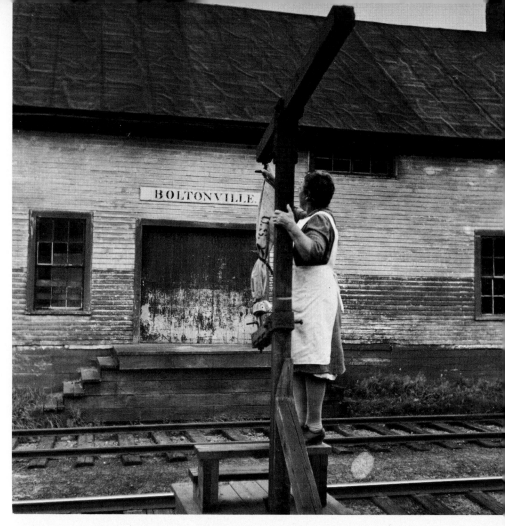

IN 1923, the Montpelier
& Wells River Railroad in
Vermont had run six
daily passenger trains over
the thirty-eight miles
between the terminals of
its corporate name.
Twenty years later its
name had been changed
to the Montpelier & Barre
and its mileage had
shrunk to fourteen. In the
years between, however,
its daily mixed had regu-
larly picked up the
U. S. Mail at Boltonville
and set it down where
the postmistress is shown
here hanging it to the
mail arm and speeding its
way cityward in No. 4.

908

THE DEEP SOUTH and deepest New England alike were the last strongholds of the daily mixed, the train of all work that delivered the merchandise and picked up the milk, set out high cars on weed-grown sidings and carried the mails, and had modest accommodations for the train crew and occasional passengers, mostly intransigents too set in their ways to acknowledge the automobile. The daily mixed was strictly a country affair, its business was in remote inaccessible pockets of resistance to progress, and it ran from yesterday to yesterday without ever emerging altogether into the twentieth century or acknowledging the universal disaster of change. Here the Rutland's No. 7, at Mooers, New York, with five refrigerator cars of upstate milk, an express car and rider coach, rolls on its smoky occasions under a spectacular summer sky in 1949. Like the photographs on the opposite page, this study in pastoral tranquility is from the ubiquitous camera of Philip R. Hastings.

THE NEWS KIOSK at St. Johns Depot, Portland, about 1912, carried as its regular stock in trade *Judge, Leslie's, Everybody's Magazine, The World's Work* and, perhaps, Colonel William D'Alton Mann's scandalous *Town Topics* for the sophisticated social trade bound for Bar Harbor. For the young it stocked Tootsie Rolls, Crackerjack, Necco Wafers and a variety of sweets known only to antiquaries in a later generation. Below: in its daytime luxury consist of parlor cars, diners and de luxe coaches painted an eye-popping canary yellow and cream for its summer-only run between Maine seacoast resorts and New York and Washington, the Boston & Maine's *East Wind* gets a wheel from Pacific No. 3710 in September 1940 just twenty-five miles south of St. Johns Station, Portland. *(Gerald Best Collection.)*

Table 5b—PORTLAND, ME., AND NEW YORK.

	No. 82	STATE OF MAINE EXPRESS.	No. 81	
......	*8 00 P M	lve...Portland....(B. & M.).arr.	*5 43 A M	......
......	8 36 P M	lve...Biddeford (Thornton St.)...arr.	5 13 A M	......
......	8 51 P M	lve.........Kennebunk.......arr.	4 58 A M	......
......	9 36 P M	lve.............Dover.........arr.	4 16 A M	......
......	10 00 P M	lve............Exeter........arr.	d3 56 A M	......
......	10 25 P M	lve........Haverhill.......arr.	h3 33 A M	......
......	10 39 P M	lve........Lawrence........arr.	*3 16 A M	......
......	*7 40 P M	lve.........Concord........arr.	†7 40 A M	......
......	8 08 P M	lve.......Manchester.......arr.	7 05 A M	......
......	8 31 P M	arr...Nashua (Union Sta.)...arr.	6 28 A M	......
......	8 55 P M	arr...........Lowell.......lve.	†6 07 A M	......
......	11 17 P M	lve...........Lowell........arr.	*2 38 A M	......
......	11 50 P M	lve.............Ayer........arr.	2 11 A M	......
......	12 40 A M	arr.......Worcester.......lve.	1 25 A M	......
......	4 25 A M	ar.New Haven (N.Y.N.H.&H.R.R.) lve.	8 55 P M	......
......	6 20 A M	arr.New York (G. C. T.) » lve.	*8 00 P M	......

LACKING the overtones of almost unearthly splendor of *The Bar Harbor Express* and terminating its run at Portland, whose St. Johns Station is shown below, *The State of Maine Express (left)* was still a long standing and institutional name train originating on the New Haven and, in summer season, not without consequential patronage, especially on weekends. There were setout sleepers for Concord, Rumford and Rockport and the cachets of the better yacht clubs and resort hotels identified the Louis Vuiton luggage in its drawing rooms and compartments. Here behind a Boston & Maine no-nonsense Pacific to give it a wheel, *The State of Maine* rolls down east as the long shadows of trackside grasses indicate the hour of sunrise. *(Left: Philip R. Hastings; Below: Everett De Golyer.)*

PRECISELY on the site of the Eastern's depot in Causeway Street and half a century after its demolition there arose as shown below the many storied Manger Hotel as part of the structural complex that included the new North Station and a sports arena. Loading where the Eastern's platforms had been is *The Gull* headed for Way Down East and the Maritime Provinces. The straitened throat tracks leading from North Station across Charlestown Estuary were much in the same pattern as they had been in the Eastern's day. (*Two Photos: Railway & Locomotive Historical Society.*)

WHEN, in 1894, the wreckers demolished the old Eastern Railroad depot in Causeway Street where, together with the Fitchburg and the Boston & Maine, it had been part of "Railroad Row," to make way for the new Union Depot, a landmark disappeared and with it much of the legend of early New England railroading. Among its component properties mourned by sentimentalists was the station bell, recovered from an ancient Spanish cathedral by one of the road's early presidents which had tolled the arrival and departure of trains. Part of the Eastern's body of legend, when it started business back in 1839 had been a salute of welcome in the *Salem Gazette* by Nathaniel Hawthorne, and the long annals of its feuding and warfare with the Boston & Maine were part of Boston's financial geology. The end was foreshadowed for the Eastern by the great Revere disaster of August 1871 in which twenty-nine died and the suits filed in consequence all but ruined the carrier. Here Jehu in an Inverness cape solicits business for his growler at the Eastern's austere portal in an atmospheric photograph from the archives of the Railway & Locomotive Historical Society.

THE *Day White Mountain Express* shown on these pages, and its opposite number *The Night White Mountain Express* with Pullman sleepers instead of parlor cars was the Boston & Maine-New Haven connection via Springfield for the resorts of its title, Fabyan's, Bretton Woods and Whitefield with their terminal at Berlin. The day train carried a broiler-buffet and parlor cars to White River Junction and the night consist included sleepers to and from Bretton Woods. *The Day White Mountain* is shown immediately above emerging from a deep rock cut at Bradford, Vermont, while at the depot of that name a trainman emplaces a flag that will protect its departure for ten minutes. In the far frame, the lights are already on at Bradford as No. 77 loads mail and head end. *(Four Photos: Philip R. Hastings.)*

AT THE RIGHT, *The White Mountain Ex* is shown near Randolph, Hampshire in 1946 heading a rare type of wooden ered bridge whose trusse protected by wo sheathing but lacks the tective roof and side of the more familiar co bridges of tradi

914

AT ROUSES POINT,
New York, where they
cross the River Richelieu,
the gantleted rails of the
Central Vermont,
corporate entity of
Canadian National in the
United States, and the
Rutland symbolized their
interlocking yet
divergent operations.
(*Philip R. Hastings.*)

FROM EARLIEST TIMES the annals of railroading from New York-Boston to the several Canadian terminals of Montreal, Quebec and the Maritime Provinces were freighted with romance and partook of the flavor of foreign adventure. The Pullmans and their luxury consists took off over wildly improbable routings for storybook destinations, often in the teeth of formidable opposition from the elements and from the New England geology, so that through sleepers for the West once rolled out of Portland for Montreal via the wooden covered bridges of the St. Johnsbury & Lake Champlain and visionaries dreamed of Portland as the nation's principal entrepot from Europe. Prone as it was to flights of elfin whimsy, New England travel in the nineteenth century produced no more enchanting eccentricity than the rare and exotic Monarch Patent parlor-sleeping car *Queen Anne* shown opposite from the collection of Andrew Merrilees. A pure sport, in the biological sense of the word, *Queen Anne* went into service between Boston and Canada over the rails of the Quebec Central Railroad and its varnished exterior is shown posed with admirers around its open platform.

Immediately below, *The Red Wing* on the Boston & Maine-Canadian Pacific overnight run between Boston and Montreal establishes continuity with the nineteenth century as it passes under the spans of a venerable wooden covered bridge in upstate New Hampshire as it nears its northern terminal. *(Two Photos: Philip R. Hastings.)*

THE MINUTE MAN, shown loading from North Station's ancient wooden low level platforms, was in reality a token luxury train rather than a veritable de luxe consist and carried but a single through Pullman for Chicago which was cut into the Central's all-Pullman *Lake Shore Limited* at Albany. It was, however, a conversation piece and a gesture of defiance in the direction of the Boston & Albany and its non-New England Vanderbilt management.

PULLMANS and parlor cars of uncertain vintage rolled on the mannered and leisurely occasions of the Boston & Maine's name trains through the New England countryside in modest numbers in the great years of rail travel, connecting with the outside world through such atmospheric runs as that of *The Minute Man* shown opposite, and *The Pine Tree Limited* depicted below in a full-dress portrait about to leave North Station for its Portland-Bangor terminals to the east. *The Minute Man* represented the B.&M.'s answer to the Boston & Albany's several daily trains for Chicago and afforded passage to the West without patronizing the B.&A. which many proper Bostonians regarded with suspicion as a property of the rascally Vanderbilts that had been forcibly ravished from its original Yankee ownership. The fact that *The Minute Man* connected via Troy and Albany with the New York Central, itself the Vanderbilt's most resounding property, was conveniently forgotten. *The Minute Man* had all the hallmarks of the grand manner, specially painted locomotives, PAUL REVERE and WILLIAM HENRY DAWES, full-length dining cars and an observation parlor car with red, white and blue awning and an illuminated train herald. *(Opposite: Rail Photo Service; Below: Everett De Golyer Collection.)*

IN THE YEARS of steam, pride of the Boston & Maine-Maine Central run between Boston and Portland-Bangor by daylight were *The Flying Yankee, The Pine Tree* and *The Kennebec Limited,* all of them full dress name trains with coaches, head end, Pullman parlor cars and diners or, in slack seasons, observation cafes or buffet cars. As flagship of the fleet with a non-stop schedule of two and a quarter hours between Boston and Portland, *The Flying Yankee* rated an assigned locomotive with its name on the smokebox and, at the other end of its consist, a tailgate herald on the observation railing. On its tight schedule over the Western Division via Dover over which, approximately a century earlier, the engine *Antelope* with a car filled with newspaper reporters had achieved the world's first mile a minute speed, *The Flying Yankee* was a thing of splendor. Above it poses with a green and gold assigned engine at North Station; at the right, its bell gets a quick polish before hitting the road. (*Above: Laurence Breed Walker Collection; Right: Rail Photo Service.*)

920

ALTHOUGH *The Bar Harbor Express* ranked all other conveyances to Mount Desert in prestige and in the public awareness, it was not the only name train to converge from Boston and New York upon the vacation focus of the Maine summer resorts. There was also the Boston & Maine's Train No. 111, *The Yankee,* a sort of advance section of *The Flying Yankee,* which left Boston's North Station at breakfast time and delivered passengers on through cars which, until Labor Day, included a broiler-buffet-parlor, to the Ellsworth connection in time for tea in Bar Harbor itself via the bus which replaced the ferry in the 1930s. There was also a parlor observation car and de luxe coaches which added up to a very respectable name train indeed. At the left *The Yankee* is shown with an assigned engine carrying white flags as evidence of a second section and below on the Boston & Maine with a burnished Pacific and ample head-end revenue to pay its way. *(Left: Laurence Breed Walker Collection; Below: John P. Ahrens.)*

ALMOST as celebrated in the folklore of New England travel as Essex Junction, immortalized in doggerel poetry as a seat of transportational chaos, was White River Junction on the Vermont-New Hampshire border where two Boston & Maine main lines from Springfield and Boston-Concord, respectively, converged on the Central Vermont for interchange on the long haul to Canada. Here the *Red Wing* by night and *Alouette* by day paused to change crews, motive power and carriers. Here the *Day White Mountain Express* and *Night White Mountain Express* set out sleepers and picked up parlor cars on their far-flung occasions. *The Ambassador's* arrival and departure was an event and here *The Washingtonian* and *The Montrealer* changed engines and head-end revenue cars. All night and all day traffic converged upon White River Junction and retreated toward far horizons at the bidding of the dispatcher. For many years knowing travelers made a point of arranging their itineraries so that mealtimes found them available to the depot restaurant there. Celebrated for its New England dishes such as pork and beans, scrodded haddock on fish days and cakes with pure Vermont maple syrup for breakfast, Stewart Holbrook also remembered that in his Vermont youth a specialty of the house to rejoice juvenile voyagers was uncommonly powerful checkermint hard candies that came in miniature brakeman's lanterns with a choice of red or green globes. Not as famous a New England landmark, perhaps, as Deacon Shem Drowne's grasshopper weather vane at Faneuil Hall, but still a reassuring artifact was the locomotive that told where the wind blew atop the cupola of White River depot. In the lower frame the Boston & Maine's *Connecticut Yankee* heads south out of White River on a flawless summer day. *(Four Photos: Philip R. Hastings.)*

922

WHILE the mists of early
morning still enshroud
the Vermont countryside, and
render the outline of White
River depot hazy (*below*) the
B.&M.'s No. 3653 awaits its
highball to leave for Berlin
while, at the left, Train No. 310
prepares to depart with Boston
for its destination. At the
left *The Ambassador,* southbound passes the venerable
White River highball signal that
established long continuity
with the railroading past.

CELEBRATED in the doggerel verses that immortalized the baffled traveler who took the wrong train, Essex Junction and the Central Vermont's covered train shed there lasted a long time in the legend of New England railroading. Originally constructed, as is shown at the bottom of the opposite page with a red brick facade, the structure was rebuilt in 1890 and a wooden sheathing applied with through passage to accommodate the increased dimensions of motive power and equipment. It is shown at the top of the page after its face lifting. Here *The Ambassador* southbound pauses at Essex Junction with Central Vermont's fine No. 600 on the head end as a daylight train in the grand manner between Montreal and Boston-New York. At the left *The Washingtonian* on the night run to the Federal City brings animation to the ancient premises in the midnight hours. (*Below, Opposite: Jim Shaughnessy Collection; Three Photos: Jim Shaughnessy.*)

925

FAMED FOR THE NINETEENTH CENTURY DOGGEREL verses that brought it celebrity when a confused traveler who had taken the wrong connecting train made it part of the enduring folklore of New England, the Central Vermont depot at Essex Junction, Vermont, as late as the middle fifties was a scene of round-the-clock activity of transport. The identical wooden train shed dating from the time when the verses themselves had been written sheltered passengers who by daylight boarded the cars of the *Ambassador* on the Montreal-Boston run and by night *The Washingtonian* between Montreal and the Federal City. Here *The Washingtonian* is pictured ready to roll southward behind a huge Canadian National 4-8-4 No. 6173 which dwarfs its ancient train shed and strains the narrow clearances that resulted in 1890 when the original brick facade was removed to accommodate the even then larger equipment. On the opposite page *The Washingtonian* loads its head-end cars with mail and express for the Federal City while waiting a highball to move out into the gelid Vermont night. Sometime during the time exposure someone moved the baggage truck in the foreground, perhaps the ghostly hand of the long dead traveler whose saddened face and battered hat in the poem told of the black despair which possessed him at this very spot. *(Two Photos: Jim Shaughnessy.)*

IN the rugged climate of
New England individualism and
religious fervor, there survived
later than elsewhere in the
land oddball characters with a
message. This prophet
of doom and his wife met all
trains at North Conway and
distributed tracts pointing
the way to salvation to the
bemused arrivals. *(Herbert H.
Harwood Collection.)*

THE LAST of the old and first of the new are represented here by the B.&M.'s summer-only *North Wind*, shown double-headed at Whitefield, New Hampshire, and the Diesel *Mountaineer* between Boston and Conway as it emerges from a primeval covered bridge to flush a barefoot country boy from the underbrush. The unit train started life as replacement for the conventional *Flying Yankee* but was found insufficient for the Boston-Portland traffic of the time. *(Philip R. Hastings; Wide World.)*

INCOMPARABLY the most celebrated of all New England railroad stations and one whose immutable Gothic architecture outranked in gloomy grandeur even the Fitchburg's Castle of Otranto premises in Boston, was the Boston & Maine's depot at Salem, Massachusetts. Its two polygonal towers of solid masonry had been reared in 1847 from the design of Gridley S. Bryant, an edifice contemporary with various Greek temples, Roman peristyles, Turkish mosques and Italianate villas that elsewhere afflicted the countryside. Salem was still a country village at the time of its construction and Nathaniel Hawthorne, its first man of letters and literary celebrity, admired the railroad inordinately. It was flanked by the town millpond and tall trees shaded its approaches where the tracks converged from north and south and passed directly through its train shed. A New England conversation piece for nearly a century, its merits of architecture were viewed by none with indifference and families were known to be divided pro and con. Esthetes, especially with the growing sophistication of the times, tended to deplore it; connoisseurs of gloom and students of Horace Walpole peopled it, in imagination, with noble ghosts from Carpathian castles of mystery. In time its adjacent waiting room and freight station were removed and the traffic of metropolis surged around its portals where trains proceeded at snail's pace through drays and trams accompanied by bells and whistles and agitated crossing tenders. Handy to its platforms, waiting rooms, lunch counters, ticket offices and baggage reception coexisted in a chaos of soot and sound which, to the fastidious, suggested a suburb of hell itself. When most of Salem was razed in a monster conflagration in 1915, excited partisans hurried from as far away as Boston on the report the depot was about to be dynamited, but it was spared at the last moment as thousands cheered. The only structure even comparable in its awful grandeur was the Fitchburg Station in Boston, but admirers until the very end hailed Salem Station, shown here in 1910, as the bravest of all monuments to vanished railroad times. (*Essex Institute.*)

SALEM Station as it was known to Nathaniel Hawthorne in the early 1860s was surrounded by the town as it had been in Colonial times with the town millpond visible in the distance and tree lined streets through which the railroad ran in an almost pastoral setting.
(*Laurence Breed Walker Collection.*)

929

ONE OF THE FEW varnish runs to be named for a tree—others were *The Palmetto* and *Royal Palm, The Pine Tree Limited* on the run between Boston and Portland carried, at various times, Pullman parlor cars, a diner or cafe car and a cafe-lounge in addition to coaches and head-end revenue. Here on the northern outskirts of suburban Boston, it rounds the long curve at Crystal Lake beside Wakefield Junction with a mile-long cloud of rolling soot to mark its going. *(Lucius Beebe.)*

930

WELL OVER a century after it had come into universal use to govern the movements of trains everywhere and to enter the American lexicon as a synonym for speed and clearance, the highball signal was still in active use throughout New England. The one shown here governed trains of three separate railroads, the Boston & Maine, Montpelier & Wells River and the Canadian Pacific at Wells River, Vermont. An even more sophisticated version *(opposite)* with night lanterns and warning bells is shown at White River Junction holding up *The Ambassador,* southbound behind Central Vermont's No. 460. Below on this page is an atmospheric view of the terminal of the Eastern Railroad at Portland when it was an autonomous operation and before the great Revere catastrophe had driven it into the hands of the waiting Boston and Maine. *(Opposite: Philip R. Hastings; Here, Two Photos: The Railway & Locomotive Historical Society.)*

INTRICATE wood and steel trusses of the Howe Patent that had been found culpable in so many of the fatal train wrecks of the nineteenth century when used for bridges and trestles, supported the depot roof at St. Albans and, when protected from the elements and not exposed to moving stresses, endured uncounted tons of snow in the structure's long lifetime. At the right the northbound *Ambassador* emerges from St. Albans train shed on its way to Montreal for a nighttime portrait by Jim Shaughnessy. *(Top: E. H. Royce.)*

932

LAST OF THE TRULY massive arching train sheds that were once part of the pattern of Victorian railroading everywhere in New England, the classic Central Vermont depot and adjoining offices at St. Albans, Vermont, never quite achieved its hundredth birthday. Built in 1866, it was found to have been so structurally weakened by age that it was demolished in 1964. Buttresses of red Vermont brick supported its 351-foot length and four arched train portals pierced its eighty-four foot bulkheads at the north and south. A venerable landmark that had withstood wintry gales of legendary ferocity, blown in from Lake Champlain, it was a monument to Yankee integrity to the end. It is shown below about 1910 without a motor car in sight and still boasting the minaret at its western extremity that disappeared in later years. At the left, snow falls gently on Train No. 332 awaiting its highball at the south portal while a setout sleeper from Boston steams quietly on an adjacent track. (*Left: Jim Shaughnessy; Below: Railway & Locomotive Historical Society.*)

AT TROY Union Station in the 1880s passengers changed cars for the last few miles to Saratoga.

A CARRIER OF limited passenger operations even though its right of way to Canada passed through some of the most spectacular scenery in the East, the Delaware & Hudson was a railroad of such pronounced character as to be felt eccentric in more conservative transportation circles. Its eccentricity derived largely from its most formidable President, Lenore Loree, himself a pronounced individualist from his name, which suggested a poem by Edgar Allan Poe, to his beard and scowl which suggested that much of the time he hated everybody, as indeed he may well have done. He was widely reputed to be an executive to whose ambitions no horizon existed, to whom fate had assigned a secondary role in life. Certainly not since Alexander Holmes of the Old Colony Railroad had, in a moment of purest Anglophilia, introduced compartment cars entered through individual doors from the side to the *Fall River Boat Train* had any American railroad assumed so English a look as did the D.&H. motive power in Loree's presidency. Here is Pacific No. 652 with the northbound *Laurentian* at Whitehall while the fireboy rakes the fuel nearer his footplate. *(Philip R. Hastings.)*

ALTHOUGH the last traces of its once unhurried
way of life were soon to disappear under the impact
of the ever more strident automotive age,
nineteenth century Saratoga, in the form of its most
resplendent hostelry, the United States Hotel,
lingered on until well into the time of
The Montreal Limited and *The Laurentian*.
Its endless verandahs and white and gold ballroom
no longer knew the tread of
Whitneys and Vanderbilts, but the horsey atmosphere
of August still maintained direct continuity
with another century. The Delaware & Hudson
yards at Saratoga were directly
under the windows of the United States Hotel
(*below*) and it was when awakened
by their nocturnal commotions that De Wolf Hopper
phoned the night clerk with his celebrated enquiry:
"Can you tell me what time this hotel
gets to Chicago?" At the left, in its years
of useful going, *The Montreal Limited* comes
to rest at Windsor Station at its northern terminal.
The time is eight o'clock and the knowing arrival
will have breakfast in the hotel of
the same name. (*Philip R. Hastings.*)

"THE CARS have rounded the last curve and speed on the home stretch for three miles, past The Geyser, whose crystal spray thrown up forty or fifty feet, glistens in the sunlight as though Undine and her troupe of fairies were showering out a welcome on the coming guests ... and now come the streets and houses of Saratoga and from the car windows we read in succession, Clarendon, Grand Hotel, Grand Union, Congress Hall ... There is an universal bustle, the whistle shrieks, the bell rings and the train slows up to the beautiful depot." Such was the lyric description of the scene depicted above when the Palace Cars of the Rensselaer & Saratoga (later the Dele-ware & Hudson) were the sole means of access to America's fastest and most moneyed summer resort, and the Mansard roofed station was in-deed a thing of beauty. Indeed so fast and gamey was the reputation of Saratoga as an abode of Vanderbilts and high fashion that James Gordon Bennett, who wasn't asked to be present, termed it "a seraglio of the prurient aristocracy." If you rode the cars further upstate on the way to Montreal, you encountered the customs inspection at Rouses Point on the border and such was the bad celebrity of this incon-venience, especially on the sleeping cars, that *Leslie's Weekly* devoted a full front page to it in 1883 as shown at the right with the caption: "A Customs Officer at Rouse's Point Searching Baggage on the Night Train."

936

FRANK LESLIE'S ILLUSTRATED NEWSPAPER

Entered according to Act of Congress, in the year 1882, by MRS. FRANK LESLIE, in the Office of the Librarian of Congress at Washington.—Entered at the Post Office, New York, N.Y., as Second-class Matter.

No. 1,429.—VOL. LV.] NEW YORK—FOR THE WEEK ENDING FEBRUARY 10, 1883. [PRICE, WITH SUPPLEMENT, 10 CENTS.

REPLACING *The Champlain* on
the daylight run between New York
and Montreal over the New York
Central-Delaware & Hudson connection
at Troy was the ten hour
Laurentian threading some of the
most spectacular scenery to be found
anywhere in the East. In ordinary
times it ran with a fine enclosed
solarium observation car on its
rear end as suggested here where the
photographer has surprised
David Morgan, editor of *Trains*
magazine in converse with the
parlor car porter at the pause
at Whitehall. In wartime, however,
The Laurentian ran bobtailed
without the glory of a tailgate
insigne through the upstate New York
heartland.   (*Left: Philip Hastings;
Below: Charles Clegg.*)

WHAT *The Bar Harbor Express* was over the decades to the Down East resort areas of the Maine seacoast, the New York Central-Delaware & Hudson's *Laurentian* was to Saratoga Springs, a name train serving one of the last great American summer resorts with aristocratic character. Its nighttime counterpart *The Montreal Limited* set out sleepers at Saratoga and, as long as the age of railroad travel lasted, a ponderable part of the Delaware & Hudson's passenger traffic in summer was in the names that made news in the society columns of the world. Aboard its cars and that of its predecessor, the Rensselaer & Saratoga came the horsey set and racing enthusiasts bound for the vast verandahs of the Grand Union and United States Hotels where the great of fashion and finance assembled in August in the years celebrated by Edna Ferber in "The Saratoga Trunk." Here the north—and southbound sections of *The Laurentian* pass in the depot of Whitehall, New York, while opposite the same train pauses in the new Saratoga Springs depot that had replaced the Mansarded glories of an earlier structure shown on an adjacent page. *(Two Photos: Jim Shaughnessy.)*

938

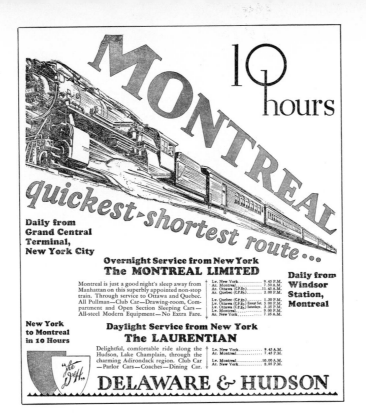

TYPICALLY Bostonian is use of the word spa to denote a refreshment booth or counter so that one of The Hub's most famous businessmen's lunch resorts achieved world fame under the style of Thompson's Spa. It only followed that a North Station news and candy kiosk should be designated the Terminal Spa and the products available served to confirm its regional character: Brigham's buttermilk, Puroxia ginger ale and hot egg and milk against the winter chill of the train shed. *(Bostonian Society.)*

THE ALL-DAY RUN through the New England countryside between Boston and Montreal aboard *The Ambassador* could be a lyric experience in auspicious seasons of the year, but chill and without cheer in the inclement months. *The Ambassador* followed the Boston & Maine's own iron to White River Junction, Vermont, where it was taken over by Central Vermont motive power to enter Canada via the Canadian National. Above it is shown on a day of heavy traffic in the 1920s, double-headed with a matronly ten wheeler as helper engine. At the left *The Ambassador* enters the identifying arched train shed at St. Albans amidst wintry gloom. Opposite, it loads at an appropriate track in Boston's North Station sometime before the structure was rebuilt to include a sports arena and modern hotel. *(Opposite: Herb H. Arey; Above: Rail Photo Service; Left: Jim Shaughnessy.)*

941

THE Boston & Maine's North Conway station whose architecture was suggested by a ranking executive after an admiring visit to Russia survived into an age when no passengers arrived or departed from the shadow of its Slavic minarets. So highly regarded was it as a landmark that a local historical society undertook its preservation as a museum. (*Railway & Locomotive Historical Society.*)

AS TWILIGHT gathered over the rails and enshrouded the roundhouses of the New England countryside where so much history had been made, nothing presaged the coming night of railroad transport with more prophetic gloom than the downgrading of once proud steam motive power to make way for Diesel expediency. Fine locomotives that had in happier times put a wheel to the *Pine Tree Limited* and *Ambassador,* aye, had even rolled the *Bar Harbor Express* to lordly destinations, ran out their final mileage in commuter runs or in milk consists such as those depicted on these pages.
Only the ghosts of Pullmans rode drawbars where once the *Flying Yankee* or *The State of Maine* had glittered. The men and the machines that had made legend in the land were gone, with them Conductor Mike Downey whose daily train out of Worcester up to Peterboro and back had come to be known as "Mr. Downey's Train" and who in fifty-two years of service on the Boston & Maine had never failed to say thank you when he took up a ticket. *(Left: Philip R. Hastings; Opposite & Below: John P. Ahrens.)*

OVER THIS superbly ballasted speedway at Rollinsford, New Hampshire, their occasions governed, as they had been for the last 100 years, by primitive highball signals, rolled the Pullmans and other luxury properties of the Boston & Maine's name trains that were channeled through Dover on their way Down East: *The State of Maine, The Gull, The Yankee* and *The Flying Yankee*. None of them paused at Rollinsford, where a branch line connected for Somersworth and Rochester, but day and night the parade of varnish runs was reported O.S. by the operator in his bow window and Rollinsford saw the great world go by in steam and glory. The Maine Central's No. 701, shown here ready to leave Portland with *The State of Maine* was one of two fast and handsomely proportioned Hudsons specially designed for candy runs, most specifically *The Bar Harbor*. On a carrier not celebrated for modernity of its motive power, they were kings of the iron with an enviable record for on-time performance with as many as twenty Standard Pullmans on their drawbar. *(Right: Boston & Maine; Below: Laurence Breed Walker.)*

ON THE Down East run from Boston to the Maritime Provinces, the Boston & Maine-Maine Central's *Gull* represented the carriers' contribution to the railroad aviary elsewhere represented by various *Eagles, Larks, Hawks, Flamingos* and *Crows*. The *Gull*, depicted here on the Maine Central with the metal smokebox flags signifying a second section east of Portland and with heavy head-end revenue, was celebrated for the complexity of its passenger accommodations in the *Official Guide* where its seasonal variations, alternating diners and cafe cars and multiplicity of setout sleepers made it one of the most complicated of all name train listings. Passengers wishing to dine at Portsmouth, New Hampshire, an on-line stop for *The Gull*, were once assured in a handbill that they wouldn't be left behind by the unannounced departure of the cars. *(Below: Rail Photo Service.)*

945

Social Distinction and the Resources of Conservative Wealth Rode The Bar Harbor Express To the Least Accessible Of All American Summer Resorts

WHAT *The Blue Train* was to traffic between Paris and Monte Carlo in the E. Phillips Oppenheim years of the Russian grand dukes, and what *The Florida Special* over the rails of the Florida East Coast was to Palm Beach before the coming of the planes, *The Bar Harbor Express* was to the Maine summer resort on a stern and rockbound coast that early in the game established itself as the seasonal capital of American social conservatism. Not as old in calendar years and the approval of the well-to-do as Saratoga Springs which dated from before the Civil War, but well enough ensconced as an enclave of wealth to regard Florida as the merest *arrivist*, Bar Harbor and, to a lesser degree, its neighboring Seal Harbor and Northeast emerged upon the general awareness in the early eighties when the Maine Central inaugurated the Mount Desert Ferry, a transfer alike of personalities and their chattels and retainers and of social destinies that was to survive until 1931 when a causeway to the mainland put an end to it forever. Fifteen years later and as though in protest against the island's availability to what its Old Guard regarded as a socially irresponsible element, Bar Harbor burned almost to the ground. It was widely regarded as an act of suttee, and when, in 1960, *The Bar Harbor Express* that had been its most celebrated agency of access ceased to run, Bar Harbor as a bastion of the aloof proprieties had itself long since ceased to exist. In the intervening three quarters of a century, however, Bar Harbor had been the most inaccessible of American resorts both in the field of logistics and in the more ephemeral realm of social acceptance. Some of the agencies which made Bar Harbor at least physically available if not an open city socially and which conveyed its devotees each summer from Beacon Street, Rittenhouse Square and Du Pont Circle are the subject matter of the pages immediately following.

946

Luxurious Bedroom Cars

WHEN it went into service in the summer of 1902,
The Bar Harbor Express originated on the New Haven and
its implications were solely those of a New York clientele.
In 1917, however, and in explicit recognition that
Bar Harbor was far more a summer suburb of Philadelphia
and Washington, it began its run on the Pennsylvania
with through Pullmans from those cities and it was on this
basis that it achieved its dimension as a convenience
of the social and economic *bon ton*. On its successive
carriers through the night, the Pennsy, the New Haven, the
Boston & Maine and finally the Maine Central its
progress was a choicely regarded jewel of their operational
crown, and its sometimes four and five sections moved
with the clockwork precision of sidereal time.
Here it is shown carrying white flags to indicate a following
section on the New Haven leg of its run at Auburn,
Massachusetts, in 1929. The photograph is
from the archives of The Smithsonian Institution.

947

FORERUNNER of such seasonal and celebrated resort trains as *The Bar Harbor Express* and *The State of Maine* was the Boston & Maine-Maine Central's first de luxe varnish run on a Down East schedule, the resoundingly named *Boston & Mount Desert Limited Express,* which went into service in the summer of 1887. Its all-Pullman consist included three superbly appointed parlor cars and a diner, all painted umber and boasting the new Sessions Patent enclosed vestibules. East of Portland, the Maine Central emplaced track pans at strategic points to facilitate a speedy run to Mount Desert Ferry where passengers embarked on successive generations of the company's steamers for the brief water passage to Bar Harbor. Here *The Limited* is depicted on the outskirts of Bangor, probably in its inaugural year in a rare photograph from the archives of the Railway & Locomotive Historical Society with Maine Central No. 14 on the drawbar.

WHEN *The Mount Desert Limited* went into service in 1887, all products of the Pullman Palace Car Company were hand crafted to the specifications of the purchasing carrier and no two cars were exactly alike. Even those built from identical floor plans differed in some detail of decor or design and the parlor cars outshopped for the Boston & Maine's first truly de luxe varnish were no exception. Pullmans on the Mount Desert Ferry run were as prestigeous as custom-built Rolls-Royces would be at a later date. Below, *The Boston & Mount Desert Limited Express* is shown in a full dress portrait behind the Boston & Maine's prideful locomotive COLUMBIA at the time of the train's inaugural. Another likeness in full color has been painted for this book by the distinguished artist Howard Fogg and appears as its frontispiece. *(Left: Pullman Standard; Below: Railway & Locomotive Historical Society.)*

BAR HARBOR EXPRESS.
Tuesdays, Wednesdays, Thursdays and Fridays, September 4th to 21st, inclusive.

Club-Lounge...New York to Ellsworth.
Sleeping Cars..Philadelphia to Ellsworth—(10 S., 2 C., D. R.).
Philadelphia to Ellsworth—(6 C., 3 D. R.).
Washington to Rockland—(8 S., 2 C., D. R.).
Washington to Waterville—(10 S., 2 C., D. R.).
Philadelphia to Rockland—(8 S., 2 C., D. R.).
Washington to Plymouth—(12 S., D. R.). (Except Saturday, September 1st.)
Washington to Ellsworth—(10 S., 2 C., D. R.).
Washington to Portland—(10 S., 2 C., D. R.).
New York to Ellsworth—(10 S., 2 D. R.).
Washington to Oquossoc—(12 S., D. R.).   (Fridays only until September 14th, inclusive.)
Dining Cars....Washington to New York.
Philadelphia to New Haven.
Portland to Ellsworth.
No Coaches New York to Ellsworth.
No baggage Philadelphia to New York.

BAR HARBOR EXPRESS.
Tuesdays and Fridays, September 25th to October 12th, incl.

Sleeping Cars..Philadelphia to Ellsworth—(10 S., 2 C., D. R.).
Washington to Portland—(10 S., 2 C., D.R.).
Washington to Ellsworth—(10 S., 2 C., D. R.).
New York to Ellsworth—(10 S., 2 C., D. R.).
Dining Cars....Washington to New York.
New York to New Haven.
Philadelphia to New York.   Portland to Ellsworth.
No Coaches New York to Ellsworth.
No baggage Philadelphia to New York.

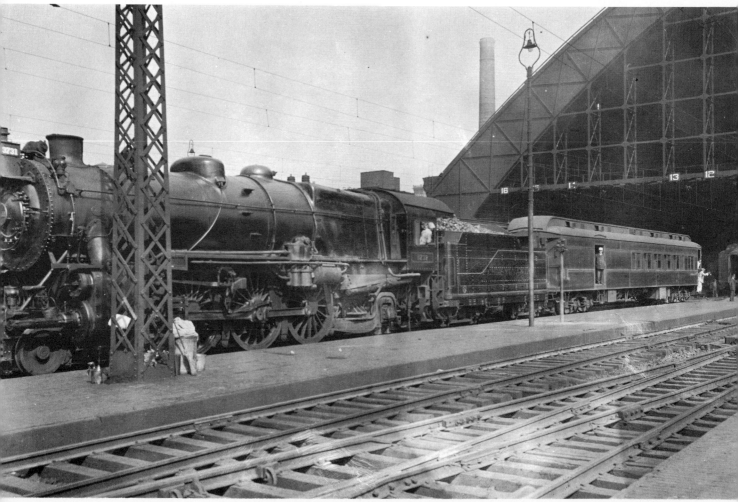

IN THE GLORY YEARS of *The Bar Harbor Express* as the most de luxe of all New England trains, some idea of the diversification of its through and setout Pullmans may be gathered from the excerpt opposite from the pages of *The Official Guide*. On the same page is depicted the Philadelphia section of "The Blue Train of America" as it was known to newspaper readers making up at Broad Street in the mid-1920s with the buffet lounge in evidence that will go all the way through to Ellsworth. Shown above at speed on the Pennsy's New York Division, *The Bar Harbor* is practically indistinguishable in its all-Pullman consist from *The Broadway Limited*. As a train of unassailable Rittenhouse Square character, it left Broad Street at three in the afternoon, an hour convenient for E. T. Stotesbury and A. Atwater Kent to finish luncheon at the Philadelphia Club and sign a few important papers before getting away from it all for the weekend. A diner ran as far as New Haven and a Maine Central diner was cut in for the breakfast trade east of Portland. One distinguishing identification of the pedigreed varnish train of its time it seems to have lacked in the form of an observation car terminating in a keystone herald with the train's name in lights. The frequent cuts and pulls to which its consist was available at New Haven, Portland and Ellsworth made this panache improbable and most of the time its confirmed patrons spent in their single bedrooms such as is shown here. (*Opposite, Two Photos: Pennsylvania Railroad; Above: Rail Photo Service; Left: Pullman Standard.*)

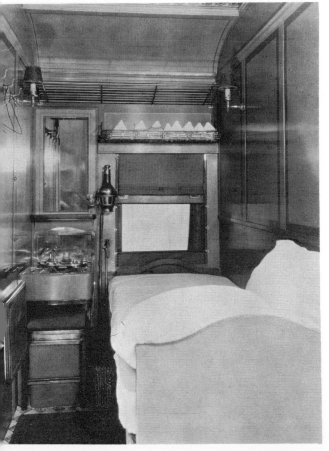

THE MOUNT Desert Ferry's hour of special glory arrived when, in August 1914, as the nations of Europe were flying to arms, the North German Lloyd liner *Kronprinzessin Cecilie*, at sea when England declared war on Germany and fearing seizure by the British Navy, sought refuge in the then neutral port of Bar Harbor. The town awoke one morning to find the sleek four stacker anchored in deep water at its front door, piloted there by an American yachtsman, Ledyard Blair. The eyes of the world turned briefly to the moment of drama before the vessel was interned. The Ferry shared in the limelight and here *Norumbega* is shown effecting the transfer of passengers to the mainland where special trains returned them to New York. Some idea of the density of passenger traffic to Mount Desert may be gathered from the Maine Central's summer schedule for 1911. (*Two Photos: Mariners Museum, Newport News.*)

MAINE CENTRAL RAILROAD

Bar Harbor and Bangor to Portland, Boston and New York

	Nos. of Trains	†110	†122	‡156	*114	*118	†120	§712	‡156	*114	*118
		WEEK DAY TRAINS						**SUNDAY TRAINS**			
	STATIONS.	A.M.	A.M.	P.M.	P.M.	P.M.	P.M.	A.M.	P.M.	P.M.	P.M.
	Manset.......	......	†8 45	*1 20	†2 30	*7 20	......	......	*1 20	......	*7 20
	Southwest Harbor.	......	†8 50	*1 30	†2 40	*7 30	......	......	*1 30	......	*7 30
	Northeast Harbor.	......	†9 05	*1 40	†2 50	*7 40	......	......	*1 40	......	*7 40
	Seal Harbor......	......	†9 25	*2 00	†3 10	*8 00	......	......	*2 00	......	*8 00
	Bar Harbor...... Steam'r lv	†6 10	†10 50	*3 00	†4 10	*9 00	......	§5 20	*3 00	§4 15	*9 00
	Sorrento.......	......	†10 30	......	*4 00	†6 30	......	......	......	*4 00	......
	Hancock Point....	......	†10 40	......	4 40	†6 40	......	......	......	......	......
	Sullivan........	†6 35	†11 05	......	*4 35	......	......	......	......	......	......
0	Mt. Desert Ferry.....	†7 00	†11 45	‡3 40	*5 00	*9 50	......	§6 05	‡3 40	*5 00	*9 50
3	Waukeag, Sullivan Ferry......	7 07	11 52	‡3 47	5 07	9 57	......	6 12	3 47	5 07	9 57
4	Hancock........	7 15	f11 55	......	5 10	......	......	6 15	......	5 10	......
8	Franklin Road....	f7 22	......	......	5 19	......	......	6 23	......	5 19	......
11	Washington Junction....	7 30	12 15	......	f5 28	......	†11 00	f6 32	......	f5 28	......
14	Ellsworth........	7 37	12 22	‡4 11	5 35	10 21	11 07	6 39	4 11	5 35	10 21
15	Ellsworth Falls......	7 42	f12 27	......	5 40	E10 25	11 12	6 47	......	5 40	E10 25
21	Nicolin.........	f7 55	f12 40	......	6 00	E10 38	f11 25	f7 00	......	6 00	E10 38
25	Green Lake.......	8 04	f12 49	......	6 08	E10 46	11 34	f7 08	......	6 08	E10 46
29	Phillips Lake.....	f8 11	f12 57	......	f6 16	E10 53	f11 41	f7 15	......	f6 16	E10 53
32	Holden.........	8 18	f1 05	......	6 24	E11 00	11 48	f7 21	......	6 24	E11 00
42	Brewer Junction......	8 38	1 24	......	6 44	E11 18	12 08	7 36	......	6 44	E11 18
43	Bangor........[ar	†8 45	†1 30	‡5 20	*6 50	*11 25	†12 15	§7 40	‡5 20	*6 50	*11 25
	Bangor........ lv	......	......	‡5 30	*8 00	*11 35	†12 40	§7 50	‡5 30	*8 00	*11 35
	Portland........ ar	......	......	‡9 25	*12 50	*3 45	†4 50	§12 20	‡9 25	*12 50	*3 45
		P.M.	P.M.	P.M.	Night	A.M.	A.M.	Noon	P.M.	Night	A.M.
182	Portland ⎰via Dover.... ⎱lv	3 35	6 00	......	......	......	†5 10	12 25	......	......	......
297	Boston ⎰ ⎱ar	6 45	9 00	......	......	......	†8 30	3 40	......	......	......
	Portland ⎰via Portsmouth lv	......	6 05	......	*1 05	*4 00	......	12 30	......	*1 05	*4 00
	Boston ⎰ ⎱ar	......	9 05	......	*5 15	*7 00	......	3 40	......	*5 15	*7 00
		P.M.	P.M.		A. M.	A.M.	A.M.	P.M.		A.M.	A.M.
	Portland........ lv	†7 20	†7 20	†9 40	......	†8 35	†8 35	......	†9 40	......	†8 35
	Haverhill........	†9 43	†9 43	......	......	†10 42	†10 42	......	......	......	†10 42
	Lowell.........	†10 39	†10 39	†12 28	......	†11 26	†11 26	......	†12 28	......	†11 26
	Worcester........	†12 17	†12 17	†2 05	......	†12 50	†12 50	......	†2 05	......	†12 50
	Springfield.......	†2 00	†2 00	†3 50	......	†2 10	†2 10	......	†3 50	......	†2 10
	New Haven.......	†3 35	†3 35	†5 33	......	†3 39	†3 39	......	†5 33	......	......
	New York........	†5 35	†5 35	†7 40	......	†5 35	†5 35	......	†7 40	......	†5 35
		A.M.	A.M.	A.M.		P.M.	P.M.		A.M.		P.M.

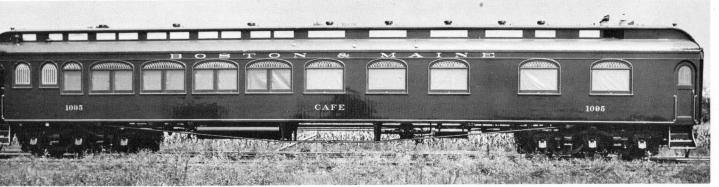

DINING aboard the cars North of Boston partook of the essential nature of the New England through which they ran and its habit, therefore, was not one of voluptuous attitudes or gastronomic debauch, but the diners and cafe cars built in 1905 for the Maine Central and the Boston and Maine and assigned to *The Bar Harbor Express* were perhaps the most beautiful of all Pullman products at the high water mark of its artistry. In the last years of its run in steam, depicted at the top of the page, *The Bar Harbor* often ran with streamlined head-end equipment and lightweight sleepers from the equipment pool of the New Haven. (*Top: Philip R. Hastings; Below: Pullman Standard.*)

COMPONENTS of the embracing panorama reproduced at the
right are both of the rival means of transport through whose
agency, until the construction of a causeway to the mainland and
the surrender of the island to motorists, Bar Harbor was
available to its once enviable residents. At the extreme right
of the photograph is visible the pier and landing facilities
of the Eastern Steamship Company aboard whose immortal
J. T. Morse generations of Bar Harbor regulars arrived from
Rockland where they had changed from the through
steamers from Boston. In the immediate foreground with the
ferry *Norumbega* in dock is the pier of the Maine Central
Railroad where a long succession of much loved steamers,
Sebenoa, Sappho, Norumbega, Samoset, Moosehead
and *Rangeley* tied up between 1884 and 1931 when a causeway
was built to the mainland. Of this noble succession, *Rangeley*
alone is still operative at Bermuda where, as the oddly
named *Chauncey M. Depew* it sees service as port tender at
Hamilton. Immediately above is the lounge, crowded in
inclement weather but otherwise little used, of *Sappho*. *Sebenoa*,
shown opposite in a builder's photograph was constructed
in 1880 as the legend suggests for the Eastern Steamboat
Company at Bath for service on the Bath-Boothbay route and
was sold four years later to the Maine Central for the
Mount Desert run where, with variations of schedule, she
remained, a summer season institution, until 1902 when she
was replaced by *Norumbega*. In its golden years, Bar Harbor was
very much a seaport.
(Three Photos: Mariners Museum, Newport News.)

STEAMER SEBENOA,
OF THE EASTERN STEAMBOAT CO.

ABOARD the Maine Central's old-time favorite with the Bar Harbor regulars *Moosehead*, names of consequence were the veriest commonplace. In June eastbound for Bar, Seal or Northeast, or headed home when the season was over, its sailing list read more like that of the *Olympic* or *Mauretania* than of a fifty minute ferry operation to a summer resort whose seawater was so cold nobody ever swam in it. *(Maine Central.)*

IN 1884 the Maine Central's Waukeag Branch, running from the main line at Washington Junction to a rock-bound coastal point designated as Mount Desert Ferry, was completed and the ferry operation itself went into service in June of that year. It was destined to be one of the most celebrated, if shortest maritime operations in the record. Here, as shown in the two rare photographs on the page opposite, the well-placed of the world descended from the overnight Pullmans, variously, from New York, Philadelphia and Washington and boarded such famous ferry steamers as *Sebenoa* and *Sappho* for the brief water passage to Bar Harbor, Seal Harbor and Northeast. The agency of their arrival at the Ferry was, of course, the immortal *Bar Harbor Express* shown here toward the end of its long and exciting life in a photograph behind Maine Central motive power near Ellsworth by John P. Ahrens. *(Opposite, Two Photos: Carl E. Henry Collection, Courtesy Maine Central.)*

FEW NAME TRAINS in the record have about them the perfumed cachet of social aloofness associated with *The Bar Harbor Express* in the years when it ran with Pullmans only from June to September in sections from Washington, Philadelphia and New York, sometimes several from each. Originating on the Pennsylvania, it ran over the New Haven, the Boston & Maine and finally achieved the Mount Desert Ferry via the Maine Central and, almost to the exclusion of lesser mortals, its sailing lists teemed with the socially and financially elect whose conservative tastes inclined them to the old fashioned manners and measured pace of Bar Harbor, Dark Harbor, Seal Harbor and other long established Maine seacoast resorts rather than the more refulgent panache of Newport or East Hampton. Regulars aboard its all-stateroom cars were lady novelist Mary Roberts Rinehart, gentleman novelist Arthur Train, physician novelist S. Weir Mitchell, clerical celebrities such as Bishop William Doane of Albany and secular celebrities such as Joseph Pulitzer, A. Atwater Kent and E. T. Stotesbury. One stateroom car on each trip was reserved exclusively for domestics and was known as "the butlers' car." On the page opposite, *The Bar Harbor Express* is shown in its all-Pullman splendor on the Boston & Maine. In the rare photograph below *The Bar Harbor Express* in 1920 is spotted at the Mount Desert Ferry while the Maine Central's fine steamer *Rangeley* strains at its moorings at the pierside. *(Opposite: Everett De Golyer Collection; Below: Carl E. Henry Collection.)*

WITH THE EXCEPTION of such notable rendezvous of members of the private car club as Palm Beach and Louisville at the time of the Kentucky Derby, no resort witnessed a greater concentration of privately owned varnish often augmented by the business cars of ranking railroaders than did the Bar Harbor run in its last fine flowering in the 1920s. On one celebrated occasion *The Bar Harbor Express* running in three sections brought in no fewer than twenty-one private cars in a single day. On the opposite page an extra section of *The Bar Harbor Express* is depicted near Brunswick, Maine, with the business car of a railroad bigwig to judge from the track lamps, perhaps General Atterbury of the Pennsy who was a notable Bar Harbor resorter in its golden age.

LEGEND AND FOLKLORE clustered in a rich aura of seacoast mythology around the Eastern Steamship Company's Rockland connection for Bar Harbor in the form of service by *The J. T. Morse* which constituted direct and unequivocal competition with the Maine Central's Mount Desert Ferry. "One of the handsomest of all Eastern Steamship vessels," according to Professor George Hilton, a ranking authority in the field, *The Morse* was a venerable sidewheeler freighted to the waterline with the social history of America's most inaccessible summer resort. It met the Boston boats, *City of Rockland* and *City of Bangor* at Rockland at the unearthly hour of four in the morning and required two hours in the cold Maine darkness for the transfer of passengers and merchandise before sailing for a crossing that could on occasion be as rough as the English Channel. *The Morse* was also celebrated for the presence of Stewardess Maggie Higgins who, for decades on end, ruled crew and passengers alike with the heavy hand of a practiced despot. "All true resorters rode *The Morse*," wrote Cleveland Amory in his definitive history of Bar Harbor, "and her passenger list included everybody from Lord Bryce to Hetty Green, while her social pitch reached that of her whistle." Like all steamships of pronounced personal character, *The Morse* had her shortcomings, one of which was a propensity for grounding if shoal water was even remotely available. One Bar Harbor cave dweller of ancestral occupancy of the Island, when she found herself stranded in Penobscot Bay after a three day rainfall, took her grievance to the captain. "I don't see how the water can be low," she proclaimed, "especially after all the rain we've had." In the below photograph *The Morse* is shown at her Bar Harbor mooring across the bonnet of a symbolic motor car whose presence was at length to relegate to the discard both the railroads and the ferry and the Boston steamers too. Eventually it was to doom the character of Bar Harbor itself. (*Four Photos: Mariners Museum, Newport News.*)

A DIRECT CONFRONTATION with the competition was afforded from the deck of *The Morse* at its Bar Harbor mooring in the form of the equally handy and even more frequently used landing of the Maine Central which was a scant fifty yards distant.

ALTHOUGH in 1911, the Maine Central scheduled four other daily through trains connecting with the Mount Desert Ferry, the big event of the day was the arrival of *The Bar Harbor Express* with its cargo of social notables that attracted the most attention. In the above photograph the arriving train has just pulled in while the ferry *Norumbega*, awaiting the transfer of its passengers, is barely visible beyond the train shed at the right. By the period represented above the eye-popping luxury of parlor cars from the original *Mount Desert Express*, shown at the left, had become more subdued, but the train's equipment represented the finest available at any given time. (*Above: Mariners Museum; Left: Railway & Locomotive Historical Society.*)

962

NOT ALL sections of *The Bar Harbor Express* which, by the mid-1930s had been shortened in general usage to the *Bar Harbor*, rolled in all-Pullman glory, perhaps with "the butlers' car" in their consist. When traffic was heavy, third and fourth sections brought up in the rear of the parade with head-end revenue cars, section sleepers and extra Pullmans added to accommodate unforeseen traffic at the last moment. On one famous night in 1923 the Maine Central turned over no fewer than 102 cars running in five sections of the *Bar Harbor* for interchange with the Boston & Maine at Portland. Above, a third section nears Ellsworth on a fine July morning in 1940, its leading refrigerator car perhaps filled with perishables for the fittingly named Bar Harbor Society Market. At the left one of the Ellsworth Pullmans, appropriately the *Cosmopolitan*, drowses through the Maine night. *(Top: John P. Ahrens; Left: Philip R. Hastings.)*

963

973